Learning through Literature

LEARNING THROUGH LITERATURE

Activities to Enhance
Reading, Writing, and Thinking Skills

CAROL SUE KRUISE

Illustrated by
Kathryn M. Vetter

1990
TEACHER IDEAS PRESS
A Division of
Libraries Unlimited, Inc.
Englewood, Colorado

Copyright © 1990 Libraries Unlimited, Inc.
All Rights Reserved
Printed in the United States of America

No part of this publication may be reproduced, stored in a retrieval system, or transmitted, in any form or by any means, electronic, mechanical, photo-copying, recording, or otherwise, without the prior written permission of the publisher. An exception is made for individual library media specialists and teachers who may make copies of activity sheets for classroom use in a single school. Other portions of the book (up to 15 pages) may be copied for in-service programs or other educational programs in a single school.

The copyright for pages 170 and 171 is held by Ann Cameron and was provided for publication in this book October 18, 1989.

TEACHER IDEAS PRESS
A Division of
Libraries Unlimited, Inc.
P.O. Box 3988
Englewood, CO 80155-3988

Library of Congress Cataloging-in-Publication Data

Kruise, Carol Sue, 1939-
  Learning through literature : activities to enhance reading, writing, and thinking skills / Carol Sue Kruise ; illustrated by Kathryn M. Vetter.
    xiii, 204 p. 22x28 cm.
    Includes bibliographical references and index.
    ISBN 0-87287-784-1
    1. Reading (Elementary)--United States--Language experience approach. 2. Language arts (Elementary)--United States. 3. Thought and thinking--Study and teaching (Elementary)--United States. 4. Children--United States--Books and reading. 5. Activity programs in education--United States. I. Title.
LB1573.33.K78   1990
372.6'044--dc20   90-36622
                                                                  CIP

CONTENTS

THE READING, WRITING, THINKING CONNECTION

LITERATURE EXPERIENCES — BOOKS TO LEARN BY

FOREWORD

In the field of education, it seems that new ideas either spread slowly, often not reaching their full impact for many years, or they spread like the proverbial wildfire, with teachers and administrators embracing them wholeheartedly from the very start. Within the same school district, or even the same school, some teachers are quick to try out a new idea or teaching approach, whereas others are more cautious, unsure — waiting to see the results brought about by this new idea.

Such is the case with the movement toward the "whole language" approach to the teaching of reading in elementary schools. Some teachers tried this approach immediately after their first exposure to it, and now swear by it; others have been more reluctant to depart from their more traditional methods of teaching reading, and they are just now starting to experiment with reading instruction that connects or integrates the teaching of reading, writing, and thinking skills through the use of literature. Whether you are an experienced literature based reading instructor or new to this approach, Sue Kruise suggests a variety of unique activities to delight your students and help them experience the joys of reading, writing, and thinking.

"Children should be steeped in good literature." Now, here is an idea that all educators embrace. When I read this sentence, I knew immediately that this book was going to fill a need. I was right. Presented in this book are ideas for good literature and practical, enjoyable learning activities that will work in any classroom, but especially where reading, writing, and thinking have been connected over a whole language framework.

I have worked with the author for three years. I was the special reading teacher, and she was (and is) the "special" librarian at the same elementary school. Her knowledge of children's literature makes her a fantastic resource for teachers who are seeking quality literature for their students to read. Whether for a phonics/basal-oriented class or for a whole language-oriented class, her suggestions for reading materials are always varied yet appropriate — for both student and teacher. The activities she includes in this text provide a variety of interesting, stimulating, and fun-filled ideas that will promote the complex learning involved in the reading-writing-thinking connection. This book is truly a labor of love for Sue. I think that each teacher who tries her suggestions for literature selections and learning activities will thank her for writing this book. She has filled that "I-need-some-help" gap and filled it well. Use this book with confidence and experience the fun and satisfaction of watching your students learn and grow.

CHERYL A. RAY
Littleton, Colorado

ACKNOWLEDGMENTS

I would like to express my appreciation and gratitude to the following people who have assisted me throughout this project:

Bonnie Brown, Chapter I Coordinator, Special Reading Program Chair, Student Program's Assistant, whose candor challenged and stimulated my thinking at the book's inception

Cheryl A. Ray, Doctoral Candidate in Social Foundations of Education at the University of Colorado Boulder and Adjunct Assistant Professor in Humanities and Social Sciences at Colorado School of Mines, Golden, Colorado, who acted as a reading consultant as the book developed

My sister, Mary Ann Brown, for her continual support and valuable criticism

My dear friend and colleague, Gloria Spannagel, whose encouragement and suggestions are a continual source of energy

Tess Giffin, Michelle Clippinger, and Ruth Wilson, my resident artists, who enhanced my knowledge of pattern and design

Judith Axelrad, librarian in the Humanities Department of the Denver Public Library, who enthusiastically helped me match paintings with stories

Cara Meier, music instructor, who after numerous "tee-tee-ta's" helped me write the rhythmic notes

All of my inestimable colleagues in Littleton District 6, resources par excellence, who willingly routed materials and suggestions upon request

Mary Lou Green whose sensitivity provided strength during difficult times

THE READING,
WRITING, THINKING
CONNECTION

Introduction

Learning through Literature: Activities to Enhance Reading, Writing, and Thinking Skills will serve as a guide for all who are involved in helping children become better readers, writers, and thinkers. The book is based on two premises. The first premise is that reading, writing, and thinking are interrelated and should therefore be developed simultaneously. The second premise is that quality literature is a vital ingredient in any effective language arts program.

Reading augments thinking and writing. Many authors tell us that they learned to write by reading. Writing requires thinking. Edward Albee is quoted as saying, "I write to find out what I'm thinking about."[1] Each skill flows directly from the other and all give each other meaning.

Much has been written about the reading/writing connection. Sometimes the thinking portion of the trio appears to be neglected. Some theorists contend that when we are reading, we are engaged in the highest levels of thinking, and thus it is unnecessary to teach creative and critical thinking skills. I would agree that when we are fully engaged in reading, we are analyzing the characters and settings, we are creating pictures in our minds, and we are making decisions and judgments about characters and events in the story, as well as about the author's style. Writing, however, requires the additional thinking skills of fluency, flexibility, originality, and imagination. When we are reading, we are not necessarily practicing these skills. For this reason, thinking skills, like reading and writing skills, must be taught. Some months ago, I attended a workshop featuring noted authors Marion Dane Bauer, Jane Fitz-Randolph, and Barbara Steiner. Each author walked us through an exercise as she developed character, plot, and setting. One shared a portion of a manuscript before and after revision. Listening to the metacognitive processes each author used reinforced for me the importance of providing opportunities for children to improve their creative and critical thinking skills, for these are the tools that authors use. Unless authors employ these skills, their stories lack color and definition.

Few, if any, would disagree that quality literature is essential to an effective language arts program. Using well-written literature with children enhances their understanding of how a story should develop and flow. It enriches their vocabulary by exposing them to vivid, colorful language. When children hear stories that excite them, their imaginations are awakened, and they are motivated to read and write. Good literature serves as a model for organizing and developing plot, character, and setting. Finally, literature is an ideal medium for teaching skills such as sentence structure, punctuation, and capitalization.

Although few question the value of using literature as a tool for teaching children to become readers, writers, and thinkers, many struggle with how to proceed once a piece of literature has been selected. Designing questions and activities that improve reading comprehension, providing meaningful opportunities for children to write, and honing creative and critical thinking skills are

---

[1]Donald M. Murray, *Write to Learn* (New York: Holt, Rinehart & Winston, 1987), 22.

extremely time consuming. This text provides new and varied ideas and can serve as a model in designing activities for use with other pieces of literature. There are numerous activities from which to choose. At no time should they all be used. We need to steep children in good literature not drown them in activities. Choose those activities that will most benefit your students. Overworking a story will cause the children to grow weary and lose interest in even the most exciting piece of literature.

The books contained in this text are intended for use in grades 1 through 3. The selections are ones that classroom teachers have used successfully with their students. I have chosen books from a variety of genre so that children can be exposed to the elements of fantasy, mystery, science fiction, adventure, and realism. The books are readable by children in grades 1 through 3; however, upper grade teachers will find many of the activities appropriate for older students. For example, *Rosie's Walk* serves as a springboard for teaching prepositional phrases, descriptive adjectives, elaboration, plot patterns, and circle stories. Teachers at all levels will find the "Think Bank" helpful in planning numerous classroom activities and projects. Each of the fifteen books developed is available in paperback should you wish to purchase multiple texts for classroom use.

This handbook presents purposeful, literature based activities that will help the printed word come alive for children. It can be used as a companion piece for teachers who use basal texts but also want their students to experience the joy of "real" literature. For those who do not use a basal text, it will serve as a source of additional ideas and activities. The text is not intended to be followed as though it were a lesson plan. As much as anything, it is an "idea book." You are the experts. You know the skills that your students need to improve. Choose projects and activities carefully. Tailor them to fit your classes and above all bring to each story your own ideas, enthusiasm, and knowledge. Together we can help children "learn through literature."

The text includes a chapter entitled "Think Bank," which defines and explains Frank Edwin Williams's creative and critical thinking skills of Fluency, Flexibility, Originality, Elaboration, Risk taking, Complexity, Curiosity, Imagination, Planning, Communication, Forecasting, Decision making, and Evaluation. Worksheets are provided to facilitate Planning, Forecasting, Evaluation, and Decision Making activities. "Think Bank" is a resource to be used throughout the text. The better we understand these skills and how they function in the writing process, the more likely we are to encourage their use as tools of creativity. It is important to understand each skill, too, in order to determine which ones the students need to improve.

The literature explored in this text includes beginning-to-read books, picture books, and novels. Each of the books begins with a Summary, which gives a brief overview of the story.

The Before Reading Activities are designed to increase comprehension by focusing the children on the story that is to follow. In addition these activities will activate children's background knowledge and increase their vocabulary thereby expanding their ability to comprehend. (Some titles referenced in a few of the activities are out of print, however, these titles are still used widely and should be easy to locate.)

The Predicting Activities help the students set a purpose for their reading and pique their interest in the story. Eliciting children's ideas and opinions prior to the reading allows them to set their own goals for reading. Research indicates that personal goal setting is extremely important in developing intelligent readers who are desirous of learning and are not just reading to answer questions posed by teachers.[2]

The Post Reading Activities allow children to respond in a variety of ways to the story. Their purpose is to develop and extend comprehension. There are numerous questions and activities from which to choose.

Thinking Activities will hone children's creative and critical thinking skills. We ask children to think and write. We expect them to be creative; these activites provide them with opportunities to

---

[2]Russell G. Stauffer, *The Language-Experience Approach to the Teaching of Reading* (New York: Harper & Row, 1980).

sharpen the skills that enable them to do so. Though we need to seize every opportunity to stimulate children's imaginations, arouse their curiosity, and challenge their reasoning, we need not try to accomplish all these tasks within the context of every story.

The Writing Activities section outlines a variety of meaningful writing exercises that provide opportunities for children to communicate and to improve their writing. Select those writing activities most appropriate for each child, for it is unlikely that all children will be in the same place at the same time in their writing development and be ready for the same writing experience.

Literature provides a marvelous springboard for meaningful activities in the areas of science, art, music, and elsewhere. The Et Cetera Activities are structured to extend the learning across the curriculum to various subject areas.

The Author Says... section makes each author come alive for both teachers and students. The authors have all been personally contacted and asked specific questions about their book used in this text. I have tried to relate details that can be shared with children to familiarize them with these authors and to help them understand how the writing process works for each of them. Although this section has been placed after the reading activities, some may prefer to relate author information before reading the story. Oftentimes, hearing about the author of the story they are about to read heightens children's anticipation about the story. The Bibliography provides a list of other books by each author. I have listed Reading Level and Interest Level (RL, IL) for each of these titles. These levels are personal assessments as a result of my experience with literature and children and are not based on any formal readability testing. The Author Activities are designed to acquaint the students with the authors' work. They provide opportunities for the students to explore the authors' style and/or illustrative technique.

The more children are exposed to good literature, the more they perceive themselves as writers, and the more they want to have their own work published. Numerous organizations, companies, and periodicals are meeting this need by giving young authors their first chance at publication. Appendix A: "Publishing Your Young Authors" lists addresses for some of these groups.

In his chapter "Enriching the Basal Reading Program with Literature,"[3] Ira E. Aaron takes issue with the often quoted statement "children learn to read by reading." In his mind the statement would be more accurate if it read "children's reading ability is maintained and enhanced by reading." He feels that reading without instruction will not produce proficient readers. By the same token, children will not become writers solely because they are given opportunities to write. We must simultaneously engage them in activities designed to develop their creative and critical thinking skills. This handbook will assist you as classroom teachers, reading teachers, remedial reading teachers, librarians, teachers of the gifted and talented, and resource teachers in your efforts to make literature come alive for children and at the same time provide you with ideas and activities that will allow children to think, read, and write more effectively and efficiently in the context of literature.

---

[3]Bernice E. Cullinan, ed., *Children's Literature in the Reading Program* (Newark, Del.: International Reading Association, 1987), 126-38.

Think Bank

COGNITIVE SKILLS

Frank Edwin Williams[1] identifies four cognitive thinking processes that facilitate productive-divergent thinking. These behaviors are Fluency, Flexibility, Originality, and Elaboration.

Fluency

FLUENCY is the ability to respond with a quantity of answers. Fluent thinkers may not generate original ideas, but they can come up with lots of ideas. Brainstorming is an effective tool for eliciting fluent thinking. When brainstorming, children should be encouraged to express themselves freely. Judgments by either teacher or students should be withheld. Negative comments squelch creative ideas quickly. Children should be encouraged to piggyback their ideas. If asked to name as many colors as they can, one child may say blue and another might say royal blue or baby blue. Many times the most creative answers surface toward the end of the brainstorming session. They spill forth when the children think they cannot come up with one more idea.

Sample activities:

1. List as many words as you can that begin with the prefix *un-*.

2. List as many kinds of shoes as you can think of.

3. How many things can you name that are round?

Flexibility

FLEXIBILITY is the ability to approach problems and ideas from different angles or points of view. Flexibility requires switching our train of thought.

Sample activities:

1. Think of different uses for a coat hanger.

2. List as many animals as you can that live in your area of the country. Categorize them in three different ways.

3. List similarities between the movie *Star Wars* and the book *The Wizard of Oz*.

---

[1]Frank E. Williams, *Classroom Ideas for Encouraging Thinking and Feeling* (Buffalo, N.Y.: D.O.K. Publishers, 1970), iii.

Originality

ORIGINALITY is the ability to generate clever or unusual answers, ideas, or solutions in unique ways. These ideas are usually colorful, but often they are not practical. Ideas may or may not be truly unique, but they may be original for the individual.

Sample activities:

1. Think up a new holiday. Decide when, how, and why to celebrate it.

2. Invent a new language.

3. Rewrite the lyrics to a song.

Elaboration

ELABORATION is the ability to expand or embellish on thoughts or ideas thus making them more exciting, complex, and/or unusual. Elaboration also can be used to clarify ideas. Elaborate thinkers are not necessarily original thinkers; they often begin with someone else's idea and add to it.

Sample activities:

1. Show the children a plain title page of a book. Ask them to make it more interesting.

2. Read a paragraph containing no adjectives. Ask the children to rewrite it using descriptive words.

3. Redesign your classroom for the year 2000.

AFFECTIVE SKILLS

Williams identifies four affective skills that need to be developed. These skills have to do with feelings, values, and motivations. The processes inherent in these skills prompt us to seek and use information. These skills are Risk Taking, Complexity, Curiosity, and Imagination.

Risk Taking

RISK TAKING involves courage. It requires opening oneself to others' views. It requires sharing ideas, expressing opinions, volunteering guesses — exposing oneself to others' criticism. If we want children to express themselves openly, it is essential that we create an environment where children value themselves and others and know that it is all right to make a mistake.

Sample activities:

1. You see your best friend shoplifting. What would you do?

2. This planet is no longer fit for habitation. You must choose ten out of fifteen people to escape from the planet. On what will you base your choices?

3. Discuss whether it is more important to be clever or honest.

Complexity

COMPLEXITY is the ability to examine a complicated situation or problem and see some order in it. It challenges an individual to find a variety of ways to approach situations.

Sample activities:

1. Create five rules that will help families get along together.

2. Suppose a giant footprint was discovered in your front yard. Speculate on how it might have gotten there and what might happen as a result of it.

3. School spirit is at an all-time low in your building. How might your class go about solving this problem?

Curiosity

CURIOSITY is the ability to question and inquire. It is a willingness to ask "who," "what," "when," "where," "why," and "how." Children need to be encouraged to puzzle and ponder. These questions fuel their imaginations and prompt them to investigate.

Sample activities:

1. Show a child a picture of someone smiling, laughing, or crying. Ask why the person in the picture might be reacting this way.

2. The punch line to the joke is "to get to the other side." What might the joke be?

3. Predict five things that will be obsolete in ten years.

Imagination

IMAGINATION is the ability to create new and unusual images and ideas, ideas not previously thought of. Imaginative people draw from the recesses of their minds. They dream the unimaginable.

Sample activities:

1. It's Halloween. Your jack-o'-lantern comes to life. Imagine what it might do and/or say and write a story about it.

2. Imagine a fairy tale character who "lived happily ever after." Write a story about this blissful existence.

3. The Town Mouse and the Country Mouse were bothered by the cat. Be creative. Design an imaginative way for them to rid themselves of the bothersome feline.

CRITICAL THINKING SKILLS

Williams identifies the following as the five Critical Thinking Skills: Planning, Communication, Forecasting, Decision Making, and Evaluation. These skills are included in the three highest levels of Bloom's Cognitive Taxonomy, that is, analysis, synthesis, and evaluation.

Planning

PLANNING is the ability to arrange the steps necessary in order to accomplish a task or achieve a particular outcome.

Sample activities:

1. Plan a dinner party for your class.

2. You want to serve cake at the party. Plan how to make a cake.

3. Plan activities for indoor recesses.

Planning requires lots of teacher assistance. Activities need to be broken down into small tasks. If the task at hand is to plan a Halloween party, the teacher might want to help the children divide this project into entertainment, refreshments, and decorations. The teacher must also assist students in listing the materials they will need and the order in which they should proceed to complete their project. It is important that children take time to analyze and list problems that might arise. Problem listing should also be teacher assisted. Lack of materials is not a valid problem; projects should not be planned for which supplies are not available. The Planning Worksheet in figure 2.1, page 10, can be used to facilitate a planning activity.

Communication

COMMUNICATION is the ability to express ourselves to others. Communication can be written, oral, or visual. It can be done through music, codes and ciphers, dance, oration, pantomime, or still pictures. It can be as simple as a nod or as complex as a lengthy story. We need to provide children with a variety of opportunities to express their thoughts, ideas, and feelings.

Sample activities:

1. One of your classmates is crying because his or her friends will not play. Explain how you can help that individual.

2. Another class put on a play for you. Write a thank you note to them.

3. Design an original product to sell to your classmates. Write and perform a cheer to entice them to buy it.

Forecasting

FORECASTING is the ability to predict, to foresee, or to speculate. Forecasting means examining "what if" situations. It involves predicting the possible cause and/or effect of a given situation. (Note that one need not be a result of the other.) Children should predict numerous causes and effects and then examine each prediction. After choosing the best cause and the best effect, they should be encouraged to give at least three reasons for their choices. The Forecasting Worksheet in figure 2.2, page 11, can be used for this activity.

(Text continues on page 12.)

Fig. 2.1

Planning Worksheet

Project/Activity _____

_____

Things we need:

1. _____   5. _____

2. _____   6. _____

3. _____   7. _____

4. _____   8. _____

Procedure:

1. _____

2. _____

3. _____

4. _____

5. _____

Problems we might have:

1. _____

2. _____

3. _____

4. _____

Fig. 2.2

Forecasting Worksheet

Statement or Situation

Causes	Effects

My best cause is _____

_____

_____

_____

_____

because:

_____

_____

_____

_____

_____

My best effect is _____

_____

_____

_____

_____

because:

_____

_____

_____

_____

_____

SCHOOL OF EDUCATION
CURRICULUM LABORATORY
UM-DEARBORN

Sample activities:

1. Suppose there were no trees. What might have caused this situation? What effect will it have?

2. What if it snowed for one month?

3. Read a picture book about a person. Speculate about what happened in the main character's life that makes the person act the way he or she does. Predict something the main character might do after the story ends.

Decision Making

DECISION MAKING is the ability to choose among alternatives. The process helps students eliminate alternatives and make choices. After identifying and stating a problem to be solved, Decision Making involves:

1. listing various alternatives or choices;

2. establishing criteria against which to judge the alternatives;

3. considering each choice and weighing it against established criteria;

4. making a decision or choice;

5. supporting or defending the final decision or choice.

The teacher may have to help children develop their criteria. Developing criteria may seem difficult at first. It helps to remind children that they base decisions on criteria every day. Each morning when they dress for school, they decide what to wear based on the criteria of what they will do that day. If they have physical education, they will wear more casual clothes than if they are to be in a special program. The weather is also a criteria for deciding what they will wear. Obviously they will dress differently during a winter storm than on a hot, sultry day. Teach the children to identify criteria by examining the decision to be made from all angles. Some factors to consider are: time, materials, safety, practicality, cost, whether you can do it, your parents' approval, and so forth. Use the Decision Making Worksheet in figure 2.3, page 14 to make decisions.

Sample activities:

1. You can go anywhere you like in the United States on a vacation. Where will you go? List some choices. While thinking about your choices, consider:
    a. climate
    b. distance from home
    c. places of interest
    d. cost to your family
    e. how long you want to be gone

2. If you could have any dog for a pet, which would it be and why? Think about the following questions:
    a. Do you like it?
    b. Can your parents afford it?
    c. Will it be easy to care for?
    d. Is it gentle?

SCHOOL OF EDUCATION
CURRICULUM LABORATORY
UM-DEARBORN

3. You get to select a musical instrument to learn how to play. List six instruments from which to choose. Consider the following criteria:

    a. cost of instrument

    b. difficulty to master

    c. popularity of instrument

    d. size of instrument

Evaluation

EVALUATION is the ability to appraise an idea's worth by examining the pros and cons. In order to avoid bias, both sides of the issue should have an equal number of points listed. When evaluating a topic remember to consider the issue from various viewpoints, differentiate between fact and opinion, and examine all aspects of the situation. The Evaluation Worksheet in figure 2.4, page 15, can be used for Evaluation activities.

Sample activities:

1. Evaluate the following statement: It is easier to be an adult than a child. Examine the advantages and disadvantages of being an adult and the advantages and disadvantages of being a child. Then make a concluding statement.

2. Debate the pros and cons of this statement: The school year should be eleven months long. What would be the advantages to this? What would be the disadvantages? Evaluate this issue from the points of view of the following people:

    a. teachers

    b. children

    c. parents

    d. administrators

Fig. 2.3

Decision Making Worksheet

A. Topic _____

_____

B. Alternatives or Solutions:

　　1. _____

　　2. _____

　　3. _____

　　4. _____

　　5. _____

C. Criteria:

　　1. _____

　　2. _____

　　3. _____

　　4. _____

D. Decision or Choice: _____

_____

_____

_____

E. I made my decision based on _____

_____

_____

_____

Fig. 2.4

Evaluation Worksheet

Topic/Issue: _____

_____

_____

_____

_____

Advantages (Pros)   Disadvantages (Cons)

1. _____   1. _____

   _____   _____

2. _____   2. _____

   _____   _____

3. _____   3. _____

   _____   _____

4. _____   4. _____

   _____   _____

Conclusion: After weighing both sides to this issue, I have decided _____

_____

_____

_____

_____

_____

CREATIVE PROBLEM SOLVING

The Creative Problem Solving process (CPS) was initially developed by Dr. Alex Osborne and Dr. Sidney Parnes.[2] The process, which combines higher level thinking skills and a variety of creative techniques, is designed to solve problems through creative thinking. The process can be used effectively with primary and intermediate level children to help them solve real life problems or generate imaginative endings for stories that they are writing. Children must be familiar with the rules for brainstorming if they are to use the CPS process effectively.

Remind the children that you are looking for a quantity of ideas, that judgments about answers or negative responses should never be made, that they should use others' answers to generate new ideas, and that even humorous and unusual ideas are welcome. With primary children each step of the problem solving process should be taught separately. Practice each step, moving slowly through the process. In the beginning, keep the problems simple. The entire process takes about one hour to complete.

Here is a simplified version of the Creative Problem Solving process for primary children:

A situation or problem is presented to the students.

Step 1:   *Fact Finding*

In this step children should ask who, what, why, when, and where type questions in order to learn important facts and details that will help them understand and solve the problem. Record questions and answers. Sample questions might be: Who is involved? What factors contributed to the problem? What resource might help solve the problem?

Step 2:   *Problem Identification*

In this step the children should clearly identify and define the problem to be solved. They should speculate about what the problem really is, examine it from several viewpoints and restate it until the statement accurately defines the problem. Their problem statements should include the who, what, when, where, and why that they established in Step 1. The problem should then be stated in a positive, solveable way. Problem statements that contain the word "not" are sometimes referred to as "knot" statements because they tie up the problem solving process. A good way to elicit positive problem statements is to turn them into questions using the IWWMW form—"In what way might we ...?" Stating problems as questions enables people to take creative steps to solve them.

Step 3:   *Idea Finding or Possible Solutions*

This step requires children to brainstorm to come up with numerous solutions to the problem. No judgments should be made during this step. Students should feel free to state their ideas. A grid can be used to list their solutions. The grid in figure 2.5 can be used for problem solving activities.

---

[2]Gary A. Davis and Sylvia B. Rimm, *Education of the Gifted and Talented* (Englewood Cliffs, N.J.: Prentice-Hall, 1985), 216-18.

Fig. 2.5

Problem Solving Grid

Problem:

Possible Solutions or Ideas	Criteria A	Criteria B	Criteria C	Criteria D	Total
1.					
2.					
3.					
4.					
5.					

Ratings: 3 = good solution

2 = fair solution

1 = poor solution

Step 4: *Solution Finding or Criteria Development*

At this point, younger children may need some assistance to develop criteria by which to evaluate their solutions. Criteria will vary according to the problem. The grid can help the children rate their solutions. With primary children happy faces can be used instead of numbers. List the criteria under A,B,C,D. List the solutions down the side with 1,2,3,4,5. You are now ready to weigh your solutions against your criteria. Be careful how you word this portion of the exercise or the children will try to make it a contest for their solutions to win. You are not pitting one solution against another. You are determining how each solution should be judged in relation to each criteria. Starting with Solution 1, move across the grid. Ask how Solution 1 should be rated on Criteria A, then B, then C, and so forth. Mark a rating of 1, 2, or 3 in each column. Then move to Solution 2 and take it across the grid. Total the ratings for each solution. The solution with the highest total wins.

Step 5: *Acceptance Finding or Plan of Action*

This step is particularly important when you are solving a real problem. The step is designed to help the children develop a plan of action by which to implement their solution. Children should outline the steps of the plan and identify resources who can help implement the plan. Problems that might arise should be discussed, as well as ways to cope with these problems. When children are using the problem solving process to develop an ending for a story, this step of the process can prove helpful to them as they generate ideas for their character's behavior throughout the story.

Sample Problem Solving Exercise

Situation: The noise level in the cafeteria is not acceptable.

1. *Fact Finding*

   Ask and record questions and answers.

   What do we know? Who is involved? When does it happen?

   All grade levels, one through five, are noisy.

   Two people currently supervise the lunchroom.

   Students and faculty agree this is a problem.

   Children like to visit while eating.

   Lunchtimes are staggered.

   Teachers have numerous duties.

2. *Problem Identification*

   What are the problems? Can they be ranked?

   Children are shouting.

   Duty teacher cannot get children to quiet down.

   Nobody enjoys lunch.

   Some children use bad manners.

   Teachers and children are upset.

What is the most important problem?

    There is too much noise in the cafeteria.

Restate the problem using the IWWMW form.

    In what way might we reduce the noise at lunchtime in the cafeteria so that everyone can enjoy eating?

3. *Idea Finding or Possible Solutions*

    Brainstorm as many ways as you can think of to solve the problem.

        Install stoplight that lights up to indicate noise level
            (red = too loud, yellow = fair, green = just right).

        Forbid talking.

        Have more lunchroom supervision.

        Ring bell when too noisy.

        Have children whisper.

        Dim lights to indicate noise level too high.

    After listing all the ideas, select the best ones. Circle them and list them on the grid under solutions.

4. *Solution Finding or Criteria Development*

    Establish criteria by which to judge your solutions. What criteria should be used?

        Is it costly?

        Is it harmful?

        Is it practical?

    Discuss each solution weighing it against each criteria. Rate each solution and put your rating in the boxes under each criteria.

Problem Solving Grid

Problem				
In what way might we reduce the noise at lunchtime in the cafeteria so that everyone can enjoy eating?				
Possible Solutions or Ideas	Criteria A Costly	Criteria B Harmful	Criteria C Practical	Total
1. Stoplight	1	3	2	6
2. Supervision	1	3	2	6
3. Whisper	3	2	1	6
4. Forbid talking	3	2	2	7
5. Dim lights	3	3	3	9

Ratings: 3 = good solution
             2 = fair solution
             1 = poor solution

5. *Plan of Action*

How will you implement your plan? What steps will you follow? Who can help?

Step 1: The principal will visit with students during an assembly and explain new procedure.

Step 2: Parents will be informed in writing of the new procedure.

Step 3: Cafeteria cooks will be informed of new procedure.

What problems might occur? How will these problems be overcome?

Problem	Solution
Students might object	Expect them to eat elsewhere
Students might not recognize proper volume	Model table conversation tone
Parents might object	Request that they supervise lunchroom
Students might continue noise	Try new solution

CONCLUSION

It is important to understand that for purposes of explanation, each skill in the "Think Bank" has been presented individually. In fact, the skills overlap. While inventing a new product an individual would no doubt be using the creative skills of originality and complexity, as well as the critical thinking skills of planning and communication.

The skills must be introduced gradually to avoid confusing or overwhelming the children. Begin with simple tasks and topics, progressing as the children demonstrate that they are ready for something more complex. Above all, remember that these are learnable skills that can be improved with practice.

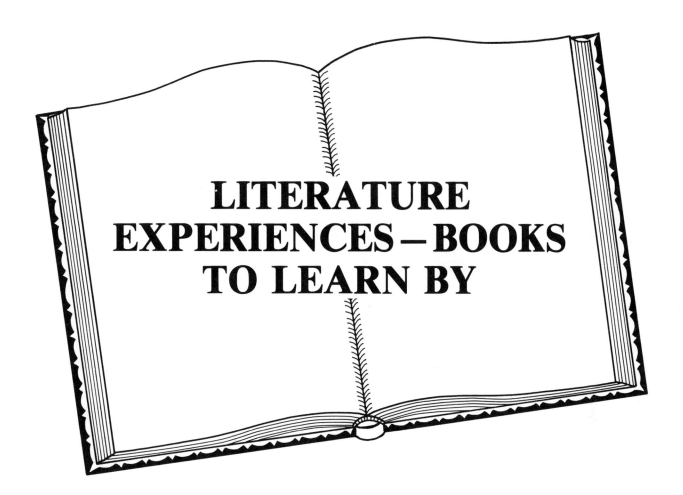

LITERATURE EXPERIENCES – BOOKS TO LEARN BY

Amigo

Byrd Baylor Schweitzer. New York: Macmillan Co., 1963.

SUMMARY

Francisco, a young Spanish boy, is lonely. More than anything, he longs for a dog. Because his parents are so poor, they explain that there are already too many mouths to feed and Francisco cannot have a dog. His mother jokingly suggests he tame a prairie dog. Simultaneously, a young prairie dog tells his family that he wants to tame a boy. In rich, poetic verse, the author colorfully describes the Southwest and tenderly shows how a boy and a prairie dog become best friends.

Possible Student Outcomes

Expand reading vocabulary.

Identify similes and metaphors.

Use descriptive words to describe a setting.

Infer the relationships that exist among the characters in the story.

Practice the thinking skills of evaluation, forecasting, fluency, flexibility, complexity, risk taking, and decision making.

** *CHOOSE A LIMITED NUMBER OF ACTIVITIES FROM EACH SECTION* **

Before Reading Activities

1. Have the children examine the book's cover. Ask them what they know about the boy from this picture and why they think that. Ask them if they know what kind of an animal the boy is looking at.

2. Have the children look at the frontispiece. Ask them where this story might take place. Ask what clues tell them this. Discuss how the area resembles or is different from the area where they live. Ask them what is following the boy. Ask what other animals they might expect to see in this area.

3. Discuss the book's title, *Amigo*. Ask what the word *amigo* means (friend). Put the word and its meaning on the chalkboard. Ask the children if they know which language this word is from. Ask the children if they know any other Spanish words. If so, list them on the board. Ask the children who they think Amigo might be. Ask why they think this. Ask the children to explain what they think this book is about.

4. Put the following vocabulary words from the story on the chalkboard:

guitar	gaze	burrows
strums	scampered	whistle
hound	coyote	nestled
cactus	prairie dog	mesquite
frowned	tame	

Read the words aloud to the children. Let them read the words with you. Use knowledge rating[1] to determine how much they know about these words. Have the children put the headings Have Seen, Have Heard, and Can Explain on a piece of paper. Have the children place the words from the board under the appropriate heading. Have them analyze what they know about the words and then discuss which words are the hardest for them, the easiest, and which most children will know. Let them predict how the author will use the words in this story. Have them categorize the words. (Some categories might be plants, animals, action words, or verbs.) Ask the children what they think the word *whistle* refers to in this story. Have them explain their answer. Let the children use the vocabulary words they know to predict what this story might be about.

Predicting Activities

1. Have the children read to the end of page 1. Francisco is sad. Have the children speculate about why he is so unhappy.

2. Have the children read to page 5, where Francisco's mother suggests he get a pet that is "small and wild and can feed itself." Have the children give examples of animals that might meet those criteria. The choices should be appropriate for the Southwest where the story takes place.

3. Have the children stop reading after the first paragraph on page 11. Francisco's mother asks, "How do you tame a prairie dog, a thing that's wild?" Ask the children how they might go about taming a prairie dog. Encourage them to discuss what they would do and how they would act if they were trying to do this. Write their suggestions on the chalkboard. After the children read through page 14, see if any of their suggestions match the author's.

4. Have the children read through page 17, where the author says, "But you still don't know— Though you very soon will—what creature was hiding—behind that hill...." Ask the children what they think the creature is. Ask why they think that.

5. Have the children stop reading at the end of page 30. Amigo is wondering how to tame the boy. Ask the children how they think he will proceed. Ask why they think that.

6. Have the children read to the end of the story.

Post Reading Activities

1. Francisco is a Spanish name for Frank. See how many children's names can be translated to Spanish. Perhaps those children whose names do not translate would like to adopt a Spanish name.

2. On page 3, Francisco says he wants a dog, a hound. Discuss what a hound is. Pictures of hounds can be found in most encyclopedias.

---

[1]The idea for this knowledge rating activity was taken from Camille L. Z. Blachowicz's article "Making Connections: Alternatives to the Vocabulary Notebook," *Journal of Reading* (April 1986): 645-46.

3. The author uses a great many similes in this story. On page 9, she says a prairie dog is "more like a ground squirrel or a mouse or a bunny than a dog...." Have the children locate other similes and metaphors in the story. Then have them use similes to describe the desert, a cactus, mountains, a prairie dog, a town.

4. Ask the children what both Francisco's father and Amigo's mother felt was the main ingredient for taming a prairie dog or taming a boy. Ask the children to explain why love is important in healthy relationships. Discuss how love manifests itself in this story and how it can manifest itself in the children's relationships.

5. Poets paint pictures with words. The author uses sound words (jabbered, shrill), hurry up words (jumped, hopped), soft words (rustle, whisper), gentle words (dreaming, wispy). Put headings for the different kinds of words the author uses on the chalkboard. Have the children locate the words in the story that go under the different headings. (Not all children will agree with each others' placement. The children should be able to justify placement by using the word appropriately in a sentence.)

6. Use this text to teach the correct use of quotation marks. Select a page from the text. Pages 9, 10, 24, 26, and 27 have clearly defined dialogue. Duplicate the page leaving out the quotation marks. Let the children put quotation marks in the correct places. A variation of this activity is to have the children locate the quotation marks in the story and explain why those passages are in quotation marks.

7. Ask the children what this story is really about (friendship). Other books about children making friends with animals are:

   Daugherty, James. *Andy and the Lion*. New York: Viking Press, 1938.

   de Paola, Tomie. *The Knight and the Dragon*. New York: G. P. Putnam's Sons, 1980.

   Galdone, Paul. *Androcles and the Lion*. Adaptation. New York: McGraw-Hill, 1970.

   Rylant, Cynthia. *Henry and Mudge*. New York: Bradbury Press, 1987.

8. Have the children discuss how Amigo and Francisco are alike and how they are different.

9. The author uses many words that end in *-ing*. Have the children pick out all the *-ing* words in the story. Place the words on the chalkboard or list them on a worksheet. Some follow-up activities might be:
   a. Have the children circle the root words.
   b. Have them underline the words that do not need to be changed in order to add the *-ing*.
   c. Have the children analyze the words and classify them by those that double the ending consonant, those that drop the *e* before adding the *-ing*, those that do not change.
   d. Have the children write sentences using these words.

Thinking Activities

1. (FLEXIBILITY, EVALUATION) On page 4, Francisco says he seldom thinks about the things he has to do without. He concentrates on what he has. Discuss the things Francisco has and the things he does not have. Have the children use the Evaluation Worksheet on page 15 to make a list of "Things I Have" and "Things I Wish I Had." Have them analyze their lists. Categorize the items on their lists. Discuss the items that meet material needs, emotional needs. Ask the children which are the most important and why. (Answers will vary.)

2. (EVALUATION) On page 7, Francisco evaluates some of the desert animals and states why he does not want them for a pet. Have the children use the other animals in the story and the

animals you identify in Et Cetera Activity 4 (page 28) to examine the advantages and disadvantages of having each animal for a pet. Use the Evaluation Worksheet on page 15.

3. (EVALUATION) Have the children evaluate the pros and cons of living in the Southwestern part of the United States. Use the Evaluation Worksheet on page 15.

4. (FORECASTING) Some people have more difficulty than others making friends. Have the children use the Forecasting Worksheet on page 11 to look at causes and effects of either of the following statements: "You have lots of friends" or "You do not have lots of friends." This activity can be done together as a class or individually.

5. (FLUENCY, FLEXIBILITY) This book is filled with rich, colorful language. Have the children brainstorm additional colorful words that describe the Southwest. These words can be used in Thinking Activity 6 (which follows).

6. (FLEXIBILITY) The author does a marvelous job of painting a picture of the Southwest, by choosing words that are descriptive of this area. Have the children select an area of the United States with which they are familiar. Have them generate words that describe this area, for example, sound words, color words, or action words. Have them paint a word picture of their area by making scenery out of words (see figure 3.1). An alternative would be to have them paint an object using words, for example, cactus words, rock words.

Fig. 3.1

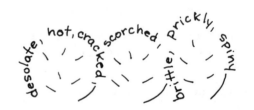

7. (FLEXIBILITY) On page 22, the author speaks of quiet sounds. She says quiet sounds are the "whisper of quail," "earthworms walking underground." Have the children create other phrases that describe quiet sounds.

8. (DECISION MAKING) On page 41, Amigo says "Mine is the *best* pet. I've tamed me a boy." Have the children use the Decision Making Worksheet on page 14 to decide which is the best pet. This can be an individual or group activity. (See Writing Activity 2 on page 27.)

9. (EVALUATION) The theme of this story is similar to the theme in Marie Hall Ets's *Play with Me* (New York: Viking Penguin, 1955). Have the children compare and contrast the two stories. Use the Evaluation Worksheet on page 15.

10. (COMPLEXITY, RISK TAKING) Analyze the reasons why Amigo and Francisco became good friends. Have the children relate their findings to their own friendships. Ask what they can learn from the relationships in the story.

Writing Activities

1. The author uses lots of sound words in this rhyming story. Have the children write a poem using sound words to describe a scene or happening. For example:

The Tom Cat

Howling, prowling
Looking for fun.
He spies his prey
Breaks into a run.

Swiftly he lunges
They roll and they yowl,
They scratch and tear
They spit and howl

Their growls can be
Heard in the still of the night
Which one will win this terrible fight?

2. Have the children write a story about the pet that they chose as the "best pet" in Thinking Activity 8 (page 26). Encourage them to use colorful language and paint pictures with their words rather than just stating facts about their animal. One way to help them plan their story might be:

   a. After they select their animal, have them brainstorm words that describe it, e.g., color words, sound words, movement words.

   b. Have them write metaphors and similes describing their animal.

   c. Have them decide on a problem their animal might have.

   d. Have them decide how the animal might solve their problem. They might want to use the Problem Solving Grid on page 17.

3. Have the children compose additional stanzas to the song that Francisco's father sings on page 1 of the story.

4. The first half of this book is written from Francisco's point of view. The second half is written from Amigo's point of view. Suggest that the children write a story from two different points of view, e.g., child/animal, parent/child, friend/friend, teacher/child.

5. Have the children research prairie dogs. Four resources to use are:

   > Alibert-Kouraguine, Daniel. *Nature's Hidden World: Prairie Dwellers*. Morristown, N.J.: Silver Burdett, 1982.
   >
   > Casey, Denise. *The Friendly Prairie Dog*. New York: Dodd, Mead, 1987.
   >
   > Eberle, Irmengarde. *Prairie Dogs in Prairie Dog Town*. New York: Thomas Y. Crowell, 1974.
   >
   > *Prairie Animals*. Chicago: Encyclopaedia Britannica, 1979.

   Using the information they find, have the children write and illustrate a story about prairie dogs. The story could be either fiction or nonfiction. One approach might be to suggest that they write a parallel plot story by dividing the page in half and having them depict life underground in Prairie Dog Town and life above ground on the prairie.

6. Byrd Baylor Schweitzer writes the story in rhyme. Have the children rewrite the story in prose.

Et Cetera Activities

1. (Choral Reading) The poetic language in this text lends itself to choral reading. The following parts need to be represented by individuals or groups.

Mother	Father
narrator	Francisco
Amigo	Amigo's mother
First Prairie Dog	aunt/uncles/cousins

    Group the children by low, medium, and high voices for the most effective reading.

2. (Art) Garth Williams's soft illustrations enhance the text. Have the children select a favorite passage from the book and draw a picture with pastels illustrating the passage.

3. (Science) Have the children plant a prairie scene in a large wooden or metal box in the classroom or have each child plant an individual prairie plant in a milk carton. Prairie seed plants can be obtained from the following sources: Applewood Seed Co., 5380 Vivian, Arvada, CO 80002; Arkansas Valley Seed, 4625 Colorado Blvd., Denver, CO 80216.

4. (Science) Francisco's mother tries to help him decide on another type of pet. She mentions several animals that live in the desert valleys and mountains, for example, birds, wildcats, tortoises, lizards, quail, coyotes, and frogs. Have the children research other animals that live in this area. Make a large map. Color in the areas that would be considered southwestern states where the flora and fauna described in this story live, i.e., western Colorado, Utah, Arizona, Texas, New Mexico, Nevada, and southeastern California. Have the children make small three-dimensional animals or tagboard animals that represent the animals that live in this area. Have them place their animals on the map.

5. (Poetry) Have the children learn the poem "Prairie-Dog Town." This poem can be found in *Time for Poetry* (May Hill Arbuthnot, comp. Chicago: Scott, Foresman, 1959).

6. (Art Appreciation) Like Byrd Baylor Schweitzer, the well-known southwestern artist Ted De Grazia loves and appreciates the harsh landscapes of the Sonoran desert. His parents were Italians who moved to Morenci, Arizona, where De Grazia was born and reared. For him "the desert was a thing of inestimable beauty, a flowing form of color, silent-sounds, and delicate movement," says his biographer William Reed. His love and appreciation of the desert Southwest is evident in his work. Show the children his painting called *Flower Boy*. Let them compare and contrast De Grazia's interpretation and painting of a Mexican child with the illustrations in *Amigo*. Discuss with them how Byrd Baylor Schweitzer uses words to describe the boy in the story whereas De Grazia uses color. Ask them if De Grazia's painting would have enhanced or detracted from this story. This painting as well as biographical information about De Grazia can be found in the book *De Grazia, the Reverent Angel* by William Reed (San Diego, Calif.: Frontier Heritage Press, 1971).

The Author Says ...

Byrd Baylor Schweitzer (1924-) was born in San Antonio, Texas. A private person, she does not particularly like to answer biographical questions. She does, however, like to talk to children about the writing process, and, when given the opportunity, she shares with them the books she has written—not so much as models for their writing, but as an illustration of the importance of writing from one's own experiences. Children should write about the things they know, the things they love. Then she says, "the words flow more easily."

Schweitzer follows her own advice. Nearly all of her work is set in the Southwest. As a child growing up on Texas ranches, she developed an appreciation for the harsh beauty of the plant and animal life. It was in this rough, dry land, watching the prairie dogs scamper about in their towns, that she conceived the idea for *Amigo*. In its original form, *Amigo* was written as two stories. Francisco's and Amigo's stories were told independently, one on the top of the page, the other on the bottom. Her publisher rejected that idea, and so she rewrote the story as we know it. Like Francisco, Schweitzer's father was a miner searching the Arizona and Mexican landscape for gold, copper, and silver.

In the *Fourth Book of Junior Authors and Illustrators*,[2] Schweitzer confesses, somewhat apologetically, that she really does not think about her audience when she begins writing. Instead she writes about experiences that excite her and treasures she holds dear. Unearthing a shattered Indian pot, discovering a turquoise bead, finding an arrowhead—these are her treasures. In *I'm in Charge of Celebrations* (New York: Macmillan Co., 1986), she describes moments she finds unforgettable—the time she saw a triple rainbow and the day she chanced upon a coyote "trotting through the bush." It was a special moment granted to her, which she now refers to as Coyote Day.

As a child, she kept a diary, which she liked to read and reread. She also enjoyed reading Rudyard Kipling's *Just So Stories*.

I asked her how the writing process works for her. When writing *Amigo* did she begin by brainstorming words describing prairie dogs and the desert setting? She said she simply began with a core idea and then the words started flowing. She does not plan her stories in her mind before she writes.

Her advice to teachers who are guiding elementary children as they learn the writing process is "Make writing fun."

Amigo is written in rhyme. I asked her if she felt children should be encouraged to write rhyme, and her answer was a definite "No." "Rhyme is much too difficult for children, other than an occasional nonsensical verse."

She does not write every day; however, when she is working on an idea, she may write day and night.

Author Activities

1. Byrd Baylor Schweitzer grew up in the Southwest. All of her books take place in this dry, desert area, which she obviously loves and appreciates. Have the children write a story set in the area of the country where they live.

2. Several of Schweitzer's books were Caldecott Honor Books: *When Clay Sings* (New York: Scribner's, 1972); *The Desert Is Theirs* (New York: Charles Scribner's Sons, 1975); *Hawk, I'm Your Brother* (New York: Charles Scribner's Sons, 1976). Explain that the Caldecott Award is given annually for outstanding artwork in children's picture books. You might want to show the filmstrip "The Man behind the Medal," available from Weston Woods, Weston, CT 06883-1199. Bookmarks containing a brief history of the Caldecott Award and a list of all past award recipients and Medalist and Honor Books can be purchased from The Children's Book Council, Inc., 350 Scotland Road, Orange, NJ 07050. After discussing the Caldecott Award, have the children read other Caldecott Honor Books and compare and contrast them to Schweitzer's books.

---

[2]Doris De Montreville and Elizabeth D. Crawford, eds., *Fourth Book of Junior Authors and Illustrators* (New York: H. W. Wilson, 1978), 31.

BIBLIOGRAPHY

Other books by Byrd Baylor Schweitzer for grades 1 through 3.

The Best Town in the World. New York: Macmillan Co., 1983. (RL 3   IL 2-5)

Everybody Needs a Rock. New York: Macmillan Co., 1974. (RL 2   IL 1-5)

I'm in Charge of Celebrations. New York: Macmillan Co., 1986. (RL 3   IL 3-5)

The Other Way to Listen. New York: Macmillan Co., 1978. (RL 3   IL 3-5)

The Way to Start a Day. New York: Macmillan Co., 1986. (RL 3   IL 3-5)

Your Own Best Secret Place. New York: Macmillan Co., 1979. (RL 3   IL 3-5)

Amos and Boris

William Steig. New York: Farrar, Straus and Giroux, 1971.

SUMMARY

Amos, a tiny mouse, loves the sea. One day he builds a boat, stocks it with supplies, and sets sail. One thousand miles from home, while lying on the deck dreaming about the beauty and splendor of the night sky, he accidently tumbles overboard. Floundering in the sea, frightened and cold, he is about to give up hope when Boris, a sperm whale, surfaces and offers to rescue him. The two mammals become beloved friends each vowing to help the other in time of need. Many years pass and the two friends go about their separate lives. One day, a terrible hurricane washes Boris upon the shore where Amos lives. Amos quickly spots his friend and, with the aid of two elephants, pushes him back into the sea.

Possible Student Outcomes

Expand reading vocabulary.

Recognize and interpret descriptive words and phrases.

Compare and contrast two or more selections in terms of similarity of theme, characters, setting, author's writing style.

Practice the thinking skills of fluency, flexibility, complexity, forecasting, planning, imagination, and evaluation.

** CHOOSE A LIMITED NUMBER OF ACTIVITIES FROM EACH SECTION **

Before Reading Activities

1. Have the children examine the book's cover and title page. Ask them what they would like to know about these pictures or about what is going to happen in the story. Questions that might elicit student questions are: Which character is Boris, Amos? What is the mouse doing in the boat? Where is he sailing? How does he get on the whale? Where is the boat?

2. Put the following vocabulary words from the story on the chalkboard:

backwashes	akin
surf	phosphorescent
navigation	bowling
sextant	driftwood
savage	treading
rodent	sound
breakers	mote
plankton	whale

   Use each word in three simple sentences to show their meaning. For example:

   Boris liked to sound, which means he liked to dive deep underwater.

   When Boris would sound, or dive underwater, Amos would fall off his back.

   Whales enjoy going underwater, which is called sound(ing).

   Ask the children to write a question or statement from their own experience that would further explain the meaning of the words. For example:

   If I were riding on a whale's back, I would jump off when the whale started to sound.

   I would not like to be riding on a whale when it sound(ed) because I might get a mouthful of salt water.

3. Put the word *sea* on the chalkboard. Have the children brainstorm words that they associate with the sea. List the words on the chalkboard. Discuss the words and place them in clusters or categories on a semantic map. Have the children label each category. Read the story and have the children identify sea words that the author uses. Add these to the list.

4. If the children have had very little background experience to help them understand the setting of this story, a filmstrip could be shown to set the stage. A set of two filmstrips about shore and ocean life that would help the children understand the author's description of the sea is "Life in the Sea" by the National Geographic Society (Washington, D.C.: National Geographic Society, 1978).

Predicting Activities

1. Have the children stop reading at the end of page 9.[1] Ask them what they think will become of Amos now that he has fallen into the sea.

2. Have the children read through page 20. Ask the children to predict what will happen if Boris takes Amos all the way to land.

---

[1]Pagination begins with the title page of the text.

SCHOOL OF EDUCATION
CURRICULUM LABORATORY
UM-DEARBORN

3. After the children have read to the middle of page 20, where Boris bids Amos farewell, ask them to predict what might happen. Ask why they think this.

4. Have the children read to the end of the story. Have them predict whether the two friends will ever see each other again.

Post Reading Activities

1. On page 3, the author says Amos loved the ocean. Have the children discuss what they love about where they live; what they do not love.

2. Once Amos decided to set sail, he worked on his boat and studied navigation. Ask the children what his behavior tells about him. Ask them if they have ever wanted something that they worked very hard for. Have them explain.

3. On page 15, Boris says he "would consider it a privilege" to take Amos home. Have the children explain what he means. Discuss other things that are a privilege.

4. On page 19, the author says Amos missed "fresh unsalty water." Ask the children to explain why he could not drink salt water.

5. The author uses extremely descriptive language in this book. Make tagboard fish shapes as shown in figure 4.1. Put one vocabulary word from the story on each fish. Glue tiny magnets to the back of each fish. Place the fish in a glass fishbowl or tank. (The tank needs to be large enough to spread the fish out to prevent the magnets from sticking to each other.) Make a fishing pole using a dowel and string. Using a paper clip for a hook, let the children fish for words and use their words in oral or written sentences.

Fig. 4.1

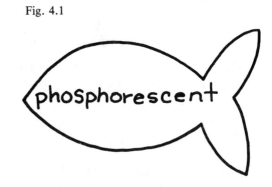

A variation of this activity would be to have the children place their tagboard fish on a chart containing the definitions as in figure 4.2.

Fig. 4.2

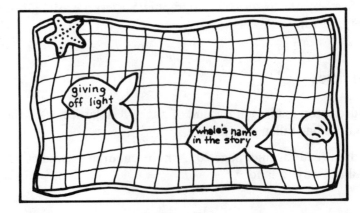

6. As a vocabulary building activity, have the children complete the crossword puzzle in figure 4.3.

Fig. 4.3. *Amos and Boris* Crossword Puzzle

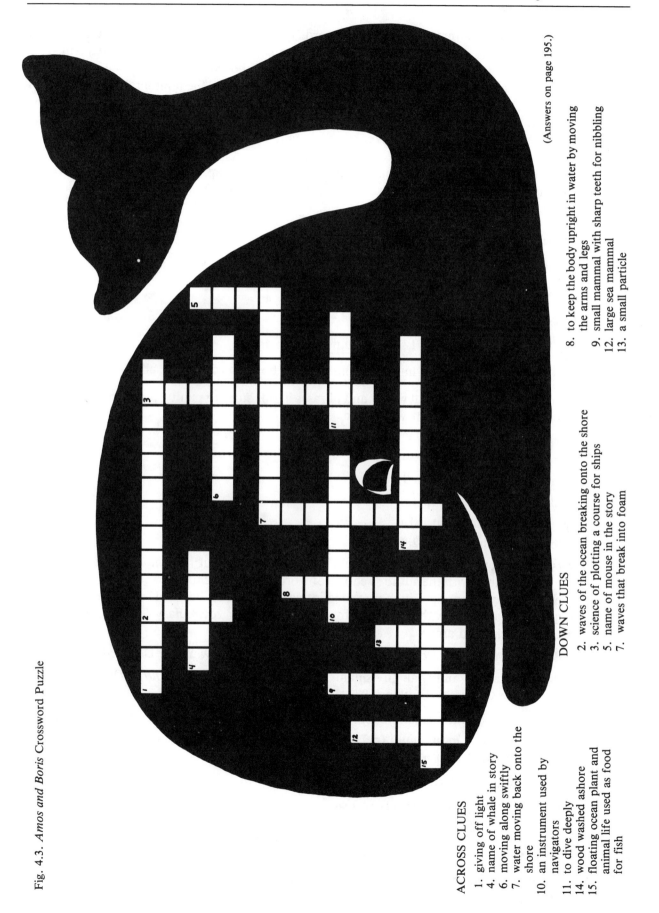

(Answers on page 195.)

ACROSS CLUES

1. giving off light
4. name of whale in story
6. moving along swiftly
7. water moving back onto the shore
10. an instrument used by navigators
11. to dive deeply
14. wood washed ashore
15. floating ocean plant and animal life used as food for fish

DOWN CLUES

2. waves of the ocean breaking onto the shore
3. science of plotting a course for ships
5. name of mouse in the story
7. waves that break into foam
8. to keep the body upright in water by moving the arms and legs
9. small mammal with sharp teeth for nibbling
12. large sea mammal
13. a small particle

7. In this story there are many homographs (words that are spelled the same but have different meanings). Ask the children to locate as many homographs as they can and explain their different meanings. Or write the homographs on the chalkboard and have the children look up the various meanings in the dictionary. The children could write the homographs on a piece of paper. Using their dictionary to find the meanings of the words as they appear in the story, the children could place the number of the correct dictionary meaning beside the word. Several homographs in the story are: breaker, surf, sound, whale, tread, suited, immensely, enterprise, bowling, and mind.

   A variation of this activity would be to write the homographs in sentences demonstrating the multiple meanings of the words. Discuss the different meanings in these sentences.

   A breaker was washed ashore by a breaker.

   The boy liked to surf on the surf.

   The scientist's job was to sound the sea where he saw a whale sound.

   The whale looked like it had been whale(d).

   As the man began to tread water, he wished he could tread on dry ground.

   My mind tells me that I should mind my manners.

   The man threw his bowling ball and it went bowling down the alley.

8. The author uses many colorful words and phrases in this story to paint a picture for the reader. Discuss the author's choice of words. For example:

   "savage strength" (p.6)

   "phosphorescent sea" (p.9)

   "immense, starry sky" (p.9)

   "dreadful questions" (p.13)

   "gemlike radiance" (p.18)

   "breaded with sand" (p.28)

Discuss other words that the author might have used. Point out how much more vividly the scenes are described with the author's choice of words. Give the children some simple sentences and let them dress them up using more descriptive language. A thesaurus could be introduced to acquaint the children with a resource for broadening their vocabulary. Two thesauruses for primary level children are:

   Bellamy, John. *The Doubleday Children's Thesaurus*. New York: Doubleday, 1987.

   Wittels, Harriet, and Joan Greisman. *The Clear and Simple Thesaurus Dictionary*. New York: Grosset & Dunlap, 1971.

9. The author uses several metaphors and similes. Have the children locate these. For example:

   "waves as big as mountains" (p.7)

   "mountain of a whale" (p.25)

   "mote of a mouse" (p.25)

Let the children make other comparisons.

Thinking Activities

1. (FLEXIBILITY) Have the children list words that describe a setting different from the story setting. Use these words in Writing Activity 1 (page 35).

2. (COMPLEXITY) On page 5, the author lists the supplies Amos loaded on his ship. Ask the children why he took water when he was surrounded by water. Discuss how the supplies might have varied if he had been going on a safari in Africa, a camping trip in the mountains, or an excursion to the Antarctic. Have the children list the factors that should be considered when planning any excursion.

3. (FORECASTING) Have the children use the Forecasting Worksheet on page 11 to forecast the effects of life without whales, without mice.

4. (PLANNING) Have the children plan other ways that Amos might have saved Boris.

5. (IMAGINATION) Sometimes whales do wash up on the shore and become stranded. Have the children invent a way to carry beached whales back to water safely.

6. (FLUENCY) Boris and Amos were both mammals. Let the children brainstorm to come up with as many mammals as they can.

7. (COMPLEXITY) Amos was stranded in the ocean. Have the children make a list of items they would need in order to survive in another hazardous situation, for example, in the mountains, in the desert.

8. (EVALUATION) Have the children use the Evaluation Worksheet on page 15 to compare and contrast this story with the fable *The Lion and the Mouse*. Discuss the theme of helping others even if you are small. Ask the children to describe situations where they have or could have helped someone older than themselves.

Writing Activities

1. The author describes the setting on page 3. Have the children use this story beginning to create a new story[2] in a different setting.

> Amos, a _____, lived by the _____.
> He loved the _____. He loved the
> smell of _____. He loved to hear
> the _____, the _____, and
> the _____.

Use the words the children listed in Thinking Activity 1 (page 34).

2. The two friends in the story missed each other a great deal. Have the children write a letter as though they were either the whale or the mouse telling each other how they feel and how they are passing their time. Ask them to be creative in thinking how they might get their letters to each other, for example, in a bottle, on a raft, or using a seagull as a messenger.

3. If a whale washed up on the shore, it would be a newsworthy event. Have the children pretend that they are newspaper reporters covering this event. Have them write a newspaper article and give it a headline.

4. One literary device that authors use is stating their main idea in the first sentence and then developing that idea in the following sentences. William Steig uses this device several times in this story. On page 19, his first sentence is: "They became the closest possible friends." He then supports that statement with details about their friendship. Have the children write that sentence on their paper and then write a paragraph giving details to support how close friends act.

---

[2]The idea for a story frame was taken from G. L. Fowler's "Developing Comprehension Skills in Primary Grades through the Use of Story Frames," *The Reading Teacher* 36 (2): 176-79.

5. Have the children do research about whales and write a nonfiction book about them. Their book might include: Types of whales (baleen, toothed), Parts of whales, History of whaling, Facts about whales, Glossary of whale terms.

Et Cetera Activities

1. (Science) On page 6, Amos launched his boat at high tide. Discuss what is meant by high and low tide. Have the children explain why Amos waited until high tide to launch. Explain what causes tides.

2. (Science) Some species of whales are nearly extinct (the blue whale, the bowhead, the right whale). For a minimum fee, students can adopt a whale. Funds raised by this project help support educational programs that provide students with information about whales. In addition, the funds help support research that is aimed at making the sea a safer place for all marine animals. For information about how your class can adopt a whale, write to: Whale Adoption Project, International Wildlife Coalition, 320 Gifford Street, Falmouth, MA 02540.

3. (Math) Amos said he was 1,000 miles from home when he fell overboard. How many nautical miles is that? It took Boris one week to get Amos home. Approximately how many miles a day did they travel? Explain the difference between a mile and a nautical mile (mile = 5,280 feet; nautical mile = 6,080 feet).

4. (Social Studies) Boris says that whales from the seven seas are going to a meeting on the Ivory Coast of Africa. Use a world map to locate the seven seas.

5. (Science) On page 13, Amos and Boris explain that they are both mammals. Make a chart that lists the characteristics of mammals or the differences between whales and fish. One source to use is *A First Look at Whales* by Millicent E. Selsam and Joyce Hunt (New York: Walker and Company, 1980).

6. (Art) Have the children fold a large piece of heavy paper in half. Draw and cut out the shape of a sea animal. Staple the paper in two or three places to prevent slipping. Using a large needle threaded with yarn, have the students whip around the outside edges of the silhouette. Stitches should be 1/4" to 1/2" apart. As they sew, have them stuff the animal with crumpled newspaper, paper towels, or tissue. See figure 4.4. Then have them paint the animals with tempera paint and hang them in the classroom.

Fig. 4.4

7. (Science) Boris is a sperm whale. Have the children research the characteristics of sperm whales and make three to five sentence strips telling important facts about these whales.

8. (Art) Have the children use crayons to draw a sperm whale swimming in the ocean. (Have them press the crayons hard to make solid lines for the best effect.) Encourage them to put some plankton and other underwater sea life in their picture. After they complete their crayon drawing, have them use blue watercolor to paint over the crayon. The watercolor does not adhere to the crayon and makes an interesting underwater effect. The sentence strips made in Et Cetera Activity 7 above can be hung from these pictures, as shown in figure 4.5.

Fig. 4.5

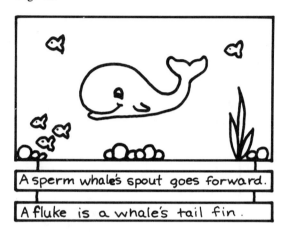

A sperm whale's spout goes forward.

A fluke is a whale's tail fin.

9. (Art) Have the children make a push-up Amos and Boris. Use tagboard to cut two whale shapes as in figure 4.6, page 38. Cut out a tagboard mouse on a long tab as in figure 4.7 (page 38). Color the whale and mouse. Cut a slit in the front whale piece. Slip the mouse tab down into the slit from the back. Glue the sides of the whale together leaving enough edge unglued to allow the mouse to move up and down on the whale's back.

10. (Social Studies) The author gives several clues as to where Amos fell overboard. Help the children locate the clues (Amos had traveled 1,000 miles; Boris offered to take him to the Ivory Coast of Africa; Elephants were quickly available to push Boris back into the sea; Amos lived on the coast). Have the children use a map of Africa and the clues to determine where Amos may have fallen into the ocean.

11. (Art Appreciation) Paintings of the sea are called seascapes. One well-known painter of seascapes is Winslow Homer (1836-1910) who was born in Boston, Massachusetts. Homer's family was always connected with the sea, for the most part as merchants buying and selling goods that sea captains brought from distant shores. Homer's painting *Summer Squall* (1904) is reminiscent of the storm that might have washed Boris ashore. Homer painted this picture over a two-week period and then put it away for eight years, at which time he felt inspired to finish it. This painting can be found in *The World of Winslow Homer* by James Thomas Flexner and the Editors of Time-Life Books (New York: Time Incorporated, 1966). The illustration at the end of the story where Boris washes up on the beach is very similar to Claude Monet's painting called *Boats on a Beach*. Monet was fascinated by the effects of light on his subjects and techniques for painting light. Much of his work is of the outdoors. For a time his studio was a boat and he painted scenes capturing nature reflecting in the water. The painting mentioned here can be found in *The Shorewood Art Reference Guide* by Matila Simon (New York: Shorewood Reproductions, 1970).

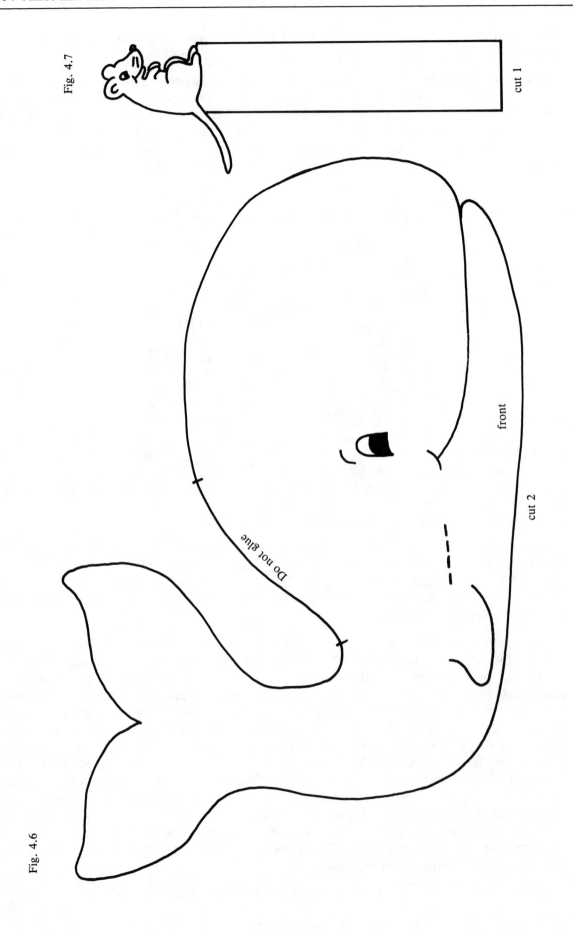

Fig. 4.7

cut 1

front

cut 2

Do not glue

Fig. 4.6

The Author Says ...

William Steig (1907-) was born in New York City. His artistic ability apparently comes naturally; both of his parents were artists, as are his three brothers, Irwin, Henry, and Arthur. Steig grew up in Manhattan and attended P.S. 53 in the Bronx. His intense interest in painting and drawing began at an early age. This prompted his oldest brother, Irwin, himself a professional artist, to begin instructing William.

In high school, Steig was an all-around athlete and while attending City College in New York, he was a member of the All-American Water Polo Team. After leaving City College, he continued his studies at New York's National School of Design.

At twenty-three, he was a cartoonist for *Life* and *Judge* magazines and later for *The New Yorker, Vanity Fair*, and others. He says that his career as a children's writer and illustrator did not begin until 1968 when his friend and publisher, Bob Kraus, of Windmill Books, convinced him that he could "make a contribution to this field." His first children's book was *C D B!* (New York: Farrar, Straus and Giroux, 1968). Since then he has written over twenty-three books for children.[3]

When asked how he begins a story, he said that after he decides it is time to write a new book, he usually begins with an idea or visual image. He then decides which animal will portray his main character and then lets the idea ramble around in his head until he discovers what will happen in the story. Steig says, "It's only when you're consciously aware of what you're doing in a book that you're in trouble." The idea for *Amos and Boris* was sparked by the image of two elephants pushing a whale into the sea. *Roland the Minstrel Pig* (New York: Harper & Row, 1968) began with the image of a pig hanging on a string. Only once did he begin with a theme in mind and that was in his book *The Real Thief* (New York: Farrar, Straus and Giroux, 1973). Here he wanted to portray a child as a victim of injustice. Despite the fact that Steig does not set out to develop a particular theme, more often than not one or two themes emerge in his work. Perhaps this is a result of his firm belief that children desperately need and want "secure, devoted families and able friends." *Amos and Boris* is the first of many of his books dealing with friendship. The strong family relationship is evident as his characters Sylvester, Abel, Pearl, Gorky, Solomon, and Irene all return home to loving families.

Steig is a very private person who does not enjoy speaking before large groups. He works most effectively in the evenings and quite often sleeps until noon. He works with his left hand and draws with "an almost incredible speed." He enjoys spending time with his family and old friends.

He loves the writing and drawing part of his work and he definitely enjoys winning awards. In 1970 he received the Caldecott Award for *Sylvester and the Magic Pebble* (Old Tappan, N.J.: Windmill Books, 1969). *Amos and Boris* was nominated for the National Book Award in the Children's category and was the *New York Times* choice of Best Illustrated Children's Books of the Year and Children's Book Showcase. These are only a few of the many honors he has received.

Steig likes magic and knows that children do also. This is what prompted him to write *Sylvester and the Magic Pebble*.[4]

As a child he loved to read and fondly remembers the tales of *Robin Hood, Robinson Crusoe*, the King Arthur series, and *Pinocchio. Pinocchio* was a particular favorite and Steig attrributes many of his own ideas to symbols that he finds in Collodi's work, sometimes incorporating the same symbolism in his own work. As an example, he says that the reason Sylvester became a rock and then a donkey again was that as a child he remembers being so impressed with Pinocchio wanting to be transformed into a boy.

William Steig is serious about his work. He is aware of the many negative influences in children's lives and wants very much to provide a positive influence by producing quality art and literature for them.

---

[3]Doris De Montreville and Donna Hill, eds., *Third Book of Junior Authors* (New York: H. W. Wilson, 1972), 277.

[4]Anne Commire, *Something about the Author*, vol. 18 (Detroit: Gale Research, 1980), 276.

Author Activities

1. William Steig was a cartoonist until he began writing children's books. Have the children draw a cartoon. Some good sources to use for this activity are:

    Ames, Lee J. *Draw Fifty Famous Cartoons.* New York: Doubleday, 1979.

    Benjamin, Carol. *Cartooning for Kids.* New York: Crowell Junior Books, 1982.

    Hoff, Syd. *How to Draw Cartoons.* New York: Scholastic, 1975.

    Hoff, Syd. *Syd Hoff Shows You How to Draw Cartoons.* New York: Scholastic, 1979.

    A variation of this activity is to cut out cartoons from newspapers or magazines. Cover the captions and let the children fill in the words. Children could also be given the words and asked to draw the cartoons.

2. The author likes to receive awards for his work. He said he buys medals in antique stores to duplicate the experience of receiving an award. Have the children design a medal for one of his books and mail it to him. He can be reached through his publisher: Mr. William Steig, c/o Farrar, Straus and Giroux, 19 Union Square West, New York, NY 10003.

BIBLIOGRAPHY

Other books by William Steig for grades 1 through 3.

The Amazing Bone. New York: Farrar, Straus and Giroux, 1976. (RL 3 IL 1-4)

Brave Irene. New York: Farrar, Straus and Giroux, 1986. (RL 3 IL 1-4)

Caleb and Kate. New York: Farrar, Straus and Giroux, 1977. (RL 2 IL ps-5)

Doctor DeSoto. New York: Farrar, Straus and Giroux, 1982. (RL 3 IL 1-3)

Farmer Palmer's Wagon Ride. New York: Farrar, Straus and Giroux, 1974. (RL 3 IL 1-4)

Gorky Rises. New York: Farrar, Straus and Giroux, 1986. (RL 3 IL 1-4)

Roland the Minstrel Pig. New York: Harper & Row Junior Books, 1968. (RL 3 IL 1-4)

Sylvester and the Magic Pebble. Old Tappan, N.J.: Windmill Books, 1969. (RL 3 IL K-5)

The Beast in Ms. Rooney's Room

Patricia Reilly Giff. New York: Dell Publishing, 1984.

SUMMARY

Richard is not looking forward to repeating second grade. All of his friends from last year will make fun of him and he certainly does not care about the new kids. Besides when you are "dumb" nobody likes you. These were Richard Best's feelings in the beginning of this story. He does not refer to himself as "Beast" for nothing. As the year progresses with help from Ms. Rooney, his classroom teacher, and Mrs. Paris, his special reading teacher, Richard begins to realize that he is not half bad. Sure he makes his share of mistakes, but he is trying.

Possible Student Outcomes

Expand reading vocabulary.

Predict what might happen next in the story.

Practice developing a character.

Practice the thinking skills of decision making, problem solving, originality, and flexibility.

** CHOOSE A LIMITED NUMBER OF ACTIVITIES FROM EACH SECTION **

Before Reading Activities

1. The title of the book is *The Beast in Ms. Rooney's Room*. Ask the children what the difference is between Ms., Mrs., and Miss.

2. After reading the title of the book, ask the children to predict what they think the book will be about. Have them examine the picture on the cover. Ask if the illustration helps their prediction. How? Use the Prediction Tree[1] in figure 5.1, page 42. Have them place the title of the book on the trunk. Ask them to write their initial predictions on the bottom branches of the tree. Suggest that they think about setting, main characters, and the problem. After they write their initial predictions ask what questions they have about the story before they begin reading. The Prediction Tree will be continued in Predicting Activities (page 43).

3. On page 2, Richard refers to himself as "a left-back." Discuss what that means and how Richard or anyone in that situation feels.

4. Richard, the protagonist in this story, thinks he cannot do many things well. Ask the children to share things they feel they do not do well. Ask them if these things affect their behavior and if so, how.

---

[1]The idea for this Prediction Tree came from Ellin Oliver Keene's "Meaningful Seatwork Alternatives." Workshop handout, 1986.

Fig. 5.1

Predicting Activities

1. Have the students read through page 4. Ask them if their initial predictions were accurate. Were they right about setting, the beast? Have the children update their Prediction Tree by adding names or details they wish to include. Ask them to predict what will happen next.

2. Have the students read through page 15 where Mrs. Paris, the new reading teacher, arrives. After reading the author's description of Mrs. Paris, ask the children to predict what kind of a person she is and how she will act.

3. Have the students read to page 47 where Emily tells Richard that they should try for the banner. Have them predict what the children might do to get it and add their prediction to the Prediction Tree.

4. At the bottom of page 51, Emily tells Ms. Rooney, "we don't know how to win the banner." Have the children predict what Ms. Rooney will tell her. Ask why they say this.

5. Have the children read to the bottom of page 59. Ask them to predict what will happen next. Ask why they think this. Update the Prediction Tree.

6. Have the children read to the end of the story.

Post Reading Activities

1. On page 2, Richard stuck the pencil eraser up his nose after the girl in the pink party dress smiled at him. Have the children discuss why he did that. Ask what this tells them about Richard.

2. After completing chapter 1, point out that none of the chapters have names. Have the children name each chapter in the book after they finish reading it. The names can be clever or they can reflect the main idea of the chapter.

3. The author uses many adjectives to describe things in the story. On page 7, she talks about "slippery gray chow mein," "a dusty kind of peanut butter sandwich." Select some nouns in the story that the author has described. Let the children use other adjectives to describe these things. This activity can be done throughout the story. For example:

    "stick-out ears" — protruding ears

    "wet-the-bed smell" — rancid smell

    "puffy brown hair" — fluffy, hazel hair

4. Have the children discuss what they know about Mrs. Paris through her actions.

5. Richard got Emily in trouble (p.28). Ask the children how they feel about the way Richard handled this situation and what they think he could have done. Have the children share times that they have gotten in trouble and how they felt.

6. Richard was supposed to locate words that had short *a*'s. He had cranberry, star, cat, cereal, and baby. Ask the children why he crumpled up the word *baby*. What other word should he have crumpled up? Have the children locate words on this page or throughout the book that have short *a*'s.

7. When Richard passed the fifth-grade room, he noticed the banner hanging in front of the classroom. Richard's reaction was that they were "lucky" (p.33). Ask the children if people win awards because they are lucky. Discuss what constitutes luck.

8. Mrs. Paris had some dried figs in her drawer (p.34). Let the children see and taste dried figs. Encourage them to describe the way the figs look, feel, and smell.

9. Richard drew a picture of an arrow and pointed out that the word *arrow* is an exception to the "bossy r" rule. Ask the children to think of other exceptions to rules. For example:

   Use *i* before *e* except after *c*. The word *their* is an exception to this rule.

   Title cards are filed in the card catalog by the first word of the title, *unless* they begin with *A*, *An*, or *The*.

   Police and emergency vehicles are exceptions to speed limits in cases of emergency.

10. Holly, Richard's sister, had to get a book at the library to do a report on James K. Polk. Ask the children what library resource they would use to find out when James K. Polk was president and what he did during his administration.

11. On page 54, Richard refused Matthew's sandwich because Matthew smells so bad. Richard says, "He hoped Matthew didn't guess why he didn't want to share his Fluffernutter." Have the children discuss whether or not Richard should have told Matthew how he felt. Ask them why or why not.

12. Discuss how Richard felt after the paper airplane incident that caused his class to lose the banner for the week. Ask the children if they remember times when they caused their class to be punished because of their misconduct. Talk about the importance of assuming responsibility for one's behavior. Even if we do misbehave, it is better to be honest and apologize and learn from our mistakes than to deny our responsibility (p.62).

13. Richard was excited when his baby teeth started to feel loose (p.76). Have the children make large teeth as in figure 5.2 to use as vocabulary cards. After they make the teeth, have the children print key vocabulary words from the story on them. These words can be identified by the teacher before the story is read or students can list the words that are unfamiliar to them as they read through the story. Place the teeth on the board by chapters. The board might be called "Beast Teeth" or "Beastly Words." Children can be asked to use the words orally in sentences or to write them in sentences. Children can work in pairs. Each pair could be assigned several words from a chapter. Be certain that the children understand the meaning of each word in relation to the story. For five minutes one student should discuss the chapter from which the words were taken using as many of the words assigned to him or her as possible. The other student should record the number of words used by the student discussing the chapter. Have the students reverse roles. After the five-minute discussions, have each student write a summary of the chapter incorporating as many of the words given to them initially as possible. Students should exchange papers and read each other's summary.

Fig. 5.2

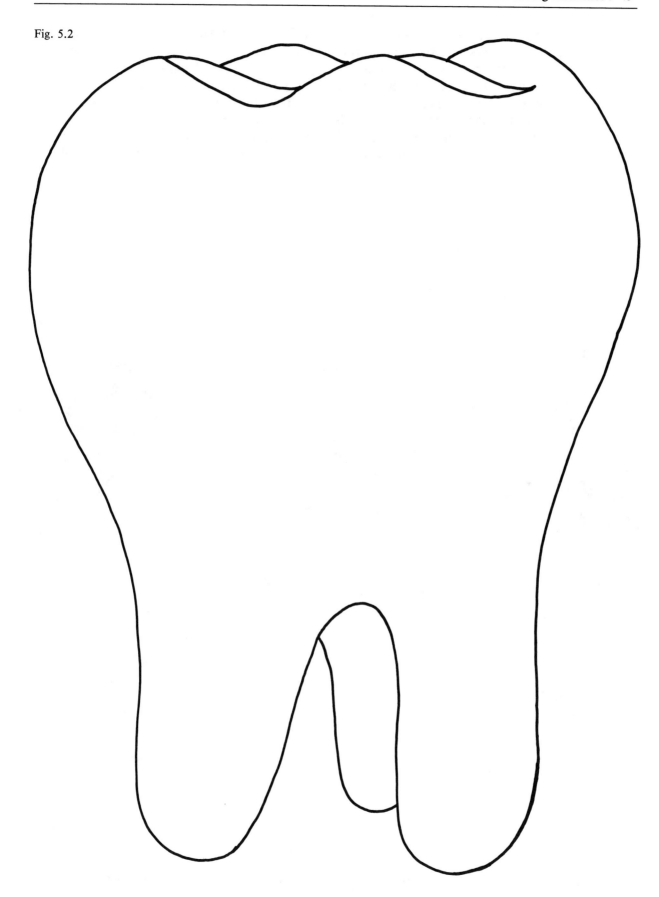

14. We know a great deal about Richard, Mrs. Paris, Emily, and Matthew. The author tells us by what these characters say, by their appearance, by their behavior, and by what others say about them. Make a semantic map[2] by putting a circle on the chalkboard with one of the character's names in the center. Have the students go through the book answering the questions extending from the circle. (See figure 5.3.) The students should be encouraged to go beyond the written text in order to answer the questions. They should look at pictures and read their own feelings into the story. This activity can be done chapter by chapter or after the entire book has been read through once. Looking at a character in this way helps the children understand how an author develops a character.

Fig. 5.3

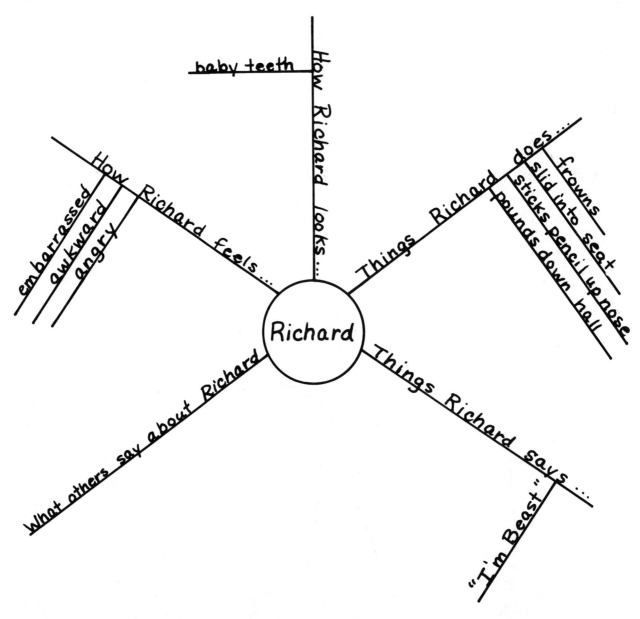

---

[2]The strategy called semantic mapping was developed by P. D. Pearson and D. D. Johnson in *Teaching Reading Comprehension* (New York: Holt, Rinehart and Winston, 1978).

Thinking Activities

1. (DECISION MAKING) Let the students decide which bulletin board in Et Cetera Activity 3 (page 49) is the best. Have the children use the Decision Making Worksheet on page 14. Criteria to use might be (1) neatness, (2) originality, (3) elaborateness, (4) cleverness, (5) most clearly explains rule.

2. (DECISION MAKING) Let the class decide which paper airplane designed in Et Cetera Activity 4 (page 49) is best. Planes could be entered in several categories, for example, complexity of design, farthest flight, most original, fastest. Criteria would have to be developed for each category. Have them use the Decision Making process outlined on page 14.

3. (PROBLEM SOLVING) Let the students determine if they could have a schoolwide contest rewarding good behavior similar to the banner award program in the story. Have them follow the steps in the Problem Solving Grid on page 17.

4. (ORIGINALITY) Let the children define some problem in their classroom or in their school. The problem might be "lack of school spirit." Ask the children to think of four unrelated objects, such as a popsicle, a T-shirt, a pencil, and a banner. Now ask the children how they might use these objects to solve the problem. For example, they might have a contest to see who can come up with good ideas to improve school spirit, and anyone offering a suggestion could be given a popsicle. Students could be given an opportunity to design a T-shirt, and the best design could be put on T-shirts and sold to the student body. Pencils could be printed with the school name and given to each student. Children could make a large banner to hang in the school foyer, and the banner could say something positive about the student body.

6. (FLEXIBILITY) Have the children list similarities between the school in this story and their school.

7. (PLANNING) The children attended the puppet show *Hansel and Gretel* (p.25). Have the children plan a puppet show using the Planning Worksheet on page 10.

8. (PROBLEM SOLVING) The children were disruptive during the puppet show (p.26). Behavior during assemblies can sometimes be a problem. Have the children design a problem statement addressing assembly behavior and use the Problem Solving Grid on page 17 to solve the problem.

9. (PROBLEM SOLVING) Drake likes to make fun of Richard (p.43). Most of us have experienced someone making fun of us at some time. Have the children design a problem statement addressing this issue and use the Problem Solving Grid on page 17 to come up with some solutions to handle this problem.

10. (EVALUATION) On page 62, Richard knew his class would not win the banner because of his misbehavior. Have the children evaluate whether Richard should have told his teacher or classmates what he had done. Use the Evaluation Worksheet on page 15.

Writing Activities

1. The class wrote a letter thanking the P.T.A. for the puppet show (p.31). Have each student write a letter to an organization or group, in or out of their school building, thanking them for something they have done. Thank-you letters say more than "thank you." Read some thank-you letters to the children as an example. The students can use the Planning Worksheet on page 10 to preplan their letters.

2. The author uses colorful verbs throughout the story. Where she could have said "run down the hall," she said "pounded down the hall" (p.1). Where she might have said "Drake hurried over," she said "Drake came charging over" (p.12). Words are wonderful tools to communicate ideas. Certain words convey our message better than others. Creative writing involves choosing the best words to communicate our meaning. Give the children some sentences and let them substitute different verbs. Talk about how these alter the meaning of the sentences. For example:

> He moved over toward them.

> He trotted over toward them.

3. Have each child select someone in the classroom to focus on as a subject for a semantic map. Imagine that this person has a real problem or have the children make up a problem that this individual might have. For example, the problem might be that the student has just flunked this week's spelling test. Have the children make a semantic map by placing their character's name in the center circle. Have the same statements extend from the circle as extend from the semantic map in figure 5.3, page 46. Have the students write descriptive words or phrases to describe the student they have placed in the center of their map. After they have described their character in this way, they can write a paragraph or story or orally tell about the person using the information on their map.

Et Cetera Activities

1. (Art, Math, Social Studies) On the frontispiece is a floor plan for Ms. Rooney's classroom. Have the children draw a floor plan for their classroom.

2. (Bulletin Board) On page 71, Richard said the book he was reading was interesting even though it was a skinny book. Have students make a "Thin Is In" bulletin board to advertise skinny books. See figure 5.4.

Fig. 5.4

Some titles to include:

> Bottner, Barbara. *Dumb Old Casey Is a Fat Tree.* New York: Harper & Row Junior Books, 1979.

Bulla, Clyde Robert. *The Chalk Box Kid.* New York: Random House, 1987.

Bulla, Clyde Robert. *The Sword in the Tree.* New York: Thomas Y. Crowell, 1956.

Bulla, Clyde Robert. *Wish at the Top.* New York: Thomas Y. Crowell, 1974.

Calhoun, Mary. *The Night the Monster Came.* New York: William Morrow, 1982.

Cameron, Ann. *Julian's Glorious Summer.* New York: Random House, 1987.

Cameron, Ann. *Stories Julian Tells.* New York: Pantheon, 1981.

Orgel, Doris. *My War with Mrs. Galloway.* New York: Viking Kestrel, 1985.

Wojciechowska, Maia. *Hey, What's Wrong with This One?* New York: Harper & Row Junior Books, 1969.

3. (Math, Language Arts, Social Studies) Richard put up a bulletin board in the special reading room (p.75) demonstrating the short vowels they had studied. Divide the class into groups. Assign each group a particular math, language arts, or social studies concept that they have learned during the year. Let the groups design a bulletin board explaining the rule(s) learned.

4. (Art) Richard used the paper on the nurse's desk to make paper airplanes (p.54). Have a paper airplane making and flying contest. Some books that describe how to make and fly paper airplanes are:

Arceneaux, Marc. *Paper Airplanes.* San Francisco, Calif.: Troubador Press, 1984.

Linsley, Leslie, and Jon Aron. *Air Crafts.* New York: E. P. Dutton, 1982.

Simon, Seymour. *The Paper Airplane Book.* New York: Penguin Books, 1971.

A special day can be designated for a paper airplane flying contest.

5. (Art Appreciation) Show the children Winslow Homer's painting *The Country School* (1871). Homer had very little formal art education. Growing up in Boston and Cambridge there were no academies or schools of art. Despite his lack of formal training, he is oftentimes referred to as "the greatest American artist." He began sketching during his teenage years and was apprenticed to a lithographer for whom he made sketches for pieces of sheet music. He came into his own around 1857 when he began painting scenes of the Civil War and country life. Let the children compare the school setting in this picture with school life in the story. Homer's painting can be found in *The American Heritage History of the Artists' America* by Marshall B. Davidson and The Editors of American Heritage (New York: American Heritage Publishing, 1973).

The Author Says ...

Patricia Reilly Giff (1935-) had an interest in books and writing at a very early age. She recalls being fascinated by a huge, tan corduroy volume with indentations in its side. She liked to put her tiny fingers in these depressions and pretend that she was playing a musical instrument. It was her father who showed her that the holes in the large dictionary had letters and gradually he began to teach her words. By first grade, she could read. From that point on, she remembers spending a good part of her time curled up with a book. Many cold winter evenings she nestled close to her father as he read her classics such as *Hiawatha* and *Evangeline*.

She majored in history at Marymount College in New York, secretly yearning to become a writer. She taught elementary school, was a reading consultant for nearly twenty years, married a detective, and had three children. She obtained a Professional Reading Diploma from Hofstra University. As both a classroom teacher and reading teacher, she worked with hundreds of children—sad children, angry children, children who had little regard for themselves or others.

There was a great deal to be said to these kids. More than anything, she wanted them to know that they are special, "that all of us are special—important just because we are ourselves."[3] At forty she still had not written a story. If she was ever going to write, she needed to begin. One morning she announced to her husband, "I'm going to write." When she arrived home from school that day, her husband was taking out a wall between two closets. When she asked him what he was doing, he told her he was making her a place to write. The time had really come for her to begin.

The problem was, she did not know how. At first she would enter her special room with tea and newspaper in hand. While her family did the dishes, she read. "She's not writing," her children would say. "Yes, she's going to write a story," her husband would reply. Desperate, she telephoned her sister and confessed that she wanted to write but had no idea how to begin. "Write about something you know," her sister advised and obviously she did. She knew about children, schools, and books and that is what her Polk Street series is all about. The school in *The Beast in Ms. Rooney's Room* is her school; the teachers and principal are people she knows and admires. Emily is her daughter. Richard is a boy she met in New Jersey. "Why don't you write about me?" he asked her. "Call me Beast," he said. "That's what everyone calls me."

She did take a formal writing class at the New School for Social Research in Manhattan. As a matter of fact, she took the same class seven times. When she first began writing, she analyzed pieces of literature she liked. One piece was Constance Greene's *Isabelle the Itch* (New York: Viking, 1973). She noted how the author developed the character and setting. She learned the importance of strong character development if your story is to be believable. In her mind, the character must be developed first and then the plot evolves. She always uses action and dialogue on the first page, a technique she learned from the well-known author Richard Peck. When she begins writing, she always has her character's problem well-defined; the plot unfolds as she writes. Sometimes she weaves herself into a corner and must begin again.

When asked how she, as a former teacher, would teach writing to her students, she said she would give them lots of time, space, and support. She also feels it is important for teachers to share their own writing with their students. When asked if she would encourage her students to write about what they know, she said not necessarily. In her experience, some of their best stories have come from their vivid imaginations.

Of all her books, *Gift of the Pirate Queen* (New York: Delacorte, 1982) is her favorite. Written for children in grades 4 through 6, the story is about courage and diabetes—her son, she says, has both.

Giff is the first one to admit that writing is hard work. When asked what is most difficult for her, she says, "getting sentences down, juggling them to make them come out right." Sometimes she spends three-quarters of an hour trying to get one sentence right. When asked if any of her submissions were rejected, she said that *Today Was a Terrible Day* (New York: Delacorte, 1984), one of her first pieces, was rejected twice before being accepted.

In spite of the fact that she spends many days on the road making personal appearances, she writes every day. Her feeling is that if you want to write you should do it every day and not put it off for a more convenient time.

Author Activities

1. There are many ways to begin a story. Some authors begin by describing the setting, others by describing a character, still others with a character saying something. Patricia Reilly Giff likes to begin her stories with action and dialogue. "Richard Best pounded down the hall of the Polk Street School," she writes. Read other story beginnings to the class where authors begin with

---

[3]Anne Commire, *Something about the Author*, vol. 33 (Detroit: Gale Research, 1983), 85.

action and/or dialogue. Using these as examples, let the students practice writing opening paragraphs showing action and/or dialogue.

2. Having been a teacher for nearly twenty years, Patricia Reilly Giff writes many of her stories about school children. Have the children keep a diary for a week. Ask them to jot down incidents that happen during the school day, incidents that they find serious or sad or humorous. Have the children select one of these incidents and write a story or paragraph about it. The setting will of course be their own school or classroom. After the students polish their stories, they could send them to Patricia Reilly Giff and ask if she might like to incorporate any of the incidents into one of her stories. Letters should be addressed to Ms. Patricia Reilly Giff, c/o Delacorte Press, 1 Dag Hammarskjold Plaza, New York, NY 10017.

3. In the end, Richard realized that he too was special. Have the children write a story about how special they are and send it to Patricia Reilly Giff.

BIBLIOGRAPHY

Other books by Patricia Reilly Giff for grades 1 through 3.

Lazy Lions, Lucky Lambs. New York: Delacorte, 1985. (RL 3   IL k-6)

Pickle Puss. New York: Delacorte, 1986. (RL 3   IL k-3)

Sunny Side Up. New York: Delacorte, 1986. (RL 3   IL k-3)

Today Was a Terrible Day. New York: Delacorte, 1984. (RL 2   IL k-3)

Binky Brothers, Detectives

James Lawrence. New York: Harper & Row, 1968.

SUMMARY

Pinky and Dinky are brothers and detectives. Pinky, the older of the two, never misses an opportunity to remind Dinky that he is in charge. When Chub, the catcher for Pinky's baseball team, hires the brothers to locate his lost mitt, it once again looks like Pinky will be out front giving orders. Unfortunately for him, he follows some clues left by members of a rival team, the Wildcats. Dinky is a little more cautious and ends up solving the case.

Possible Student Outcomes

Expand reading vocabulary.

Predict what might happen next in the story.

Relate the sequence of events in the story.

Practice the thinking skills of: fluency, flexibility, elaboration, complexity, and decision making.

*** CHOOSE A LIMITED NUMBER OF ACTIVITIES FROM EACH SECTION ***

Before Reading Activities

1. Have the children examine page 3. Ask them if they see any problem with the sign that Dinky is making. Suggest that they compare this page with the title page or the book cover.

2. Put the following passage on the board. Ask the children to fill in the blanks with words they think might be in this story. Write the various words the children suggest in the blanks.[1] Read the passage over together. Encourage the children to discuss what they think this book will be about.

> Chub looked _____. "Someone _____ my catcher's mitt," he said. This was bad news. Pinky and Chub had a _____ game after lunch. "How do you know someone _____ your mitt?" Pinky asked. It was _____ on a nail in our _____," said Chub. "Now it is _____. This _____ was on the nail." "Leave the _____ with me. I will get to work on this _____ right away," said Pinky.

3. Ask the students to brainstorm to come up with as many baseball words as they can. After listing the words, have the students categorize them. Suggested headings might be players, equipment, rules, playing field.

4. On page 8, Dinky reminds Pinky that he always has to be "boss." Ask the children what it means to be "the boss" and why some people dislike the idea of someone else being "the boss." Have the children share situations where someone has been their "boss" or accused them of having to be "the boss." Have them discuss situations where a boss is needed, not needed.

Predicting Activities

1. Have the children look at the pictures on pages 12 and 13 and discuss what is happening. After the children read page 12, ask them to explain why Pinky said "Hot Dog! Here comes lots of business!"

2. Have the children read to the bottom of page 20 where Pinky says, "Don't rush me, I will think of something." Ask them to predict what Pinky might do.

3. Have the children read through page 30. Ask them to predict where the glove might be hidden.

4. Have the children read to the end of the story.

Post Reading Activities

1. The author uses the following contractions in the story: can't, don't, what's, it's. There are many other places in the story where children could use contractions. Teach the children the following contractions and let them locate places in the story where these can be used.

---

[1]This activity is based on a strategy called OPIN developed by Frank Greene of McGill University (Frank Green, "Radio Reading" in C. Pennock, ed., *Reading Comprehension at Four Linguistic Levels* (Newark, Del.: International Reading Association).

you're (pp.11, 26)   doesn't (p.32)

I'll (pp.20, 37, 45)   I'm (p.50)

you'll (p.22)   didn't (p.60)

we'll (p.24)

2. Have the children look at the picture on page 17 and explain why the message has a picture of a skull and crossbones in the corner. Ask them where else they might have seen a skull and crossbones. Ask them what a skull and crossbones means.

3. On page 41, the author says Pinky "yelled" and "hollered." Ask the children to suggest other words that the author might have used. These words are synonyms. Have the children list synonyms for the following words in the story:

    hot dog (p.12)   smart (p.21)

    upset (p.14)   laughed (p.23)

    bad news (p.14)   hurried off (p.34)

    took (p.15)   chuckling (p.37)

    gone (p.16)

4. On page 50, the author describes Pinky's face as "getting red." Ask the children to explain what Pinky was feeling. The author chose not to say that Pinky was embarrassed. Instead he painted a picture with words describing how Pinky felt. Have the children select one of the sentences below and use words to paint a picture as the author did.

    Joe is bossy.

    Spike acts smart.

    Pinky is mad.

    Dinky is hurt.

5. Have the children look at the illustrations on page 63 and explain why Dinky is covering his eyes. Ask the children how the illustrator shows the pitching problem.

6. The title of the book is *Binky Brothers, Detectives*. There is a comma after *Brothers* because the word *detectives* explains what the Binky brothers are. Place the following sentences on the board and ask the children which parts of the following sentences should be set off by commas.

    Dinky Pinky's brother found the mitt.

    Patsy Ann a friend lost her turtle.

    Chub the catcher drank four lemonades.

    Melvin Krantz shortstop hid the mitt.

    Spike Brown and Joe Parker Wildcats liked to act smart.

7. Throughout the story, *Wildcats* is capitalized because it is the name of the team. Words are also capitalized when they begin sentences. Write some sentences on the board. Ask the children to explain why the underlined words are or are not capitalized. For example:

    We saw a wildcat in a tree.

    The Wildcats hid the mitt.

    Pinky climbed up to the Wildcats tree house.

    Wildcats are dangerous animals.

8. Have the children use the Story Map in figure 6.1 to outline the main characters, the problem, the events, and the resolution in this story.

9. An analogy is a way of comparing two things by suggesting that they are alike in some way. Analogies are helpful in developing children's thought patterns. Have the children make the following analogies.

    Touchdowns are to football as _____ are to baseball. (home runs)

    Quarters are to baseball as _____ are to baseball. (innings)

    Bat is to batter as _____ is to catcher. (mitt)

    A sweeper is to soccer as a _____ is to baseball. (shortstop)

    A referee is to soccer as an _____ is to baseball. (umpire)

Thinking Activities

1. (FLEXIBILITY) On page 7, Pinky says his name should go on the sign first because he thought up the idea to be detectives. Oftentimes there are several names on signs. Ask the children to decide other ways to determine the order in which names could be placed on a sign (alphabetically, most important person, oldest person, biggest contributor to work, person with most money).

2. (FLUENCY) Have the children list as many team sports as they can think of.

3. (FLEXIBILITY) Have the children categorize the sports listed in Thinking Activity 2 (above) in a variety of ways, for example, winter, summer; indoor, outdoor; use ball, do not use ball; team, individual.

4. (ELABORATION) Divide the class into thirds. Give each group a beginning story line. Have each child in the group elaborate on the story line with the last person bringing it to a close. Story starters might be:

    "I was walking down the sidewalk minding my own business when all of a sudden ..."

    "One dark, rainy night I was lying in bed listening to the wind howling at my window when suddenly I heard ..."

    "I was almost home when I realized I'd forgotten my math book. Since I had an assignment due tomorrow, I ran back to school. When I entered the classroom, I saw ..."

5. (COMPLEXITY) Mysteries often contain clues. Here are some clues. Have the children speculate about what crime might have been committed.

    You come home from school and find

    > dirt on the floor
    > the curtain blowing
    > the temperature dropping in room.

    (broken window, robbery)

    You witness a child in the classroom

    > going through his pockets and desk
    > talking to the teacher
    > crying at 12:00 noon

    (money stolen, tickets stolen)

Fig. 6.1   Baseball Story Map

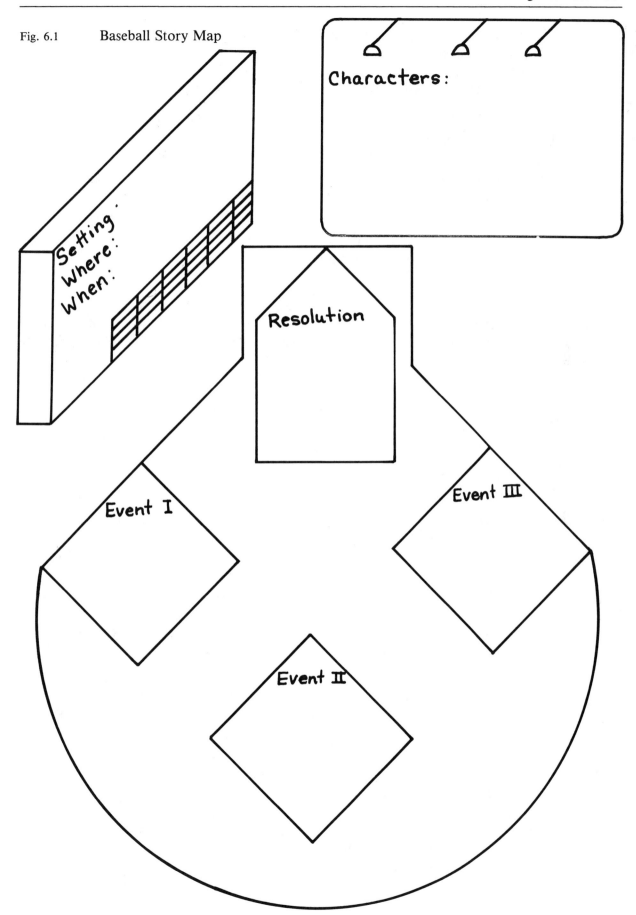

It is early in the morning. A man is in his yard

> scratching his head
> looking in his neighbor's yard
> angrily going into his house

(newspaper missing)

6. (COMPLEXITY) Below are several crimes that children might experience. Have the children discuss appropriate ways to deal with these happenings.

    Your bicycle is stolen.

    Your library book is taken.

    Your lunch disappears.

    You see writing on the bathroom wall in the school.

    You witness a classmate stealing from another child's desk.

    You see a classmate cheat on a test.

7. (COMPLEXITY) Detectives often rely on eyewitnesses to help them solve crimes. In figure 6.2 a crime is being committed. Have the children look at the picture carefully for three minutes. After three minutes, have them turn the picture over and see how many of the following details they can remember.

    What time was the crime committed?

    What was the crime?

    How many people were in the store?

    On what aisle was the merchandise stolen?

    What was the shoplifter wearing?

    Where did he hide what he stole?

8. (DECISION MAKING) Have the children read three other mysteries and decide which one they like best and why. This activity can be done as a class, group, or individual activity. The children can use the Decision Making Worksheet on page 14. Other mysteries they might read are:

    Bonsall, Crosby. *The Case of the Cat's Meow*. New York: Harper & Row Junior Books, 1978.

    Boyd, Selma, and Pauline Boyd. *Footprints in the Refrigerator*. New York: Watts, 1982.

    Kellogg, Steven. *The Mystery of the Missing Red Mitten*. New York: Dial Books Young, 1974.

    Lexau, Joan M. *The Dog Food Caper*. New York: Dial Books Young, 1985.

    Sharmat, Marjorie W. *Nate the Great*. New York: Putnam Publishing Group, 1972.

Writing Activities

1. Two notes were found in the story. People write notes for lots of reasons. Parents write notes to remind their children to do things; they write notes giving children directions on how to do something. Children often write notes to their friends. Have each child select someone to whom they would like to write a note. Give the note to the person and have the person write a reply. Both parties could share their notes orally with the class.

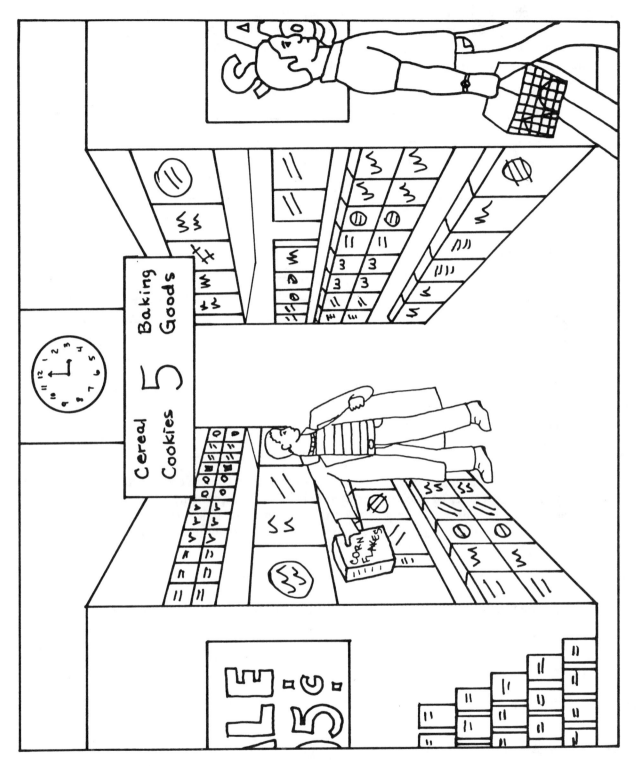

Fig. 6.2

2. Have the children write a mystery story. The children might want to use the Story Map in figure 6.1, page 55, as a guide for this writing activity. Some children might need more structure to complete this activity. After discussing the Story Map in figure 6.1, they could use the following story frame to write their story.

The Case of the _____

This story takes place in _____

_____ .

The detective on the case is _____ .
                                              (Name)

_____ is _____
    (Name)

_____ .

The problem is _____

_____

_____ .

Next, _____

_____

_____ .

At last the problem is solved when _____

_____ .

The story ends when _____

_____ .

3. Pinky did not treat Dinky very nicely in this story. Have the children pretend that they are Pinky and write a letter of apology for their behavior. Discuss the fact that a letter of apology should say more than "I'm sorry." Ask the children to verbalize the reasons Pinky should apologize to Dinky. Read a letter of apology to the class. Use the following chart to plan this writing activity.

Letter of Apology

Event or activity	Way each person felt	What you plan to do differently
1.	1.	1.
2.	2.	2.

Et Cetera Activities

1. (Art) Pinky and Dinky sold lemonade and ran a detective agency. Discuss some jobs that children might have, for example, car wash, delivery service, house cleaning. Have them design a sign for a business.

2. (Math) Pinky and Dinky had several mathematical equations to solve in this story. Let the children complete the math problems in figure 6.3.

Fig. 6.3

Binky Brothers, Detectives Mitt Math

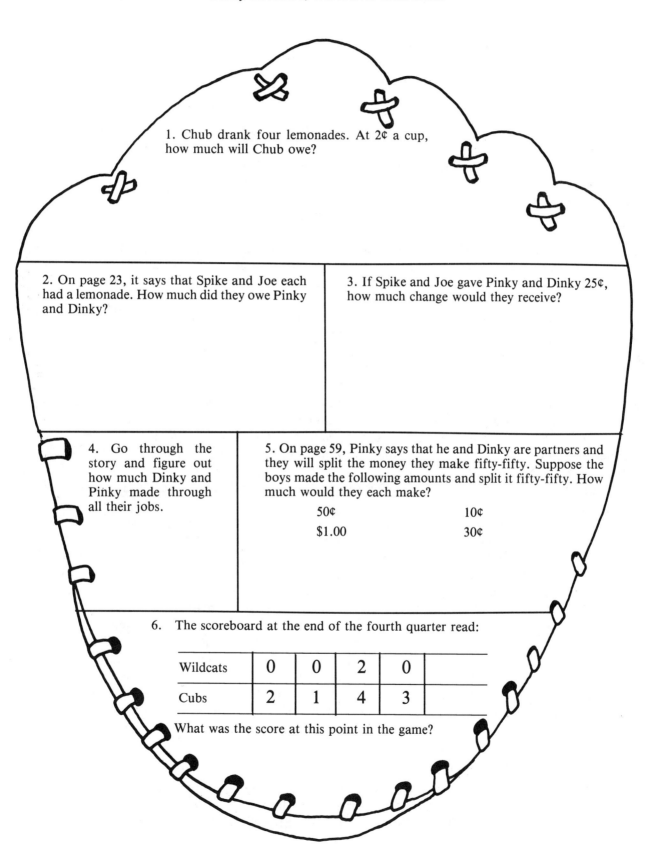

1. Chub drank four lemonades. At 2¢ a cup, how much will Chub owe?

2. On page 23, it says that Spike and Joe each had a lemonade. How much did they owe Pinky and Dinky?

3. If Spike and Joe gave Pinky and Dinky 25¢, how much change would they receive?

4. Go through the story and figure out how much Dinky and Pinky made through all their jobs.

5. On page 59, Pinky says that he and Dinky are partners and they will split the money they make fifty-fifty. Suppose the boys made the following amounts and split it fifty-fifty. How much would they each make?

50¢   10¢

$1.00   30¢

6. The scoreboard at the end of the fourth quarter read:

Wildcats	0	0	2	0	
Cubs	2	1	4	3	

What was the score at this point in the game?

3. (Vocabulary Expansion) Select three sports the children know something about. Have the children brainstorm to come up with words about each sport. Have each child select one of the sports and make an illustrated sports dictionary defining words appropriate for that sport. The dictionaries could be shaped like a ball, bat, glove, or helmet. Each page could contain several vocabulary words with an illustration. All words should be in alphabetical order. The students' dictionaries could be put on display.

The Author Says ...

James Lawrence (1918-) wanted to be an author for as long as he can remember. As a child growing up in the twenties and thirties, he recalls reading the Oz books, Fu Manchu, Tarzan, and works by his favorite historical novelist, Rafael Sabatini. He feels very strongly that children should be encouraged to read all kinds of literature, not just "the classics." In his opinion, children, like most of us, read for enjoyment. It is very difficult to dictate what one should enjoy reading. If kids will read comic books, cartoon strips, the Hardy Boys—Lawrence says let them read.

He began his career writing commercial and educational film scripts for companies that produced technical films. He also wrote radio scripts and magazine and newspaper articles. In 1954, Lawrence learned that Stratemeyer Syndicate (creators of juvenile books) wanted to issue a series on Tom Swift, Jr. His application to write for this series was accepted and he eventually accepted a position as writer-editor with this group.

Lawrence likes to outline an entire story in his mind before he begins writing. "Some authors compose as they write, but I'm fearful that my stories will ramble," he says. His writing process may be influenced somewhat by doing series work; oftentimes the series creators will give the author an outline from which to work.

When he began *Binky Brothers, Detectives*, he had the idea of the big brother bossing the little brother. Somehow he wanted to trick the big brother. Rarely does an idea for a story "hit me like a bolt of lightning," Lawrence says. "It usually requires hard work and lots of floor pacing."

He writes every day despite the fact that often he has to push himself to do so. "No matter how much you enjoy writing," he says, "I don't know many authors who will tell you that it's not difficult to sit at a typewriter all day."

Lawrence also writes comic strips. One series on James Bond ran for years in the *London Daily Express*.

When asked what advice or trade secrets he would like to share with children, he answered by quoting Steven Spielberg, "It all begins with a good story." Kids are natural storytellers and we should be receptive to the stories they have to tell. As teachers, we should "imbue them with a desire to tell stories." At the same time, children must be taught grammar and punctuation. Most important, he said, is to teach them to be concerned with exact meanings of words. In his opinion, some authors do not seem concerned enough with the best choice of words for the story.

When asked what frustrates him as an author, he says no one ever writes as well as they would like to—everyone would like to write immortal books. Much of what one writes is dictated by the machinery of the publisher. He believes that children prefer books with action—books that have a story to tell, hence the popularity of mysteries. Oftentimes editors are more concerned with in-depth character development than with action. The conflict between what publishers feel will sell and authors want to write is leading some authors to publish their own books.

Author Activities

1. Authors enjoy hearing from children about their books. Have the children write a letter to James Lawrence. Letters should be sent through his publisher to Mr. James Lawrence, c/o Harper & Row Junior Books Group, 10 East 53rd Street, New York, NY 10022. Before writing

their letters, they should hold a group discussion regarding appropriate letter content. Authors find it difficult to answer letters from students who are writing because their letter is an assignment.

2. James Lawrence has written several educational film scripts. Have the children choose a non-fiction topic. It could be a sport, animal, place, or other. Ask your library media specialist to locate materials on these topics at appropriate reading levels for the children. List the topics on the board. Put the topics in categories, for example, specific animals will be in the animal category, and so forth. Each child should research a particular topic locating five to ten facts about the subject. Have the children work in groups. Give each group a roll of paper. Have the children put together a script for an educational film. Each child should illustrate his or her topic on the roll of paper, one illustration under the other. Their program should be given a title and names of the students working on that program should be listed. After the roll of paper is illustrated, use masking tape to attach each end to a wooden rod so the paper can be rolled. Cut a square hole in a box that is big enough for the class to see. Place one rod through the top of the box, the second rod through the bottom so that by turning the rods, the paper will roll and produce the effect of a television screen. See figure 6.4. The children could record their script on a cassette tape. Appropriate music could be played softly in the background for a more finished product. The tape can be played while the paper is being rolled to produce an educational television production.

Fig. 6.4

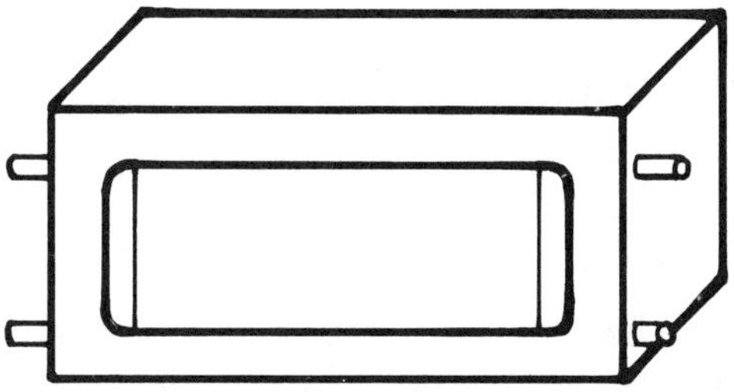

3. James Lawrence also writes comic strips. Have the children write and design a comic strip.

4. Much of James Lawrence's work is done under a pseudonym. Series like The Hardy Boys and Nancy Drew are written by numerous authors even though Franklyn W. Dixon's and Carolyn Keene's names appear on the covers. Discuss other authors who wrote under a pseudonym, for example, Samuel Clemens (Mark Twain) and Dr. Seuss (Theodore Geisel).

BIBLIOGRAPHY

Another book by James Lawrence for grades 1 through 3.

Binky Brothers and the Fearless Four. New York: Harper & Row, 1970. (RL 2   IL 1-3)

Cherries and Cherry Pits

Vera B. Williams. New York: Greenwillow Books, 1986.

SUMMARY

Bidemmi loves to draw and to tell stories. Each new colored marker her friend brings her is an occasion for a new set of stories. In this book, all the characters Bidemmi creates are enjoying cherries, delicious red cherries. They all savor the flavor and spit out the pits. All, that is, except Bidemmi. When she becomes part of her story, she saves the pits and plants them in her drab city neighborhood and eventually her entire block is filled with cherry trees laden with cherries.

Possible Student Outcomes

Expand reading vocabulary.

Identify similes and incorporate them into the writing of a character description.

Recognize some ways that illustrators communicate with the reader.

Practice the thinking skills of: fluency, flexibility, evaluation, and attribute listing.

** CHOOSE A LIMITED NUMBER OF ACTIVITIES FROM EACH SECTION **

Before Reading Activities

1. Bring in several kinds of cherries, for example, maraschino, bing, sour. Let the children taste them. Discuss each kind of cherry—do the children like them, how they are used, how they grow. (See Thinking Activity 5 on page 64 for a Flexibility idea.) Tell the children that they are going to read a story called *Cherries and Cherry Pits*. Ask them what they think this story might be about.

2. Put the following vocabulary words from the story on the chalkboard. Go over the words with the children. Ask the children to predict how these words might be used in the story. After reading the story come back to the words and see which predictions were correct.

Bidemmi	switches	banister
subway	leans	geranium
wrinkle	strap	beret
thick	twisted	escalator
muscles	cherry	sprout

3. There are many references to the subway in this story. Discuss subways with the children. Explain that the prefix *sub-* means under. Ask what other words they know that begin with *sub* (submerge, submarine, subheading). Be certain that they understand what a subway is. Ask them why some cities do not have subways and others do. Discuss alternate means of transportation and the advantages and disadvantages of subways. In order to determine how much the children know and understand about subways, have them draw a picture of a subway station. Encourage them to include as many details as they can. Let them share their pictures and discuss them in order to clear up any misunderstandings they have about subways. When they

read the story, the children can locate words that are subway words and see how many of these they have included in their drawing.

Predicting Activities

1. Have the children read to the end of page 9.[1] Ask them what the man might be carrying in the small white bag and what he is going to do with its contents.

2. Have the children read through page 15. Ask the children what might be in the brown paper bag in the lady's purse. Ask where she is taking them and for whom.

3. After the children read through page 29, ask them why they think Bidemmi is putting the pits in her pocket. Ask why they think that.

4. Have the children read to the end of the story.

Post Reading Activities

1. Ask the children where this story takes place and what clues the author uses to tell this.

2. Have the children draw a picture of the person who is telling this story. Discuss their pictures. Ask what they know about this person and why they describe the person as they do.

3. Ask the children why the author uses the three dots (ellipsis) on pages 7, 10, 13, and 21. Explain that this is a device to show the reader that there is more to come—that something is going to follow. Have the children explain why the author repeats phrases such as "and there they sit eating the cherries and spitting out the pits, eating the cherries and spitting out the pits" and "And I tell the pits to grow ... grow and grow." Explain that the author uses this technique to give the feeling of time passing, something going on and on.

4. Ask the children why the first letter of each page is made with red dots. Explain that this typographic clue is a clever device to remind the reader of the importance of cherries to the story theme.

5. Ask the children how the author emphasizes the beginnings of Bidemmi's stories. Ask how this changes the way they read those sentences.

6. The person telling the story says she or he would like to ask Bidemmi questions about her stories. Ask the children to share questions they would like to ask Bidemmi about her stories. Ask why they think she moved from one story to the next so quickly.

7. After they finish reading the story, ask the children to close their eyes and try to visualize how the neighborhood might look with a "whole forest of cherry trees right on our block." Have them describe what they see. Discuss the changes that might occur as a result of this happening.

8. The reader can learn a great deal from the illustrations in a story. Have the children examine the pictures of Bidemmi where she is drawing. Ask what the illustrator tells us about Bidemmi by her posture, her facial expression. Discuss the illustrations on pages 37 through 40. Help the children see how the illustrator uses a collage to show multiple happenings. This technique allows the illustrator to convey a busy or hurried effect, to depict multiple happenings. Ask the children why Williams used such vivid, bright colors and how this affects the tone or mood of the story. Have the children explain the illustration on the last page of the book.

---

[1]Pagination begins with the title page of the text.

9.   Bidemmi lives in a city. Ask the children if they think Bidemmi would like to live where they live. Ask them why or why not and on what they base their decision.

10.   Discuss how the children's lives are alike or different from Bidemmi's. Discuss what she has that they do not have and vice versa.

Thinking Activities

1.   (ELABORATION) Bidemmi likes to draw by starting with a dot and drawing lines out from the dot. Have the children elaborate on all the shapes in figure 7.1. Have them select one drawing and write a story about whatever they created.

2.   (FLEXIBILITY) See how many ways the children can find to use cherries in recipes. Have each child bring in a different food and have a tasting party.

3.   (EVALUATION) Give prizes for the various cherry recipes. A prize could be given for the most unusual recipe, the sweetest, sourest, most delicious, and best looking.

4.   (FLUENCY, FLEXIBILITY) Have the children brainstorm to come up with as many things as they can that are naturally red. See how many different items they can identify and then let them generate words that best describe the shades of red, for example, scarlet, ruby, blood, deep, bright. Point out that their list of objects can be used to construct similes, for example, as red as a ruby.

5.   (FLEXIBILITY) As the children taste the cherries in Before Reading Activity 1 (page 62), see how many words they can use to describe the taste, texture, and smell.

6.   (FLUENCY) The man's children all had names that began with the letter *D*. See how many names the children can list that begin with the letter *D*, how many words.

7.   (FLUENCY) Have the children list the compound words in the story.

8.   (EVALUATION) Two other books with the theme of beautifying the world are *Miss Rumphius* by Barbara Cooney (New York: Viking Penguin, 1982) and *Johnny Appleseed* by Aliki (Englewood Cliffs, N.J.: Prentice-Hall, 1963). Share these books and ask the children to compare and contrast them with *Cherries and Cherry Pits*. Have them look at characters, setting, theme. Ask them which story they like best and why. Discuss other ways to beautify the world besides planting things. Ask how they could improve their school, neighborhood, community.

9.   (ATTRIBUTE LISTING) Have the children choose something that they think needs improving, for example, cafeteria food, playground equipment, the library. Using a chart similar to the one below, let them plan how they might improve the item.

For example: How might we improve the cafeteria food?

Making an Improvement

Parts to improve	Attributes	Ideas for Improvement
Menu	Monotonous	Vary
		Poll children for ideas
Vegetables	Limp, soggy	Steam them

Fig. 7.1

Look at the unfinished shapes on your paper. Turn each shape into something.

Writing Activities

1. On the dedication page, the author has written a letter to her father thanking him for all the stories he told her. Have the children write a letter thanking someone for something special that person has done for them.

2. Bidemmi always begins her stories with "THIS." Have the children use "THIS" as a beginning to a story. A variation of this activity might be to have several objects available to use as story starters. The children could use these to begin their story, for example, "This is an eraser_____"; "This is a jar of jelly_____"; "This is a pear_____."

3. Have the children write a cookbook featuring all their cherry recipes. (See Thinking Activity 2 on page 64.)

4. Bidemmi describes each of her characters in the same way. She describes their location or setting, their appearance, and where they are going. Let the children use the same format to describe a character. Have them use the Planning Sheet in figure 7.2 to plan a story.

5. Bidemmi focuses her stories on cherries. Ask the children what food or topic they would focus on if they were telling the stories. Have the children use the planning sheet completed in Writing Activity 4 to write a story that is patterned after this one by Vera Williams.

6. Help the children write a poem about cherries. First give each child a cherry to eat. Have them brainstorm for words that describe the way the cherry looks, feels, smells, tastes, and any sounds they can imagine, such as what it sounds like when you bite a cherry or pick a cherry. Help them put together a poem using these five senses. For example:

    I reach inside the brown paper bag

    My fingers feel the firm, round circles,

    Cherries, deep red cherries

    They shine like patent leather

    They taste sweet and fleshy

    Their skin feels smooth and tight

    I like the way they pop when I bite them.

7. Bidemmi wanted to make her drab world more beautiful by planting the cherry trees. Have the children write about some place that they would like to improve, for example, home, school, community. The children could do Thinking Activity 8 (page 64) before beginning their writing.

Et Cetera Activities

1. (Math) Place enough cherries in a bag to make cherry pies for the entire class. Let the children estimate the number of cherries in the bag. Count the cherries to see how close they came to the correct amount.

2. (Cooking) Let the children make cherry pies using prepared cherry pie filling.

3. (Science) Have the children plant the cherry pits from the Before Reading Activity 1 (page 62). Use glass jars for planting containers so the children can observe their plant's root system as Bidemmi did. Other seeds such as bean seeds can also be planted. Have the children keep a notebook illustrating the plant's progress. Children can also observe the amount of water and sunlight the plants need to grow.

Fig. 7.2.

Cherries and Cherry Pits Character Planning Sheet

Think about the person you are going to describe. Write the answers to the questions in the shapes below.

1. Who is the person and what is the person's name?

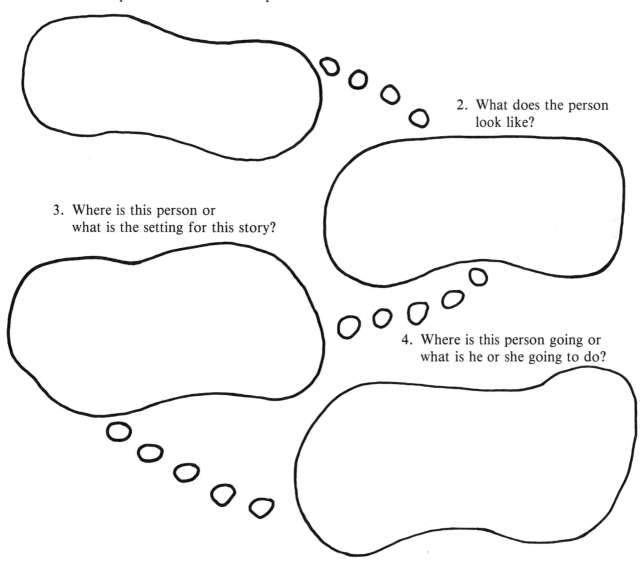

2. What does the person look like?

3. Where is this person or what is the setting for this story?

4. Where is this person going or what is he or she going to do?

The author uses similes when she describes her characters. Select some items from number 2 (above) and write some similes to describe your character's appearance.

4. (Science) Have the children research the topic of cherries. They could record their findings on an octagon similar to the one used by Williams on page 36. They might include country of origin, areas where grown in the United States, uses of cherries, types of cherries.

5. (Poetry, Drama) Have the children learn the humorous poem "'Let's Marry!' said the Cherry." The poem can be found in the book *Let's Marry Said the Cherry* by N. M. Bodecker (New York: Atheneum, 1974). Different students could be assigned the various fruit and vegetable parts. The children could make simple costumes such as masks or headpieces to portray the vegetable they represent. Students could read their parts and use facial expressions and hand movements to make their characters come alive. (In order to prevent their parts from becoming singsongy, students should mime their characters and write down things their characters might say as preparation for getting into their parts.)

6. (Math) Ask the children to name their favorite fruit. Graph the results. See figure 7.3.

Fig. 7.3

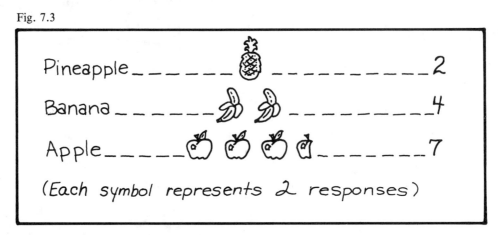

7. (Social Studies) Bidemmi says when the cherries are ripe, there will be enough cherries for everyone "even for their friends from Nairobi and Brooklyn, Toronto and St. Paul." Let the children use maps to locate these places.

8. (Music) Teach the children the Old English ballad "Billy Boy." The music and lyrics can be found in The Metropolitan Museum of Arts book called *Go In and Out the Window: An Illustrated Songbook for Young People* (New York: Henry Holt, 1987).

9. (Art Appreciation) Sometimes artists use fruits and vegetables as subjects in their paintings. This type of painting is called a still life. Paul Cezanne (1839-1906) was a French artist who liked to paint landscapes and still lifes. One of his paintings is called *Still Life with Cherries and Peaches* (1883-1887). This work can be found in *The World of Cezanne* by Richard W. Murphy and the Editors of Time-Life Books (New York: Time Life Books, 1968). Cezanne preferred painting still lifes for two reasons. One because his subjects found it difficult to sit quietly for the long periods of time he required to paint them and two because he had difficulty relating to people. Pablo Picasso (1881-1973) painted a still life called *Still Life with Cherries* (1943). Let the children compare the two paintings. It is interesting to note that between 1900 and 1904, Picasso made several trips to France where he studied the works of Cezanne. A black and white reproduction of Picasso's painting can be found in *The Shorewood Art Reference Guide* by Matila Simon (New York: Shorewood Reproductions, 1970).

10. (Art Appreciation) Artists sometimes capture the beauty of flowering trees in their paintings. Show the children Paul Klee's painting the *Young Tree*. This work is found in Ernest Raboff's book *Paul Klee* (Garden City, N.Y.: Doubleday, 1969).

11. (Social Studies) Bidemmi loved the idea of using cherry trees to beautify her neighborhood. Explain to the children that the beauty and fragrance of the cherry tree is appreciated by nearly everyone. Every spring the people in Washington, D.C., celebrate the Cherry Blossom Festival. The cherry trees were planted in 1912 by Mrs. William Howard Taft. The trees were a gift from the mayor of Tokyo, Japan.

The Author Says ...

Vera B. Williams (1927-) is a woman with a cause. To understand her cause is to understand her writing and her illustrations. She has spent her life planting and cultivating seeds of understanding and appreciation of all people. Continually working to improve people's quality of life, she has devoted time to such causes as nonviolence, children, women, and the environment. She has even been jailed for peacefully demonstrating against social injustice. She is committed to these causes because she sees evidence that some people's lives have been made better by others having the courage to do what she is doing. As a mother, grandmother, a lover of children, she feels very strongly that she must try to preserve our planet and make it a better place for all.

Williams was born in Hollywood, California, but grew up in New York City during the Depression. Like most families of that time, her parents were extremely poor. She vividly remembers the unpleasantness of being placed in a foster home and in a children's home for a time. In spite of the hardship and pain that she and her sister, Naomi, experienced, she says she "grew up in a hopeful climate." Her parents were constantly involved in causes designed to better the human condition. They believed that all people should be treated with dignity and respect and worked very hard to make this a reality. Despite their difficulties, Williams remembers her parents undying faith in her. Her parents had high expectations and felt that both of their girls had "special talents and were always on the lookout for educational opportunities." At an early age the girls were routed to the Clinic for Gifted Children at New York University. Here they began art classes, traveling alone on the subway every Saturday morning to study in the city. Williams continued her art studies through high school and college.

She graduated from Black Mountain College in North Carolina where her educational program was a combination of liberal arts and practical work. Here she met and married Paul Williams. Together they founded an "intentional community" at Stony Point, New York, where she lived and worked for seventeen years. Her days were spent gardening, baking, and teaching art, writing, and nature studies in the Barker School, which she and her husband helped establish. The closing of this school in 1970 brought a radical change in her life. She divorced and moved to Canada where she ran a bakery, lived in a houseboat, and wrote and illustrated her first children's book, *Three Days on the River in a Red Canoe*. This story was based on her five-hundred-mile canoe trip on the Yukon River. In 1979, she moved to New York City.

Her illustrations are purposely reminiscent of the pictures she painted in her childhood. She says, "In all of my children's books, I've worked from these early artistic impulses." Sometimes she draws a scene over and over and then selects the picture that most accurately portrays the feeling tone of the story. Sometimes she cuts and pastes pieces from several drawings. Whatever her method, she always has a message to convey—a thought, a feeling from her own life that she wants to share.

Asked how she researches her drawings, she said that she occasionally uses a live subject; however, most often she uses library books and pictures. She experimented with an accordion while writing *Music, Music for Everyone*. The more she experiences her topic, the better she can convey her meaning to her audience.

A Chair for My Mother was written in memory of her mother. It is a story of a little girl's love and consideration for her mother. Williams says it was her attempt to alter the past and make it more beautiful than it was. In fact, her own mother was only able to purchase a chair on the "installment plan."

Williams paints people of all colors and races. She hopes to demonstrate how alike we are, regardless of our backgrounds. This Williams does in brilliant simplicity. Her stories are full of love, kindness, and hope. She says, "I find living mysterious, difficult and wondrous. I hope that this is in my books somehow."[2]

Author Activities

1. The little girl telling this story says she would like to ask Bidemmi some questions about her stories. Have the children write questions that they would like to ask the author, Vera Williams, about this story.

2. The dedication page tells us that the author's father told her lots of stories. Ask the children to tell or write a story that their parents or another relative told them.

3. Vera Williams used watercolor to do this book. Have the children use watercolor to illustrate the character they describe in Writing Activity 4 (page 66).

4. This story is about a little girl's dream to improve her world. The author uses this theme a lot in her stories. Initiate a discussion with the class about things that need improving in their homes, schools, communities, the world. Ask them how they can help improve conditions in these areas of concern. Have them work individually or in groups and adopt a project at one of these levels. Let them use the Planning Worksheet on page 10 to plan how they might improve the area in question. They could write an article or story about their project and send it to Vera Williams. She can be reached through her publisher: Ms. Vera Williams, c/o Greenwillow Books, 105 Madison Avenue, New York, NY 10016.

BIBLIOGRAPHY

Other books by Vera Williams for grades 1 through 3.

A Chair for My Mother. New York: Greenwillow Books, 1982. (RL 3   IL k-3)

Music, Music for Everyone. New York: Greenwillow Books, 1984. (RL 3   IL k-3)

Something Special for Me. New York: Greenwillow Books, 1983. (RL 3   IL k-3)

Three Days on a River in a Red Canoe. New York: Greenwillow Books, 1984. (RL 3   IL 2-3)

---

[2]Anne Commire, *Something about the Author*, vol. 52 (Detroit: Gale Research, 1983), 191.

Chester the Worldly Pig

Bill Peet. Boston: Houghton Mifflin Co., 1965.

SUMMARY

Chester is an unhappy pig. After all, what is there to anticipate other than becoming sausage, ham, or bacon? Taking charge of his fate, he learns to stand on his snout. Equipped with his newly cultivated talent, he runs off to join the circus. His career as a performer is short-lived. He flees the circus only to be chased by a bear and captured by tramps. Narrowly escaping with his life, he returns to the farm seemingly resigned to his fate. As luck would have it, an observant carnival owner spies the outline of the six continents in Chester's hide. He puts him on exhibit and Chester becomes a star at last.

Possible Student Outcomes

Expand reading vocabulary.

Describe characters in a selection after examining both implicit and explicit character traits of the individuals.

Identify the base word for words ending in the suffix -*ly*.

Practice the thinking skills of fluency, flexibility, evaluation, complexity, decision making, risk taking, planning, originality, and communication.

** CHOOSE A LIMITED NUMBER OF ACTIVITIES FROM EACH SECTION **

Before Reading Activities

1. Place the outline of a pig on the chalkboard. Ask the children to think of as many words as they can that relate to "pigs." Have the children generate categories for the words listed, for example, food, description, habitat, behavior. Have the children list these categories on a piece of paper and then place the words on the chalkboard in the correct categories. Have the children share their placements orally. Discuss where they have placed each word, making changes if necessary. Explain that they are going to be reading a story about a pig. Ask them to watch for the words they have listed to see if they appear in the story.

2. Place the word *circus* on the chalkboard. Ask the children to think of as many words as they can that relate to the "circus." Have the children categorize these words. Categories might be: performers, animals, equipment. Explain that the pig in the story goes off to join the circus. Discuss the fact that they will meet many of the words they just generated in the story. Go over all the words making certain that each child understands their meanings.

3. Have the children look at the title page. Ask them what questions they have about what is happening. Ask them why the pig is dressed the way he is. Ask where they think this story takes place.

4. Put the following vocabulary words from the story on the chalkboard.

pig	worldly	clown
circus	tramp	train
star	bear	snout
racing	geography	balance

Go over the words with the children. Be certain that they understand the word meanings.[1] Use the connect two process to predict how the words will be used in the story. Have the children select any two words and tell how they might relate them. For example, a child might select the words *tramp* and *train* and say that tramps ride on trains to get where they are going. Explain that all these words are in the story they are going to read.

Predicting Activities

1. Have the children look at the illustration on page 3 and predict what Chester is feeling. Have them read the first sentence and tell which word verifies that Chester is angry and unhappy.

2. Have the children read to the end of the first paragraph on page 3 where Chester says, "I intend to try and amount to something." Ask them to predict what he might do to accomplish his goal. Ask why they think that.

3. Have the children read to the end of page 19 where the author says that "glorious dream" has turned into a "nightmare." Ask them to predict what might happen.

4. Have the children read to the end of page 27. The page ends with an incomplete sentence. "He was only one jump away when all of a sudden...." Ask the children to predict what might happen to Chester next. Ask what makes them think that.

5. After they read to the bottom of page 39, ask the children to predict what Chester will do next. Have them justify their answer.

6. After they read to the bottom of page 45, ask the children to explain the meaning of the word *geography*. Ask the children to predict what the gentleman who purchased Chester might do with him. Suggest that they examine the pig carefully before answering. Ask why they think that.

7. Have the children read to the end of the story.

Post Reading Activities

1. Ask the children to describe Chester. Ask what they know about him from his actions and speech. Have them use the letters in his name to write words that describe him. For example: C lever, H uge, E normous, S mart.

2. *Worldly* is an adjective describing Chester. Explain that the base word is *world* with the suffix -*ly* added to it. Put the following vocabulary words from the story on the chalkboard.

surely	quickly	frilly
finally	merely	plainly
carefully	suddenly	spotlessly

Ask the children to identify the base word in each of the above words.

---

[1]The idea for this connect two activity was taken from Camille L. Z. Blachowicz's article "Making Connections: Alternatives to the Vocabulary Notebook," *Journal of Reading* (April 1986): 646.

3. Chester had several physical characteristics that helped him become special, for example, his nose, his body markings. Ask the children to discuss other characteristics he had that helped him. Each of us has special characteristics. Initiate a discussion with the children about things that are special about each of them. Encourage them to share special things about each other.

4. On page 7, the author says that despite his hundreds of tumbles, by nightfall Chester's "spirits were high." Have the children discuss Chester's satisfaction. Ask why he was pleased with himself. Ask what makes their "spirits high." Discuss the importance of continued perseverance, as well as the importance of telling ourselves we did well rather than always relying on other people's praise.

5. Pages 14 and 15 show the circus people setting up the circus tents. Point out that there are wagons with rubber wheels parked beside the tents. Ask the children how these arrived, since the circus came by train. After the children speculate about this, have them examine the illustration on the back cover, which shows the wagons loaded on flatbed cars. Ask them if they have seen trains carrying trucks on flatbed cars.

6. Pages 10 and 11 show "the train's elegant red coaches." Discuss what it means to travel by coach on a train or airplane. Ask the children to think of other coaches they have heard about such as a stagecoach or Cinderella's coach.

7. Have the children compare and contrast a circus and a carnival.

8. As a vocabulary building activity have the children fill in the blanks on the Railroad Words worksheet in figure 8.1, page 74. All the words can be found in the text.

9. Select certain pages in the text. Have the children read the pages either silently or orally. Ask them to examine the illustrations on the pages they read and point out those words or phrases that the author has chosen to illustrate.

10. Have the children explain the following colorful expressions used by the author.

"He turned this around and around in his head." (p.3)

" So far so bad." (p.7)

"He was all set to be discovered." (p.8)

"He settled down to a good steady dogtrot." (p.13)

"The poor pig had turned almost the color of the clown's needle nose." (p.22)

"The bear was close on his trail, eating up the distance in long easy strides." (p.27)

"Lucky thing that the pig was light on his feet." (p.36)

Fig. 8.1

Chester the Worldly Pig Railroad Words

The following vocabulary words can be found in *Chester the Worldly Pig*. Fill in the blanks with the correct words. Place the numbered letters in the train cars at the bottom of the page and you will spell another word from the text.

1. Trains run on ___ ___ ___ ___ ___ ___.

1

2. The piece on the front of the train to push things off the track is a

   ___ ___ ___ ___ ___ ___ ___ ___ ___ ___.

2

3. A big car that pulls the train is a ___ ___ ___ ___ ___ ___ ___ ___ ___.

3

4. The cars that carried the poles and tents are ___ ___ ___ ___ ___ ___ ___.

4

5. The tramps rode on the ___ ___ ___ ___ ___.

5

6. The last car on the train is the ___ ___ ___ ___ ___ ___ ___.

6

7. A covered car that holds people is a ___ ___ ___ ___ ___.

7

8. The window ___ ___ ___ ___ ___ ___ were drawn to keep out the light.

8

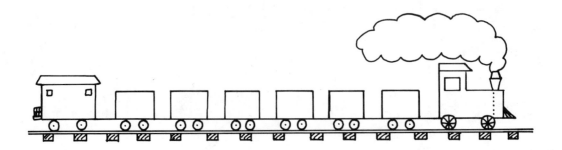

(Answers on page 195.)

11. As a vocabulary building activity, let the children play the game "Chester's Big Adventure." Duplicate figure 8.2, page 76, for the game board and duplicate figure 8.3, pages 77-80, to make the thirty Question Cards, five Bad Luck Cards, five Good Luck Cards, pieces for the children to move around the board, and the answer sheet the players will use (page 81). The game is designed for two players. In order for more children to play, more questions would need to be designed. The object of the game is to draw a question card from the stack and answer it correctly and move to the end of the game board. The player reaching the last square first wins. A player does not have to get the exact number of spaces to land on Chester's Adventure End in order to win.

Rules for
"Chester's Big Adventure"

1. Each player selects a marker and places it on the START square.

2. Shuffle the question cards. Put them beside the game board with the question side down.

3. Shuffle the Good Luck Cards and Bad Luck Cards and put them in two separate stacks face down.

4. The player whose last name begins with a letter closest to the beginning of the alphabet begins. Then the game continues in clockwise order.

5. The first player picks up a question card, reads it *aloud* and *answers it aloud*. The player across the table checks the answer sheet to be certain the answer is correct. If the answer is correct, the player moves the number of spaces specified on his question card. If the player answers incorrectly, or fails to read both the question and answer aloud, he or she does not move. If a player lands on a darkened square, he or she draws a Good Luck Card or Bad Luck Card, reads it *aloud*, and follows the directions. All used cards are placed on the bottom of the appropriate card stack.

6. The player reaching the END square first, wins.

SCHOOL OF EDUCATION
CURRICULUM LABORATORY
UM-DEARBORN

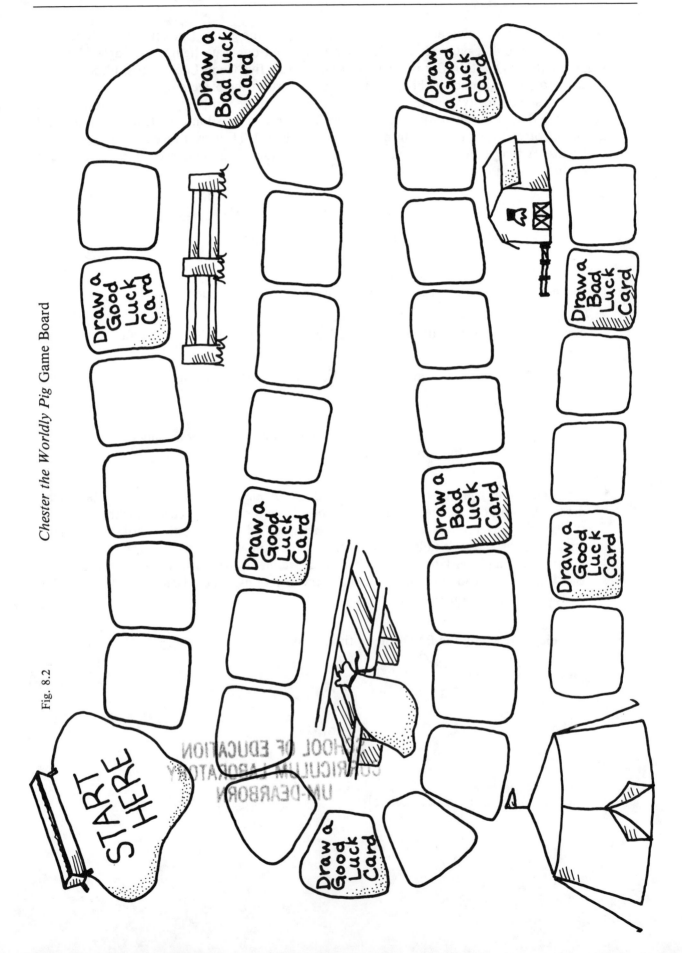

Fig. 8.2.   *Chester the Worldly Pig* Game Board

Fig. 8.3

Chester the Worldly Pig Question Cards

Card 1

If someone *grumbled*, that person is probably

    (happy, sad, mad)

Go ahead 2 spaces.

Card 2

A *trough* is used
    — to sit in
    — to eat from
    — to stand on

Go ahead 1 space.

Card 3

A *snout* is another name for:
    — a pig
    — a nose
    — a train car

Go ahead 3 spaces.

Card 4

The *locomotive* is usually at the _____ of the train.

Go ahead 1 space.

Card 5

Which word means the same as *elegant*?

    (ugly, lovely, plain)

Go ahead 3 spaces.

Card 6

What part of the train is the *coach*?

Go ahead 4 spaces.

Card 7

Chester moved down the track in a *dogtrot*. He moved:
    — very fast
    — very slowly
    — at medium pace

Go ahead 2 spaces.

Card 8

The circus _____ are made of *canvas*.

Go ahead 3 spaces.

Card 9

What do *roustabouts* do in the circus?

Go ahead 2 spaces.

Card 10

What does an *acrobat* do in the circus?

Go ahead 2 spaces.

(Figure 8.3 continues on page 78.)

Fig. 8.3—*Continued*

Card 11

Ringmaster is to circus as _____ is to class.

Go ahead 3 spaces.

Card 12

If you are a *spectator* you are:
      (acting, watching, running)?

Go ahead 1 space.

Card 13

Where is the *caboose* located on the train?
      (back, front, middle)

Go ahead 2 spaces.

Card 14

Geography is the study of:
      (living plants, the earth's surface, prehistoric animals)?

Go ahead 3 spaces.

Card 15

Europe, Africa, Asia, North America, South America are all
_____?

Go ahead 3 spaces.

Card 16

When you *boost* someone, you move them:
      Ahead, up, to the side?

Go ahead 2 spaces.

Card 17

What two words make up the word *pigpen*?

Go ahead 2 spaces.

Card 18

How many syllables are in the word *parade*?

Go ahead 2 spaces.

Card 19

Give two meanings for the word *star*.

Go ahead 3 spaces.

Card 20

A plume would be:
      hard, soft, sticky?

Go ahead 2 spaces.

Card 21

What is a *tramp*?

Go ahead 3 spaces.

Card 22

What color is *soot*?

Go ahead 3 spaces.

Card 23

How would you use an *aisle*?

Go ahead 3 spaces.

Card 24

How many syllables are in the word *lemonade*?

Go ahead 2 spaces.

Card 25

Give a synonym for the word *performance*.

Go ahead 4 spaces.

Card 26

Something that is *cumbersome* is: light, heavy, hard?

Go ahead 3 spaces.

Card 27

If you are *weary*, you want to: rest, run around, laugh?

Go ahead 2 spaces.

Card 28

What do you do with *sausage*?

Go ahead 2 spaces.

Card 29

Chester *teetered* on his nose. What does that mean?

Go ahead 3 spaces.

Card 30

What are *turnip greens*?

Go ahead 3 spaces.

(Figure 8.3 continues on page 80.)

Fig. 8.3—*Continued*

BAD LUCK CARDS	GOOD LUCK CARDS

1. The clown is mean to Chester.

    (Lose a turn)

2. A bear chases Chester.

    (Go back 2 spaces)

3. Tramps catch Chester.

    (Go back 3 spaces)

4. Chester sleeps in an alley.

    (Lose a turn)

5. The farmer is going to eat Chester.

    (Go back 4 spaces)

1. Chester learns to stand on his snout.
    (Move ahead 3 spaces)

2. Chester escapes from the circus.
    (Move ahead 2 spaces)

3. Chester becomes a star.

    (Move ahead 4 spaces)

4. The carnival man buys Chester.

    (Take an extra turn)

5. The carnival man sees the map on Chester.
    (Go ahead 2 spaces)

GAME MARKERS

Answers to Question Cards

Card 1   mad
Card 2   to eat from
Card 3   a nose
Card 4   front
Card 5   lovely
Card 6   car to carry people
Card 7   at medium pace
Card 8   tents
Card 9   set up the tents
Card 10   perform tricks on a trapeze, a high wire, or the ground
Card 11   teacher
Card 12   watching
Card 13   back
Card 14   the earth's surface
Card 15   continents
Card 16   up
Card 17   pig   pen
Card 18   two
Card 19   a heavenly body, a famous actor, or to mark with a star
Card 20   soft
Card 21   a person who travels on foot
Card 22   black
Card 23   to walk up and down
Card 24   three
Card 25   act, show
Card 26   heavy
Card 27   rest
Card 28   eat it
Card 29   moved unsteadily back and forth
Card 30   the green tops of a turnip that stick up out of the ground

Thinking Activities

1. (FLEXIBILITY) Pigs' noses are sometimes called "snouts." Have the children identify other kinds of noses such as a trunk, beak, proboscis, blowhole. This activity could be used in conjunction with Writing Activity 1 (page 82).

2. (FLEXIBILITY, COMPLEXITY) Have the children outline the physical and personal qualities that contributed to Chester's success in the circus.

3. (FLUENCY) Have the children list as many expressions or uses of the word *pig* as they can think of (pig out, pig in a poke, pig-headed, piggy bank, etc.).

4. (EVALUATION, DECISION MAKING) Read other pig stories with the same theme to the children. Have them use the Evaluation Worksheet on page 15 to compare and contrast the stories. The children's concluding statement might explain which pig story is most like *Chester the Worldly Pig* and why. Other similar pig stories are:

    Jeschke, Susan. *Perfect the Pig*. New York: Holt, Rinehart and Winston, 1981.

    Kings-Smith, Dick. *Pigs Might Fly*. New York: Viking Penguin, 1982.

    White, E. B. *Charlotte's Web*. New York: Harper & Row Junior Books, 1952.

5. (DECISION MAKING) Hold a "Chester Look-Alike Contest." Let the children bring in pigs that are stuffed, ceramic, slippers, banks. Establish criteria by which to judge the pigs. Use the Decision Making Worksheet on page 14 to decide which pig should win the prize.

6. (RISK TAKING, COMMUNICATION) The farmer on page 45 laughed because he thought he had tricked the carnival man into buying the "fattest pig." Discuss the farmer's behavior. Ask the children if he deceived the carnival man. Ask if his behavior was dishonest. Pose questions such as: Do we always need to be totally honest? Is not telling everything you know a lie?

7. (PLANNING) According to *Chase's Annual Events 1990*, March 1 is National Pig Day. Let the children plan a celebration using the Planning Worksheet on page 10. *Chase's Annual Events 1989* can be ordered from Contemporary Books, Dept. C, 180 North Michigan Avenue, Chicago, IL 60601.

8. (ORIGINALITY) The carnival man saw the shape of the various continents on Chester's hide. Have the children find various alphabet or geometric shapes in things around them. For example, a saxophone looks like the letter *J*, or the chalkboard is shaped like a rectangle or square.

Writing Activities

1. Chester's nose was one thing that he used to make himself become "something special." Have the children use the book *Whose Nose Is This?* by Richard Van Gelder (New York: Walker and Company, 1974) as a model to put together a book of noses. They could draw an animal's nose on one page and draw the animal's face or whole body on the back or they could cut and paste magazine pictures of animals' noses and faces. On the page picturing the whole animal, have the children write something about how the animal uses its nose.

2. Examine the author's choice of words as he describes the various characters, such as the carnival man. The author describes "a dignified white-whiskered man with a broad-brimmed hat and fancy frock coat." Let the children practice using other words to describe the man. Select other characters in the story and have the children analyze their actions, appearance, and speech. Then ask them to write descriptive phrases or paragraphs about these characters.

3. *The Book of Pigericks* by Arnold Lobel (New York: Harper & Row Junior Books, 1983) is a book of limericks about pigs. Share the book with the children. Teach them the rhythm and rhyme pattern for limericks. Suggest that they write a limerick about another pig. The pigs in the books listed in Thinking Activity 4 (page 82) could be their subjects. For example:

Chester's Limerick

There was a young pig who was sad

Thought his life on the farm was all bad.

He went searching for fame

But oh what a shame

He met up with a terrible cad.

Et Cetera Activities

1. (Art) Have the children examine the circus poster on page 4. Discuss the name of the circus as it relates to "Barnum and Bailey." Let the children design a circus poster advertising in words and pictures a circus they have seen or would like to see.

2. (Bulletin Board) Put up a "Pig Out on Books" bulletin board. Have the children make book jackets to advertise books they read. One end paper of the book jackets should contain a summary of the book and the other should contain comments written by several classmates advertising the books.

3. (Art) Have the children design an award for the pigs they bring for Thinking Activity 5 (page 82). The award could be a ribbon, trophy, or certificate.

4. (Art) Have the children make a poster or billboard advertising Chester's circus act.

5. (Geography) The circus poster on page 4 says that the circus is coming to Vincennes on May 15. Vincennes is in the state of Indiana. Use a map to locate this town near Chester's home.

6. (Art Appreciation) Show the children Henri de Toulouse-Lautrec's famous painting *In the Circus Fernando: The Ringmaster* (1888). The painting can be found in Ernest Raboff's *Henri de Toulouse-Lautrec* (Garden City, N.Y.: Doubleday, 1970). Two childhood accidents left Lautrec crippled. He used a walking stick and was less than five feet tall. He began painting at eight years of age. Three of his favorite subjects were clowns, acrobats, and horses. His father and art teacher took him to the circus often "to see the horses." This painting was his first attempt at using several figures to create motion.[2] Ask the children how he shows movement in this painting.

The Author Says ...

Every now and then we come to know someone whose warm, friendly manner makes us wish that we could know him personally. This describes my experience with Bill Peet.

He was born January 29, 1915 in the small town of Grandview, Indiana. When he was three, his family moved to Indianapolis. Their home was on the outskirts of the city and he and his two brothers enjoyed exploring the open countryside that was only a three-minute hike from home.

---

[2]Douglas Cooper, *Toulouse-Lautrec* (New York: Harry N. Abrams, 1985).

He has fond memories of his trips to his grandfather's farm in southern Indiana. En route the family passed through the town of Vincennes. The circus poster that catches Chester's eye in *Chester the Worldly Pig* advertises the circus as coming to Vincennes. Peet remembers as a child "being happily delayed by a circus parade coming through town." The farm held a particular fascination for him as the woods around it were filled with squirrels, chipmunks, weasels, opossums, raccoons, and red foxes. Animals have always fascinated him. He remembers well his first trip to the Cincinnati zoo. He had saved his money, earned from selling newspapers, and purchased a small box camera in anticipation of photographing all the animals. The camera malfunctioned and none of the pictures turned out. A lesson well-learned, from then on he always carried his sketch pad and pencil and drew the animals. To this day after selecting an animal for a story, he uses real animals as models. He says he likes to sketch them at the zoo where he can get acquainted with them, and then he develops his version to fit the personality.

Drawing has always been one of his favorite pastimes. As far back as he can remember, he was always drawing anything and everything. He remembers his classroom teacher taking his tablet away from him because he was drawing when he should have been listening. He particularly remembers one of his teachers marching him to the front of the room saying, "I want you to see what William has been doing!" With that she let the class see his work, returned his tablet, and said, "I hope you will do something with your drawing some day." I asked Peet what suggestions he would give teachers who are helping primary level children learn to write and draw and he said, "Give them freedom to express themselves so that their natural individual approach isn't hindered by too much instruction." When asked what advice he would give to children as they begin their writing and illustrating career, he said, "Don't worry about what others think of your work. Do it your way. Please yourself first—then be concerned later about others' opinions." Peet has followed this advice. He continued drawing through high school and was awarded a scholarship to the John Herron Art Institute in Indianapolis where he studied drawing, painting, and design for three years.

After leaving school, he accepted a position with Walt Disney as an animated film artist and eventually became Disney's top writer-illustrator. His last two films for Disney were *One Hundred and One Dalmations* and *The Sword in the Stone*. He attributes his storytelling ability to all the practice he got telling bedtime stories to his two sons, Bill and Steve. After twenty-seven years with Disney, he left to write and illustrate picture books. At forty-four his first book, *Hubert's Hair-Raising Adventure* (Boston: Houghton Mifflin, 1959), was published. Since then he has done thirty-five books. After this many, he says he has no favorites. When I asked if his family appears in any of his books, he reminded me that *Capyboppy* (Boston: Houghton Mifflin, 1966) is his one true-to-life animal story. The giant rodent was a family pet for a couple of years. His family is pictured in this story.

In relating how the writing process works for him, Peet said he "usually has the whole story visualized and when he feels that it is something he can enjoy illustrating, he does the writing." Most of his stories are "dreamed up," he says—products of his imagination.

I asked him to share one thing that he would like children to know about him and he said, "Through hard work—perseverance, I was able to have two careers which gave me a chance to use my talents as artist and writer."

Author Activities

1. Bill Peet enjoyed telling stories to his two boys when they were young. Storytelling is nearly a lost art. Talk about storytelling with the children. Explain the importance of selecting a story that *you like*, and the need to read the story over and over until it becomes "your story." Have the children work with their librarian and select a story to tell to their class.

2. At one point in his career, Bill Peet designed greeting cards. Have the children design a card using animal illustrations. Bring in greeting cards as samples. Read and discuss the messages they contain as examples for the children.

BIBLIOGRAPHY

Other books by Bill Peet for grades 1 through 3.

Big Bad Bruce. Boston: Houghton Mifflin Co., 1972. (RL 3   IL k-3)

Buford the Little Bighorn. Boston: Houghton Mifflin Co., 1967. (RL 3   IL k-3)

Caboose Who Got Loose. Boston: Houghton Mifflin Co., 1971. (RL 3   IL k-3)

Cowardly Clyde. Boston: Houghton Mifflin Co., 1979. (RL 3   IL k-3)

Encore for Eleanor. Boston: Houghton Mifflin Co., 1981. (RL 3   IL k-3)

Fly Homer Fly. Boston: Houghton Mifflin Co., 1979. (RL 3   IL k-3)

The Gnats of Knotty Pine. Boston: Houghton Mifflin Co., 1975. (RL 3   IL k-3)

Huge Harold. Boston: Houghton Mifflin Co., 1961. (RL 3   IL k-3)

Jethro and Joel Were a Troll. Boston: Houghton Mifflin Co., 1987. (RL 3   IL k-3)

The Kweeks of Kookatumdee. Boston: Houghton Mifflin Co., 1985. (RL 3   IL k-3)

The Luckiest One of All. Boston: Houghton Mifflin Co., 1982. (RL 3   IL k-3)

No Such Things. Boston: Houghton Mifflin Co., 1983. (RL 3   IL k-3)

The Wump World. Boston: Houghton Mifflin Co., 1970. (RL 3   IL k-3)

Zella, Zack and Zodiac. Boston: Houghton Mifflin Co., 1985. (RL 3   IL k-3)

Chicken Little

Retold by Steven Kellogg. New York: Mulberry Books, 1985.

SUMMARY

While walking to school Chicken Little is hit on the head by a mysterious object. Without investigating, she immediately jumps to the conclusion that "the sky is falling." Her frantic cries for help summon a variety of passersby. Each chimes in declaring, "the sky is falling." Unbeknownst to the frantic fowls, the fox is lurking in the bushes waiting for the precise moment to capture them. Disguised as a police officer, he makes his move shoving his victims into his truck. He carelessly tosses the acorn up into the sky. The flying acorn jams the sky patrol helicopter rotor blade and Sergeant Hippo Hefty falls to the ground and captures the fox. A trial is held and the fox is punished.

Possible Student Outcomes

Expand reading vocabulary.

Make judgments about characters' behavior.

Identify the characteristics of and write a cumulative tale.

Compare and contrast this version of the story with a more traditional version.

Practice the thinking skills of fluency, flexibility, complexity, evaluation, risk taking, planning, and decision making.

*** CHOOSE A LIMITED NUMBER OF ACTIVITIES FROM EACH SECTION ***

Before Reading Activities

1. Before showing the children this book, ask them if they have ever misjudged or misunderstood a situation because they only had part of the story. Have them share their experiences. Discuss the fact that we can make serious mistakes by not getting all the facts. Explain that the story they are going to read is about a character who did not get the facts straight and because of that she caused many problems for a lot of people. Ask the children if they know who that character might be.

2. Ask the children if they know what the word *poultry* means. Write the word on the chalkboard. If they are unable to explain the word, tell them that chickens, ducks, geese, and turkeys are all poultry and then let them attempt to explain the word. Explain that they need to understand this word's meaning in order to understand parts of the story.

3. Ask the children if they have ever seen a "Wanted" poster. Discuss where they might have seen posters, their purpose, and history. Bring in a Wanted poster for the children to see. Point out the poster on the book's frontispiece. Ask the children why the illustrator might have drawn it in the beginning of the book.

4. Put the following vocabulary words from the story on the chalkboard.

poultry	disguise	beaned
chicken	police	trial
acorn	escape	fox

Have the children say each word and then ask them to relate everything they know about each word. After discussing all the words, ask them how they think the words might fit together in this story or how these words might be used in the story.

Predicting Activities

1. Have the children look at the frontispiece where Chicken Little is looking at the Wanted poster. Ask the children where Chicken Little might be going. Ask why they think that. Ask what she might be thinking.

2. Have the children read to the bottom of page 13[1] where the fox says he is going to "avoid a scuffle by outsmarting those foolish fowl." Have them predict how the fox will outsmart them. Encourage them to use clues from the beginning of the story to answer this question.

3. After they read to the bottom of page 21 where the fox tosses the acorn up in the air, have the children predict what might happen.

4. Have the children read to the end of the story.

Post Reading Activities

1. Discuss reasons why a fox is often portrayed as a villain.

2. Ask the children how Chicken Little is feeling on the title page of the story. Ask what visual and verbal clues tell them this.

3. The author uses many colorful verbs throughout the text. Put some sentences on the chalk-board or on an overhead transparency. Ask the children to substitute other words for the ones the author uses. For example:

    "Poultry coming," <u>announced</u> Foxy Loxy, as he <u>spotted</u> Chicken Little <u>skipping</u> down the road."

    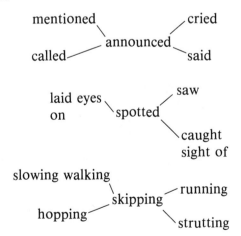

    Discuss the importance of selecting the appropriate words to best convey our meaning.

4. Ask the children what time of year it is in this story. What visual clues did they use to determine this answer?

---

[1]Pagination begins with the title page of the text.

5. On page 6, the Fox says that the hen "has a *plump pair of drumsticks* and they'll be mighty tasty *southern-fried*." Have the children explain these two expressions. Discuss why chicken legs are called drumsticks.

6. On page 10, the fox says, "I'll toast the bite-sized one as soon as I get home...." Ask the children to name other things that are "bite-sized." Have them relate where they have heard this expression.

7. Ask the children why the words *The Sky Is Falling* continue to get larger throughout page 11. Explain that this is a typographic clue used to show that all the characters are speaking at once and growling increasingly excited.

8. On page 13, the author says that the turkey and goose look "like pretty tough birds." When speaking about birds, the word *tough* can have two different meanings. Ask the children to explain the two meanings. Words that sound the same but have different meanings are called homographs. Have the children locate other homographs in this story, for example, spring, charge, toast, pop.

9. In order to fool the birds, the fox alters the sign on his truck. Ask the children to look at page 14 and explain what he has done incorrectly. Suggest that the children select other words from the text and use the first three letters to form other words just as the fox did with the word poultry. For example:

	servant
	serpent
service	sergeant
	series
	serf

    A variation of this activity would be to have the children select words from the text and let them find other words within that word. For example:

	of
	off
Officer	office
	ice

10. The illustrations in this book convey a lot of emotion. Even if there were no text, in many instances the reader would know what the characters were saying, thinking, and feeling. Have the children examine the double-page spread on pages 16 and 17 where the fox is shooing the animals into the truck. Let the children describe the characters' thoughts and feelings and speculate about what they are all saying. Have them justify their opinions.

11. The author uses a variety of words to describe the sounds the animals make, for example, shrieked, cried, chuckled, cackling, squawked, wailed, whispered, murmured, laughed. Discuss how varying the words enlivens the story. Each of these words has a slightly different connotation. Have the children demonstrate each sound by imitating the sound or describing how and when you might hear or use the sound. Place the following sound words on the chalkboard: whisper, murmur, chuckled, laughed, cried, shrieked. Have the children list the words in order from softest to loudest.

12. Use the words found in Before Reading Activity 4 (page 86) to make the following vocabulary game. Put each word on a card and place the cards in a box or bowl called the "Word Pool."

Let various children pick a card and structure a question that would have that word for its answer. For example:

| Answer | Question |

acorn   What hit Chicken Little on the head?

The teacher should select other words from the story and add them to the pool of words.

Thinking Activities

1. (EVALUATION, DECISION MAKING) There are many versions of this familiar tale. Read several to the children. Let them use the Evaluation Worksheet on page 15 to compare several versions.

    Bishop, Gavin, illus. *Chicken Licken*. New York: Oxford University Press, 1987.

    Burgess, Beverly C. (orig.) *Chicken Little*. Tulsa, Okla.: Harrison House, 1987.

    Byer, Carol, illus. *Henny Penny*. Mahwah, N.J.: Troll Associates, 1981.

    Dolan, Ellen M., and Janet L. Bolinske, retellers. *Henny Penny*. St. Louis, Mo.: Milliken Publishing, 1987.

    Galdone, Paul, illus. *Henny Penny*. Boston: Houghton Mifflin Co., 1984.

2. (FLUENCY) Ask the children to name as many stories as they can where a fox or wolf is the villain. The titles listed can be used in Writing Activity 2 (page 90).

3. (FLUENCY, FLEXIBILITY) The fox mentions numerous ways to fix chicken. Have the children brainstorm to come up with as many ways of cooking chicken as they can (roast, bake, barbecue, etc.).

4. (EVALUATION, DECISION MAKING) In its original form, this story was one of three or four thousand stories called *Jataka* tales. These stories originated in India and served to explain the origin of Buddha. According to legend, Buddha took the form of many different animals before he was ultimately transformed into the Enlightened One. Through each reincarnation, he learned a different lesson. An earlier version of this tale is Marie Shedlock's fable called "The Hare That Got Away," which can be found in *Eastern Stories and Legends* (New York: E. P. Dutton, 1920). In this story Buddha (to be) was born a lion. He brings a foolish hare to her senses when she thinks the Earth is falling in after being hit on the head by a piece of fruit. An updated version of the hare story is *Foolish Rabbit's Big Mistake*, revised by Rafe Martin (New York: Putnam Publishing Group, 1985). Share one of these versions with the children. Have them compare the stories and use the Decision Making Worksheet on page 14 to decide which one they like best and why.

5. (COMPLEXITY) Have the children analyze the fox and Chicken Little and list words that describe both characters. They should use words from the text, as well as words that they feel describe the characters.

Character Description

Chicken Little	
Physical description	Behavior
small	foolish
little	silly
feathery	dim-witted
yellow	featherhead

6. (FLUENCY, FLEXIBILITY, COMMUNICATION) Chicken Little is on her way to school. One of her books is an A-B-C book. Have the children write and illustrate an alphabet book for Chicken Little. Each letter could represent a word that might prove helpful to Chicken Little. For example:

> *A* is for *apple* that grows on the trees in the barnyard.
>
> *B* is for *barn* where many farm animals live.
>
> *C* is for *coop*. All chickens live in a coop.

Chicken Little's other book is a number book. The children could create either a counting book or a math book of equations that Chicken Little needs to know. For example:

> Chicken Little finds seven bugs. Three more bugs crawl beside her. How many bugs does she have all together? (7 + 3 = 10)

7. (COMPLEXITY) This story could be classified as a fable. Have the children decide on a moral to the story.

8. (FLUENCY) Have the children brainstorm to come up with ten things to do with an acorn.

9. (COMPLEXITY, RISK TAKING) Discuss with the class Chicken Little's reaction to the falling acorn. Ask the children to identify better ways for the birds to have handled this situation. Ask them to relate times that they have jumped to conclusions and been sorry.

Writing Activities

1. Have the children write this story in the form of a rebus. Encourage them to use pictures, letters, and symbols to represent characters, scenes, or objects in the story. For an example, see figure 9.1.

Fig. 9.1

The Story of Chicken Little

[rebus] as opposed to Chicken Big [rebus]

1 day, [rebus] set out for [rebus]. As she skipped along, she passed under a [rebus].

Suddenly an [rebus] hit [rebus] on her [rebus]. "The sk-[rebus] is falling," she said. "The

sk-[rebus] is falling." "[rebus] some-1 please help me?"

2. Chicken Little first sees the fox on a Wanted poster. Have the children design a Wanted poster for other literary "bad guys." Some of these characters might be the villains they listed in Thinking Activity 2 (page 89). Other characters they might choose are Goldilocks, Hansel and Gretel's stepmother, the Queen in Snow White. Children should brainstorm for words that describe the characters. Students could use the outline of the Wanted poster in figure 9.2 for this activity.

Fig. 9.2   *Chicken Little* Wanted Poster

WANTED

FOR _____

_____

WARNING: _____

_____

_____

IF YOU SEE _____

_____

SCHOOL OF EDUCATION
CURRICULUM LABORATORY
UM-DEARBORN

3. *Chicken Little* is a type of cumulative or repetitional tale where the story progresses as the characters travel and meet other characters on the way. Read several cumulative tales to the children such as:

> Aardema, Verna. *Bringing the Rain to Kapiti Plain*. New York: Dial Books for Young Readers, 1981.
>
> Grimm, Jacob, and Wilhelm K. Grimm. *Bremen Town Musicians*. Mahwah, N.J.: Troll Associates, 1979.
>
> Zolotow, Charlotte. *Mr. Rabbit and the Lovely Present*. New York: Harper & Row Junior Books, 1962.

> Have the children write an original cumulative tale. The planning worksheet in figure 9.3 might be helpful to the children in planning their story.

4. This is a modernized version of an old tale. Let the children discuss the changes in characters and events. Several authors have written updated versions of fairy tales. Read some of these to the children and let them select a different fable or fairy tale and rewrite it with modern day characters and events. The following books can be used as examples:

> Briggs, Jim. *Jim and the Beanstalk*. New York: Putnam Publishing Group, 1980.
>
> Cole, Babette. *Prince Cinders*. New York: Putnam Publishing Group, 1987.
>
> Myers, Bernice. *Sidney Rella and the Glass Sneaker*. New York: Macmillan Co., 1985.
>
> Scieszka, Jon. *The True Story of the 3 Little Pigs*. New York: Viking Kestrel, 1989.

5. The fox was obsessed with recipes using the various birds in the story. Have the children write recipes using chicken, duck, goose, and turkey and compile a class book entitled *Foxy Loxy Poultry Recipes*. The cookbook can include imaginative recipes that the children create or actual recipes that they bring from home. The children's book could include a table of contents like the one on page 22 in the story.

6. Have the children imagine that they are newspaper reporters covering this story. Have them write an article covering the events. Read several newspaper articles to the children before making this assignment. Analyze the articles and point out how newspaper articles include the who, what, when, where, and how of stories.

Et Cetera Activities

1. (Rhythm) Teach the "Chicken Little Rap" in figure 9.4, pages 94-96 to the children.

2. (Drama) Have the children make puppets of the various characters in the story. The children can use the outlines for puppets in figures 9.5 and 9.6, pages 97 and 98, or they can design their own puppets. Have the children write an original script and put on a puppet show.

3. (Art) The title page is a landscape of a rural area. Have the children draw a landscape. If possible, take the children outside on the lawn or on a nature walk. Otherwise, children can look at pictures of landscapes to have a scene to draw.

4. (Art, Sequencing) Ask the children to fold a piece of 12" × 18" paper into eight squares. Have them illustrate the eight major events in the story. Have them write the moral of the story on the bottom of their pictures. These pictures can be glued to a stiff background, laminated, and cut up for picture puzzles. Children could cut the laminated pictures into eight squares and place them in proper sequence. If the pictures are to be used for sequencing, the moral of the story should be left off of the original drawing.

(Text continues on page 99.)

Fig. 9.3

Chicken Little Planning Worksheet

Use this planning worksheet to write a cumulative tale.

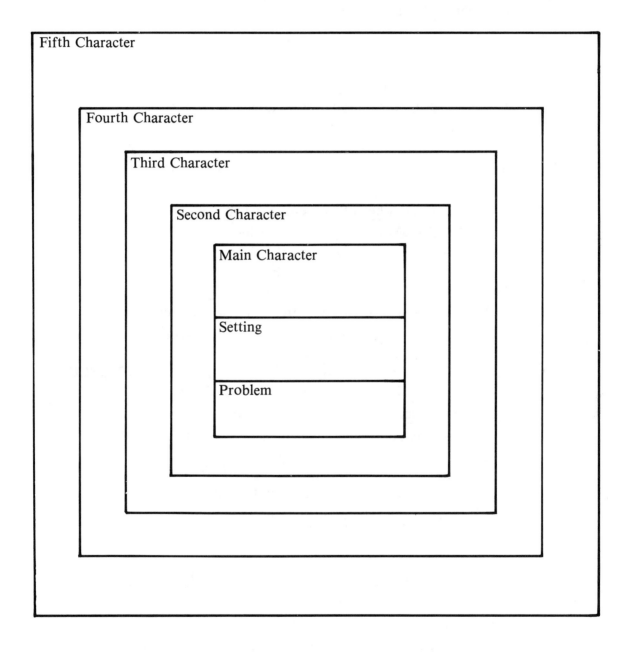

Fig. 9.4

Chicken Little Rap

This rap can be done by a group in unison or it can be done by a group with parts being assigned to Chicken Little, Henny Penny, Ducky Lucky, Turkey Lurkey, Foxy Loxy, and the Judge.

There was <u>once</u> a little chicken,
Chicken <u>Little</u> was her name.
She got <u>bopped</u> on her head (Tap head) and that <u>lead</u> to her
fame.
I said she got <u>bopped</u> on her head and that <u>lead</u> to her fame.
Now I <u>know</u> you're probably <u>wondering</u> how this <u>incident</u>
occurred
Because the <u>whole</u> thing sounds <u>terribly</u> absurd
Yes the <u>whole</u> thing sounds <u>terribly</u> absurd.

(CLAP)

Seems the <u>chick</u> was <u>a-walkin'</u> down the <u>path</u> one morn,
When something <u>fell</u> from a <u>tree</u> — it <u>was</u> an acorn
Yes, something <u>fell</u> from a <u>tree</u> — it <u>was</u> an acorn.

(PATSCH)

It <u>hit</u> Chicken Little on the top of her <u>head</u>
The <u>poor</u> thing, she thought she was <u>dead</u>
Yes, the <u>poor</u> thing, thought she was <u>dead</u>.

(CLAP)

"The <u>sky</u> is falling she began to <u>shout</u>!
"The <u>sky</u> is falling can you <u>help</u> me <u>out</u>! "

Her <u>cries</u> were heard by a <u>friendly</u> bird
Henny Penny was her <u>name</u> and she said,
"<u>My</u> word, <u>my</u> word, <u>my</u> word.
What's <u>wrong</u> with <u>you</u> Chicken Little, my <u>child</u>?
You <u>sound</u> just like you're <u>going</u> wild."

"The <u>sky</u> is falling," Chicken Little said.
"A piece of it <u>hit</u> me on the <u>head</u>."

With that the two began to shout,
"The sky is falling, can you help us out?
The sky is falling, can you help us out?"

x/ x/ x/ x/ x/ x/ x/ x/ x/ x/   (PATSCH)

Their cries were heard by another bird
Ducky Lucky was his name and he said,
"My word, my word, my word.
What's wrong with you two,
You sound like you belong in the zoo."

"The sky is falling," the two girls said.
"A piece of it hit Chicken Little on the head."

With that the three began to shout,
"The sky is falling, can you help us out?
The sky is falling, can you help us out?"

x/ x/ x/ x/ x/ x/ x/ x/ x/ x/   (CLAP)

Their cries were heard by a lady bird
Goosey Loosey was her name and she said,
My word, my word, my word.
What's wrong with you three,
You sound like you belong in a tree."

"The sky is falling the three birds said
A piece of it hit Chicken Little on the head."

With that the four began to shout,
"The sky is falling, can you help us out?
The sky is falling, can you help us out?"

x/ x/ x/ x/ x/ x/ x/ x/ x/ x/   (PATSCH)

This time Turkey Lurkey came up the path.
"Be quiet," he said.
"You're much too loud.
Besides that, you're drawing a crowd."

"The sky is falling" the four birds said.
"A piece of it hit Chicken Little on the head."

(Figure 9.4 continues on page 96.)

Fig. 9.4—*Continued*

With that the five birds began to shout,
"The sky is falling, can you help us out?
The sky is falling, can you help us out?"

x/   x/ x/   x/   x/ x/   x/ x/ x/   ⌐   (CLAP)

This time Officer Loxy came on the scene.
He'd been listening to the silly birds scream.
"I'll be glad to help you," he said with a smirk.
And with that, he gave them a terrible jerk.
Threw them into his truck—threw the acorn up high
What he didn't know was that up in the sky
Was the sky patrol with Sergeant Hippo (Raise right fist)

The helicopter crashed, the fox was caught
The judge said, "After giving this thought,
You'll go to jail, you nasty beast.
You'll never have fowl for a feast."

x/   x/ x/   x/   x/ x/   x/ x/ x/   ⌐   (PATSCH)

So that's the story of the silly bird (Both palms up)
Who started to shout before she thought things out
The lesson is clear for all to see (Lower voices)
Listen while we tell it to thee!

GET THE FACTS, MAN! (Loud voices)

(CLAP)

Fig. 9.5

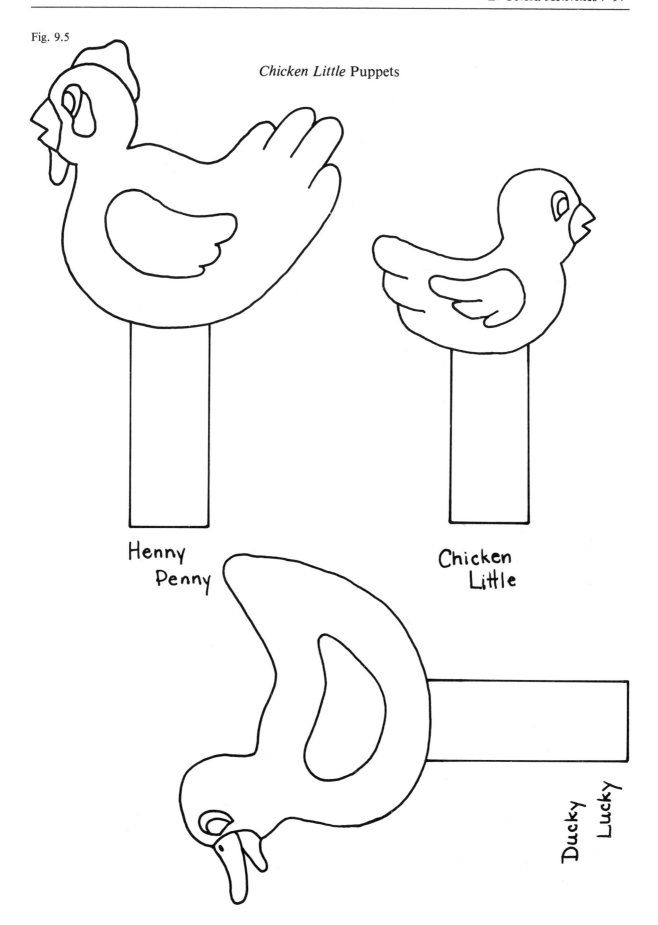

Chicken Little Puppets

Henny
Penny

Chicken
Little

Ducky
Lucky

Fig. 9.6

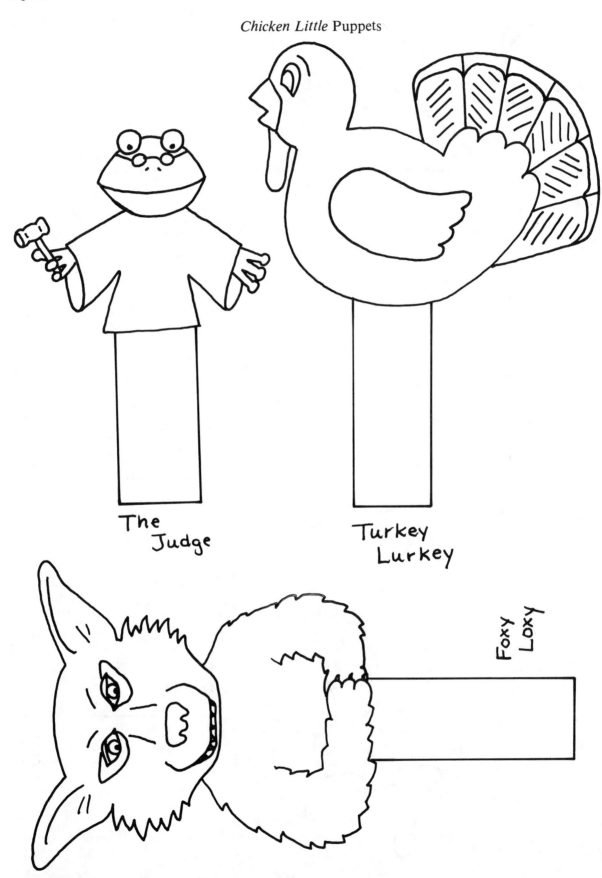

Chicken Little Puppets

The Judge

Turkey Lurkey

Foxy Loxy

The Author Says ...

Steven Kellogg was born on October 6, 1941, in Norwalk, Connecticut, a country town outside of New York City. As far back as he can remember he has wanted to write and draw. As a youngster, he drew stories for his sisters using their stuffed animals as the main characters. His sisters said he was "telling stories on paper."

He particularly liked drawing animals and birds and confesses that his room had the appearance of a "crayoned aviary-bestiary" because the walls were adorned with drawings of wildlife.

It was his grandmother who had the most influence on his early writing career. She was his best friend and confidante. It was she who taught him to love and appreciate the trees, plants, and animals in the nearby woods. She shared her love of nature and taught him to appreciate the "treasures that comprised the Victorian clutter of her room." He says he often finds traces in his work of the things the two of them shared.

Kellogg studied at the Rhode Island School of Design and as a senior was awarded a European Honors Fellowship, which afforded him the opportunity to study in Florence, Italy. He later took graduate classes at American University in Washington, D.C., and exhibited his work in the Washington area. He also began submitting his work to a variety of publishers of children's books. In 1966, he illustrated *Gwot!* (New York: Harper & Row, 1967) by George Mendoza. This was the beginning of a long and successful writing and illustrating career. He often illustrates for other authors. One of his favorites is *The Boy Who Was Followed Home* by Margaret Mahy (New York: Dial, 1983).

When he is creating a book, Kellogg often walks in the woods and fields outside his home. The quiet sounds of the wooded area help him sort through his ideas.

He finds children an "observant and responsive audience." He delights in his work and has won numerous awards. Both *Can I Keep Him?* (New York: Dial Books for Young Readers, 1971) and *The Orchard Cat* (New York: Dial Books for Young Readers, 1983) were selected for inclusion in the American Institute of Graphic Arts' Children's Book Show in 1971-1972. The New York Times selected *There Was an Old Woman* (New York: Dial, 1974) as one of the ten Best Illustrated Books of the Year in 1975. *The Mystery of the Missing Red Mitten* (New York: Dial Books for Young Readers, 1974) was in Children's Book Showcase in 1975 and *Yankee Doodle* (New York: Parents' Magazine, 1976) was an ALA Notable Book in 1976.[2]

Author Activities

1. Steven Kellogg has illustrated numerous books by other authors. Authors and illustrators seldom communicate with one another when a work is in progress. Publishers employ both authors and illustrators. When an author submits a manuscript, the publisher selects the illustrator they feel will best communicate the story in pictures. Let the children illustrate a classmate's manuscript. The author can select someone to illustrate his or her work, or, as in the "real world," the teacher can select the illustrator. This activity could be done as a cooperative project with an upper grade class. Fifth graders could illustrate primary children's manuscripts.

2. As a youngster, Steven Kellogg loved to write and illustrate stories using his sister's stuffed animals as the main characters. Set up a display of stuffed or ceramic animals brought in by the children. Have each child select an animal to write and illustrate a story about. Copies of the stories can be given to the animal's owner.

---

[2]Doris De Montreville and Elizabeth D. Crawford, eds., *Fourth Book of Junior Authors and Illustrators* (New York: H. W. Wilson, 1978), 208-9.

3.   Steven Kellogg has illustrated filmstrips, as well as books. Let the children put one of their stories on filmstrip. Blank filmstrip kits for making filmstrips can be purchased from companies such as Brodart Co., 1609 Memorial Avenue, Williamsport, PA 17705.

BIBLIOGRAPHY

Other books by Steven Kellogg for grades 1 through 3.

Aster Aardvark's Alphabet Adventures. New York: William Morrow, 1987. (RL 3   IL k-up)

Best Friends. New York: Dial Books for Young Readers, 1986. (RL 3   IL k-3)

Can I Keep Him? New York: Dial Books for Young Readers, 1971. (RL 3   IL k-3)

The Island of the Skog. New York: Dial Books for Young Readers, 1973. (RL 3   IL 1-3)

Much Bigger Than Martin. New York: Dial Books for Young Readers, 1976. (RL 3   IL k-3)

The Mysterious Tadpole. New York: Dial Books for Young Readers, 1977. (RL 3   IL k-2)

The Mystery of the Flying Orange Pumpkin. New York: Dial Books for Young Readers, 1980. (RL 2   IL 1-3)

The Mystery of the Missing Red Mitten. New York: Dial Books for Young Readers, 1974. (RL 2   IL 1-3)

The Mystery of the Stolen Blue Paint. New York: Dial Books for Young Readers, 1982. (RL 2   IL 1-3)

The Orchard Cat. New York: Dial Books for Young Readers, 1983. (RL 3   IL 1-3)

Pecos Bill. New York: William Morrow, 1986. (RL 3   IL 1-3)

Pinkerton, Behave! New York: Dial Books for Young Readers, 1979. (RL 3   IL 1-2)

Prehistoric Pinkerton. New York: Dial Books for Young Readers, 1987. (RL 3   IL 1-2)

Ralph's Secret Weapon. New York: Dial Books for Young Readers, 1983. (RL 3   IL 1-3)

A Rose for Pinkerton. New York: Dial Books for Young Readers, 1981. (RL 3   IL 1-2)

Tallyho, Pinkerton! New York: Dial Books for Young Readers, 1982. (RL 3   IL 1-2)

Won't Somebody Play with Me? New York: Dial Books for Young Readers, 1972. (RL 3   IL k-3)

The Cloud Book

Tomie de Paola. New York: Holiday, 1975.

SUMMARY

When we look up in the sky, we often see clouds of various sizes, shapes, and descriptions. This book helps children understand what clouds are and how to identify the different kinds of clouds.

Possible Student Outcomes

Understand what clouds are.

Understand that there are different kinds of clouds and how to distinguish one from the other.

Explain several meanings for the word *cloud*.

Practice the thinking skills of flexibility, fluency, evaluation, complexity, and forecasting.

*** CHOOSE A LIMITED NUMBER OF ACTIVITIES FROM EACH SECTION ***

Before Reading Activities

1. Build a concept ladder on the chalkboard. Place the word *cloud* in the center of the ladder as in figure 10.1. Place questions on the ladder. The questions can be both teacher and student generated.[1]

    Fig. 10.1

    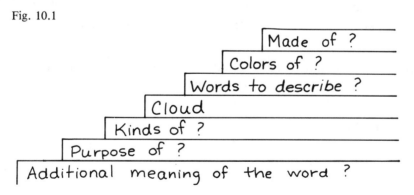

    Discuss *clouds* before reading the text. Ask the children if they can answer any of the questions on the ladder before reading the book. Write in their responses. After reading the text, fill in the ladder revising previous answers where necessary.

2. Have the children list as many words as they can think of that describe clouds. Put the headings Shape, Color, Size, and Texture on the chalkboard. List the children's words under the appropriate headings. See how many of their words the author uses and how many words they have that the author did not use. After reading the story see if they can substitute any of their words in the story without changing the author's meaning.

---

[1]The idea for this concept ladder was taken from Camille L. Z. Blachowicz's article "Making Connections: Alternatives to the Vocabulary Notebook," *Journal of Reading* (April 1986): 648.

3. Put the following vocabulary words from the story on the chalkboard. Discuss the words before reading the story. Ask the children if they have any ideas about how the author might be going to use these words in the story.

atmosphere	mare	lofty
cirrus	cauliflower	fleecy
cumulus	drizzle	halo
stratus	flurries	mackerel
feathery		

Predicting Activities

1. After the children read page 5, ask them what they think clouds are.

2. After they read through page 7, ask the children if all clouds are the same. Ask how they are different.

3. After they read through page 17, ask the children what *fog* is.

4. Before the children read page 19, ask them why there is a picture of a snake on this page.

5. Have the children read to the end of the story.

Post Reading Activities

1. Because weather played such an important part in our ancestors' lives, they were always trying to locate signs to predict the weather. The most reliable observations were passed down from generation to generation and were recorded in reference books such as *The Farmer's Almanac*. Show the children the weather section of a current *Farmer's Almanac*, as well as an older edition if possible.

2. The author has included an index in *The Cloud Book*. Teach the children how to use the index. Explain the difference between the use of a hyphen and a comma in an index. Let the children complete the Index Worksheet in figure 10.2.

3. The author says that in olden days people observed the clouds and found various shapes in them. People still do this for amusement. Take the children on a walk and let them observe the clouds and see if they can find shapes in them.

4. The author uses metaphors and similes to describe clouds. He says cirrocumulus clouds are "moutons"; cirrostratus clouds are "bed-sheet clouds"; cumulus clouds are puffy and look like "cauliflowers." Have the children use other similes and metaphors to describe other weather phenomenon such as lightning, thunder, tornadoes, and hurricanes.

5. The author explains that fog is a cloud that is low to the ground. Teach the children Robert Sandburg's well-known poem "Fog." The poem can be found in *The Golden Treasury of Poetry* compiled by Louis Untermeyer (New York: Golden Press, 1959).

Fig. 10.2

The Cloud Book Index Worksheet

1. How many pages tell about cumulus clouds? _____

2. On what page will you find information about stratus clouds? _____

3. Look up *cirrocumulus* clouds in the index and answer the following question.

    Where are cirrocumulus clouds located in the sky? _____

    _____

4. Look up *altocumulus* clouds in the index and answer the following question.

    What color are altocumulus clouds? _____

5. Look up *cirrostratus* clouds in the index and answer the following question.

    Why are cirrostratus clouds sometimes called "bed-sheet clouds"? _____

    _____

    _____

6. In order to reinforce the characteristics of the various types of clouds, make a semantic feature analysis grid[2] to help the children analyze the clouds described in the book. The grid can be as simple or complex as you choose to make it. See figure 10.3.

Fig. 10.3

Semantic Feature Analysis Grid

Cloud	High in sky	Fair weather	Low in sky	Puffy/ fleecy	Bad weather
cirrus	+	+	–	–	–
cumulus	–	+	+	+	+
stratus	–	–	+	–	+
cirrocumulus	+	+	–	+	–

7. Many words have more than one meaning. The author shows us that a *boa* is a snake. Mountain people say a cloud wrapped around a mountain is a "boa cloud." A boa is also a woman's feather or fur wrap that can be draped around her shoulders. Make a list of words that have several meanings. Words such as *fog, cloud, blue, hog,* and *steamed* could be on the list. Have each child pick a word and make a mobile to show that he or she understands the various word meanings. See figure 10.4.

Fig. 10.4

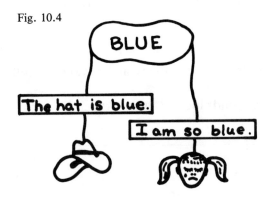

8. The author explains the idiomatic expressions "She has her head in the clouds" and "He's in a fog." Other cloud expressions are:

"on cloud nine" — extremely happy

"cloud-cuckoo-land" — imaginary situation or state of affairs

"clouded crystal ball" — a poor or mistaken view of what is going to happen

"under a cloud" — under suspicion, not to be trusted, or bad things continually happening

"in the clouds" — in a dreamworld

"every cloud has a silver lining" — good things often follow bad things

Have the children illustrate these sayings both literally and figuratively.

---

[2]The idea for the semantic feature analysis grid was taken from D. D. Johnson and P. D. Pearson's *Teaching Reading Vocabulary*, 2d ed. (New York: Holt, Rinehart and Winston, 1984).

9. Write the characteristics of cirrus, cumulus, and stratus clouds on the chalkboard. Point out that cirrocumulus clouds are named by combining "cirrus" and "cumulus." Help the children pick out the characteristics from each cloud that are combined to make the new cloud.

10. Have the children explain the weather sayings on pages 24 through 27 in their own words.

Thinking Activities

1. (FLEXIBILITY) Have the children think of as many things as they can that the weather affects (clothes, work, recreation, mood, crops, travel).

2. (FLUENCY) Have the children brainstorm to come up with as many words as they can that describe clouds (fluffy, billowy, dense).

3. (EVALUATION) People have many notions about how to forecast the weather. For example, some people say that previously broken bones ache when the weather is changing, or that children become restless when the barometric pressure is dropping. List as many weather predictors as you can find. Have the children conduct a survey of parents, teachers, and friends to determine the accuracy of these predictions. After locating several people who feel they can predict weather by the indicators listed, assign children to check with these people over a certain period of time. After collecting data, evaluate the results. Determine if these are accurate predictors.

4. (FLEXIBILITY) Have the children brainstorm to come up with a list of people to talk with and discuss how the weather affects them. Your list might include campers, firemen, athletes, automobile drivers.

5. (COMPLEXITY) This book has an index but no table of contents. Divide the children into small groups and give each group a book that has both a table of contents and an index. Let the children examine both parts of the book and explain the differences. Differences should include:

Table of Contents	Index
Located in front of book	Located in back of book
Arranged by chapters in the book	Arranged in alphabetical order
Lists chapters	Lists details found in chapters

Have the children create a table of contents for this book by grouping the information into subjects. Sample chapters might be:

Types of Clouds 1
Legends about Clouds 20
Cloud Sayings 24

6. (PLANNING) Have the teacher and children plan an experiment to illustrate how clouds are formed, how rain is made, and how frost is made. Use the Planning Worksheet on page 10. As you discuss the process of how clouds are formed, let the children generate ideas about what might be needed to plan these experiments. Children need to know that warm air can carry more water vapor than cold air. They will need to decide what materials they will need to simulate or produce warm air (hot plate, pan of water) and how they can produce cold air (ice, tin can). See Et Cetera Activity 3 (page 107).

7. (FLUENCY) Have the children list as many examples as they can that demonstrate water vapor being changed to clouds (breath on a cold day, steam from a tea kettle or pan of boiling liquid, exhaust from a car, air coming from an opened freezer door, fog on a lake).

8. (FLEXIBILITY) Have the children list as many materials as they can think of to simulate clouds (styrofoam, cotton, shaving cream, angel hair). These suggestions can be incorporated into the science activity in Et Cetera Activity 1 (page 107).

9. (ORIGINALITY) Have the children speculate about the following statement: All of the clouds turn green. Why?

10. (FORECASTING) Have the children forecast the effects of having no clouds. Use the Forecasting Worksheet on page 11.

Writing Activities

1. Sometimes expressions are made up to explain weather phenomenon. For example "thunder is a sack of potatoes rolling" or the children's chant, "It's raining; it's pouring; an old man is snoring." Have the children make up an original explanation for such weather happenings as clouds, lightning, fog, dew, sleet, or smog.

2. Have the children write and illustrate a weather book entitled *Fact or Fable*. Using the information in *The Cloud Book* and other weather information that they can gather, they can arrange their information into statements that are either fact or fiction. For example:

   Clouds are heavier than air. (Fact or Fable?)

3. Haiku is a type of Japanese poetry that paints a picture in the reader's mind. Seventeen syllables long, the poems most often describe something in nature. Have the children select one type of cloud mentioned in *The Cloud Book* and write a haiku about their cloud. For example:

   Clouds, low down, puffy
   Always changing in the sky
   Flat bottoms, fluffy.

   (Cumulus)

4. Have the children compose riddles about particular types of clouds. For example:

   I'm high up in the sky but hard to catch your eye. What am I? (Cirrocumulus)

5. The author quotes numerous weather sayings that have been passed down for generations. List the weather generalizations that follow and have the children write their own weather rhymes. For example:

   When ladybugs cling together
   There's going to be fair weather.

   or

   Chickens scratching in a group
   Means they should be heading for the coop.

Generalizations:

Rain comes if:

   there is a ring around the sun or moon

   sheep stand close together

   small birds and animals are noisy

   hair sags

   your nose itches

   bees stay near their home

   there's thunder in the morning

Fair weather if:

 ladybugs fly together

 if it thunders at night

 bees fly far from home

 insects fly together

Expect storms if:

 chickens cluster together and scratch

 owls hoot

 cows use their tails to swat flies

Weather rhymes and generalizations can be found in the following books:

 Caney, Steven. *Kids America.* New York: Workman Publishing, 1978.

 Davis, Hubert, comp. *A January Fog Will Freeze a Hog.* New York: Crown Publishers, 1977.

 Schwartz, Alvin, collector. *Cross Your Fingers, Spit in Your Hat.* Philadelphia: J. B. Lippincott Company, 1974.

6. Tomie de Paola writes a silly cloud story at the end of the book. Let the children write their own cloud story.

Et Cetera Activities

1. (Science) Have the children select one type of cloud and illustrate the kind of weather produced by that cloud. The picture should include people who are dressed appropriately and activities and other details that would communicate information about the weather this type of cloud would bring.

2. (Science) Have the children listen to and record the weather forecast for two weeks. Have them record the weather to see how accurate the forecast is. Ask them what they learn from this experience.

3. (Science) Clouds are droplets of water clustered together. Ask the children where the water comes from. (Explain how the sun warms puddles, ponds, oceans. The water in these areas warms and appears to disappear. Actually it is changing into a gas called water vapor. The water vapor rises and becomes an invisible part of the air. As it rises, it cools and changes into tiny drops of water. These droplets bunched together are clouds.) Perform the following experiments to demonstrate how frost, rain, and clouds are formed. (You will need a tin can, ice, rock salt, a pan or tea kettle, a tall jar or glass, and a fireplace match.)

Experiments

 Fill a tin can with layers of ice and rock salt. Observe what happens to the can. Ask the children to explain why this happens. (Frost forms on the outside of the can because the warm air is cooled and moisture in the air condenses or changes form into frost.)

 Hold the can over a pan of boiling water or over a boiling tea kettle. Observe what happens to the frost. Ask the children why this happens. (The frost turns to water droplets or "rain" because warm air can carry more water vapor than cold air. The warm steam hits the cold can, the warm air is cooled and as a result it cannot hold all of its water and "rain" droplets appear.)

Fill a tall jar or glass half full with hot water. Light a fireplace match and hold it over the top of the jar. Blow out the match, allowing the smoke from the match to go into the jar. Place the can on top of the jar and observe what happens inside the jar. (A cloud appears inside the jar. The can gets very frosty and the cloud turns to rain because again the warm air in the jar hits the cold air above it.)

4. (Art) Have the children select several weather generalizations in Writing Activity 5 (page 106) to illustrate on a page and let their friends see if they can predict which type of weather they have illustrated.

5. (Music) The author of the following poem is unknown. Using the melody to "Baa, Baa, Black Sheep Have You Any Wool?", teach the children the following lyrics:

> White sheep, white sheep
> On a blue hill,
> When the wind stops
> You all stand still
> When the wind blows
> You walk away slow
> White sheep, white sheep
> Where do you go?

6. (Art Appreciation) John Constable (1776-1837) was a well-known English landscape painter whose ability to capture the sky was unequalled. His predecessors painted the countryside, but he was more concerned about the sky and the effects of light on his subjects than he was on the scenic details. Many of his works, such as *Stake-by-Nayland* (1836) and *The Hay Wain* (1824), feature beautiful airy clouds. Constable's paintings can be found in N. W. Janson's *History of Art: A Survey of the Major Visual Arts from the Dawn of History to the Present Day* (New York: Harry N. Abrams, 1969).

The Author Says ...

Tomie de Paola (1934-) was born in Meriden, Connecticut. He considers it his good fortune to have been brought up pretelevision and has fond memories of listening to the Saturday morning radio show "Let's Pretend." Two important influences on his choice of careers were this program and his mother's intense love of books and the hours she spent reading to him and his brother.[3] As a child he loved to read. When asked if he had a favorite title, he replied, "I was very fickle. I fell in love with each and every book I picked up."

His stories often include people and events that are meaningful to him. His rich Italian heritage is evident in many of his books, particularly the many delightful tales of Strega Nona and his beautiful piece *The Clown of God* (New York: Harcourt, Brace Jovanovich, 1978). *Watch Out for the Chicken Feet in Your Soup* (Englewood Cliffs, N.J.: Prentice-Hall, 1974) is reminiscent of his grandmother's chicken soup recipe, which included chicken feet. He said that the idea for *The Cloud Book* came to him as he was looking at clouds one day.

When asked what advice he can give to children as they begin their writing and illustrating careers, he said, "Practice" and "Be professional."

As a child he loved to draw. He began formal art classes at Pratt Institute in 1952 specializing in children's book illustrating. He completed an M.F.A. at California College of Arts and Crafts in

---

[3]Anne Commire, *Something about the Author*, vol. 11 (Detroit: Gale Research, 1978), 70.

1969 and was honored with doctoral equivalency at Lone Mountain College in 1970. A highly acclaimed artist, his work includes designing for the theater and designing flower shows. In the spring of 1989, he designed the annual Dayton's/Bachman's Spring Flower Show in Minneapolis. The show was visited by 125,000 people. His work has been displayed in several one-man shows and his murals can be found in Catholic churches and monasteries in New England. When asked which artists most influenced his style, he mentioned the Siennese painters as well as Giotto, George Rouault, Fra Angelico, and Ben Shahn.

When asked how teachers could be most helpful to their students in the areas of writing and illustrating, he stressed the importance of reading to children for enjoyment, keeping activities to a minimum, and the need to surround children with "loads of books in the classroom."

Writing nonfiction is different from writing fiction. Obviously it is important for the author to research his topic thoroughly before beginning. I asked de Paola if he could offer any further advice for children to assist them in their nonfiction writing. He said, "Read encyclopedias from A to Z over and over again. That's what I did as a child."

Author Activities

1. Tomie de Paola has written several nonfiction books. (See bibliography following this section.) Read several of these books to the children. Note how the books are organized. Have the children select a nonfiction topic and write a book on one of these subjects. Point out the importance of researching your topic so that you have your facts correct. Children's Press has a series entitled New True Books. These are excellent resources for small children to use to gather information about nonfiction topics.

2. The author creates many different characters using the same shape for the face. By changing the facial expression, he makes people happy, sad, surprised. Let the children experiment with different facial expressions. Put a basic face shape on the chalkboard. Also put various expressions, hairdos, hats on the board. See figure 10.5. Let the children create a variety of people. Have them write a sentence or paragraph describing their character's feelings and actions.

Fig. 10.5

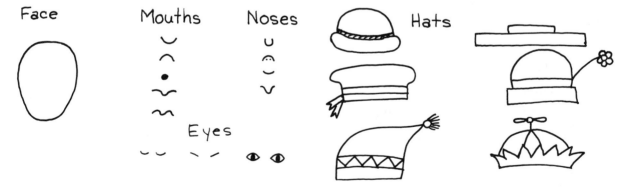

3. Tomie de Paola's books include people and events in his life. *Charlie Needs a Cloak* (Englewood Cliffs, N.J.: Prentice-Hall, 1974) was easy for him to write because he himself is a weaver. Have the children write a story about one of their hobbies or a story that includes someone close to them.

BIBLIOGRAPHY

Other nonfiction books by Tomie de Paola for grades 1 through 3.

Charlie Needs a Cloak. Englewood Cliffs, N.J.: Prentice-Hall, 1982. (RL 3   IL 1-3)

The Family Christmas Tree Book. New York: Holiday, 1980. (RL 3   IL 2-3)

The Kids' Cat Book. New York: Holiday, 1978. (RL 3   IL 2-3)

The Quicksand Book. New York: Holiday, 1977. (RL 2   IL 1-3)

Things to Make and Do for Valentine's Day. New York: Franklin Watts, 1976. (RL 3   IL 1-3)

The Fallen Spaceman

Lee Harding. New York: Bantam Skylark Books, 1973.

SUMMARY

An alien, Tyro, is outside his spacecraft repairing a faulty camera. Suddenly, without warning, his starship starts its engines and speeds away. The sudden jolt sends the lone alien spinning toward Earth where he crash-lands. Two young brothers discover the spaceman encapsulated inside an enormous spacesuit. Curious, Erik climbs inside and is trapped. When he comes face to face with Tyro, the two realize that each is equally frightened of the other and even though they cannot speak to one another, they understand each other's feelings.

Possible Student Outcomes

Expand reading vocabulary.

Identify characteristics of a science fiction novel.

Recognize the author's use of personification.

Describe key characters in the story.

Practice the thinking skills of fluency, flexibility, forecasting, evaluation, planning, and decision making.

** CHOOSE A LIMITED NUMBER OF ACTIVITIES FROM EACH SECTION **

Before Reading Activities

1. Ask each child to brainstorm to come up with a list of words about the genre of science fiction. Place these words on the chalkboard. Ask the children if any of the words listed do not fit. Circle the questionable words. Ask the children to examine the words that are not circled and

then explain the elements of science fiction (stories that emphasize scientific laws and technology, stories that describe human beings and other beings involved with futuristic machines and technology, such as robots, spaceships, talking computers). Explain to the children that science fiction is a type of fantasy. It differs from pure fantasy in that fantasy describes the impossible while science fiction deals with things that are possible. Science fiction is believable while fantasy is not. Ask the children to explain why the circled words do not fit.

2. Explain to the class that they are going to read a science fiction novel. Put the following paragraphs up on the board and ask them to fill in the blanks with the words they think will best fit. After they complete this activity, discuss the words they chose. Read the first page of the story and compare the children's choice of words with the author's.

The alien _____ circled Earth many times before the _____ fell.

The _____ inside the starship looked a little like _____, but they were different in many ways.

They came from another _____ in a _____ part of the galaxy.

They were _____, like children, with tiny _____ and _____.

They had large _____ and pale _____ and no body _____ at all, not even an _____. The tops of their _____ were _____ as apples.

Their _____ were strange. To our ears their _____ would sound more like _____.

3. Ask the students to pretend that an alien is visiting their classroom. This is his first trip to Earth. Their job is to describe Earth people to him. Each child could brainstorm to come up with adjectives that might be used to describe Earth people. After sharing their adjectives, they should explain or demonstrate why their words are good describing words. Explain that the author describes his perception of Earth people in this story. After reading the story come back to the words the children listed and see how many the author used. Have the children compare their descriptions with the author's.

4. Ask the children if they have ever traveled in a foreign country, different state, or if they have spent an extended period of time in someone else's home. Ask them how they felt, for example, welcome, apprehensive, lonely. Ask them what contributed to their feeling the way they did. Discuss the difficulties we face when we are not at home. Ask the children how they would like to be treated in such a situation. Explain that this is a story about an alien stranded on Earth who has many of the same feelings they described. This discussion should help them identify with Tyro's feelings and help set the stage for the story.

Predicting Activities

1. Have the children stop reading after the second paragraph on page 5. Ask whether they think the spaceman should continue to drift around Earth waiting to be rescued or land. Ask what things they think he needs to consider before making a decision.

2. Have the children read through page 11, where Tyro's ship has landed and he is unconscious, and have them predict what they think will happen next and why.

3. After the children read through page 18, ask them to predict what Erik will do now that he has discovered the spaceship. They need to justify their opinion. Ask them if they are basing the opinion on an incident in their own life where they either found something or were first to see or experience something.

4. Have the children read to page 31 where Erik has found a tiny opening on the back of the spacesuit. Ask the children to predict if he will enter it. Encourage them to describe what they think will happen.

5. Have the children stop reading at the end of page 44 where Tyro hears a strange sound. Have the children predict what he will do and explain their prediction.

6. After they read to the end of the first paragraph on page 77, ask the children to predict the way the story will end.

7. Have the children read to the end of the story.

Post Reading Activities

1. On page 1, the author says the starship "came from another world in a distant part of the galaxy." Ask the children to explain what the galaxy is, the solar system.

2. The author uses a simile to describe the aliens' heads. He says, "their heads were as smooth and as polished as apples" (p.1). Explain how similes help the author paint a picture for the reader. Have the children list the similes in the story. Let them rewrite the similes.

3. Have the children explain the sentence on page 2 that says "In this way they were most like us."

4. On page 4, the author says that Tyro felt alone and afraid. Ask the children to describe a time that they have experienced these same feelings.

5. Have the children explain the statement on page 8 that says "The great oceans threw back the sunlight and dazzled his weak eyes." Have the children rephrase the sentence to make certain that they understand that the sun was reflecting off of the water and hurting Tyro's eyes.

6. On page 10, the author says, "Gradually the spacesuit steadied as the *dazed* computer realized what had happened." Ask the children if a computer can be "dazed." Sometimes authors give human traits to inanimate objects. This is called *personification*. Encourage the children to find other examples of personification in the story. For example:

rockets coughed (p.10)	air screamed (p.10)
purr of the control (p.20)	forest felt warm and kind (p.22)
light winked (p.39)	anxious helicopters (p.84)
starship had thrown open arms (p.92)	

   Have the children write some phrases using personification. As preparation for this activity select one of the words the author uses, such as *purr*. Have the children brainstorm to come up with as many things as they can that could be described as "purring." This activity should help them generate phrases such as "The motor sounded as though it were purring."

7. In order to help us visualize the events in the story, the author selects his words carefully. He wants us to both see and hear the spaceship as it rips through the forest. One sound device used by authors is the *onomatopoeia*—words that sound like their meaning, for example, hissed, buzzed, creaked, roared, thundered. Have the children locate examples of onomatopoeia in the story.

8. In order to help the children internalize the characters and events in the story and expand their vocabulary, have them make a picture outline of the story.[1] The outline can include the main characters and setting. (See figure 11.1.)

---

[1] A graphic organizer. See D. W. Moore et al., *Prereading Activities for Content Area Reading and Learning* (Newark, Del.: International Reading Association, 1982).

Fig. 11.1

Tyro

spaceman
kind
weak
curious
timid
intelligent
anxious to learn
wanted to make good
    impression

Erik

brave
curious
foolish
kind
caring
afraid of Tyro
sick from space
    ship air

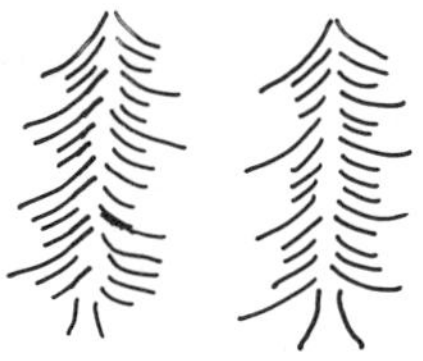

Forest

green
rich
dense

Father (John)

intelligent
trusting
father of boys
frightened
gets help

Spacesuit

gigantic
70 feet tall
computerized
broken
seat belt
out of order

Earth people

warlike
loud voices
fighting among themselves

9. Have the children discuss why the voice on page 90 is telling Tyro, "You have done well." Encourage them to relate this statement to their own lives and share incidents when someone might have said this to them or when they wished someone would have said this to them. Remind them of the importance of telling ourselves that we have done well and not always relying on others to tell us this.

10. Tyro said he would return to Earth when wars had ceased and people on Earth treated each other like brothers. Have the children discuss how they might proceed to make the necessary changes for Tyro's return.

11. As a vocabulary building activity, put up a bulletin board similar to the one in figure 11.2, page 114. Use vocabulary words from the story to make one or several constellations. Put dots on the board in the shape of a constellation. Put a construction paper outline of the constellation as seen by early man. Write vocabulary words on strips of paper and put them in a construction paper spaceship pocket on the bulletin board. Children can take words from the pocket. As they demonstrate an understanding of the vocabulary words by using them in a sentence or writing out their meaning or illustrating them, the children can take yarn from dot to dot, thus slowly forming a constellation. A variation of this game might be to give each child laminated posterboard squares containing dot-to-dot drawings of various constellations. Children could take vocabulary words from the bulletin board and as they demonstrate an understanding of the words, they could use washable pen to draw from dot to dot on their own posterboard square, thus forming a constellation.

Fig. 11.2

12. Let the children complete the "Galaxy of Words" puzzle in figure 11.3, pages 115 and 116, using the vocabulary words from the story. The children can reread the pages indicated on each question and fill in the blanks on the galaxy with the correct word from the story.

Thinking Activities

1. (FLUENCY, FLEXIBILITY) Encourage the children to brainstorm to come up with ways to use robots.

2. (FORECASTING) Have the children forecast the cause and effect of a spacecraft landing on the school playground. Use the Forecasting Worksheet on page 11.

3. (EVALUATION) Use the Evaluation Worksheet on page 15 to evaluate the following statement: Robots should replace people in the following lines of work: teaching, nursing, space flight, firefighting, and music.

4. (PLANNING, ORIGINALITY) Have the children plan and design a spacecraft. Use the Planning Worksheet on page 10.

5. (PLANNING, ORIGINALITY) Have the children plan and design an earth home for Tyro. They should consider everything they have learned about him physically and emotionally.

6. (DECISION MAKING, EVALUATION) Make the following statement to the children: Suppose you were asked to accompany Tyro back to his planet. You are told that you can take five things with you. What would they be? Use the Decision Making Worksheet on page 14 to decide. Discuss the pros and cons of the trip.

7. (EVALUATION) Have the children use the Evaluation Worksheet on page 15 to discuss the advantages and disadvantages of computers, robots.

Fig. 11.3

The Fallen Spaceman

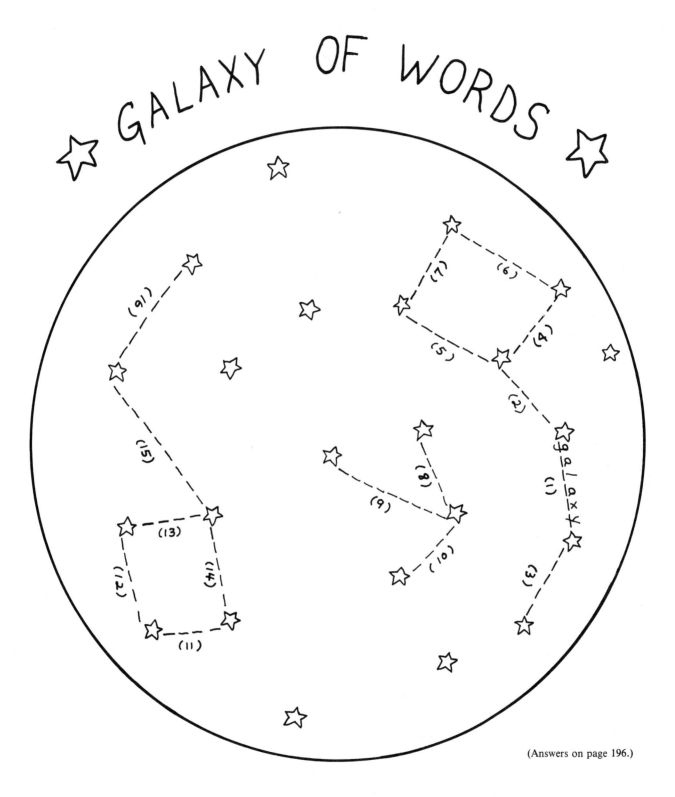

(Answers on page 196.)

(Figure 11.3 continues on page 116.)

Fig. 11.3 — *Continued*

Galaxy of Words Puzzle Questions

Read the questions below. Sometimes you will be asked a word meaning. Sometimes you will be asked for an analogy. Each question has the page number in *The Fallen Spaceman* where you can find the correct word. As you identify the word, fill in the blanks on the galaxy above to form three different constellations. Blanks between the stars indicate the number of letters in each word. The first one is done for you.

1. A word that means a group of stars (p.1).

2. Slight coloring of the alien's face (p.66).

3. A word describing the circles of color in the rocks (p.27).

4. A word that describes the force of the wind against Tyro's spacesuit (p.9).

5. A word describing the spacesuit's jerky movement (p.10).

6. Seat belt is to car as _____ is to spacesuit (p.6).

7. A two-legged creature (p.23).

8. The high-pitched sound of the falling spacesuit (p.12).

9. Transparent is to windshield as _____ is to faceplate (p.23).

10. The body of the ship where Tyro was working (p.2).

11. Wires that are wound around to enable the computer to speak (p.21).

12. A word to describe what the spacesuit walked on (p.48).

13. Stair is to staircase as _____ is to ladder (p.62).

14. The hole cut in the trees by the fallen spacesuit (p.29).

15. A mass of stone or metal fallen to earth (p.13).

16. A synonym for immediate action (p.69).

8. (FLUENCY, EVALUATION) Have the children brainstorm to come up with as many things as they can that are computer controlled. Then have them evaluate society's current dependence on computers. Use the Evaluation Worksheet on page 15.

9. (EVALUATION) Have the children debate the pros and cons of Erik's leaving Tyro after Tyro had worked to save his life (p.88).

10. (FORECASTING) Have the children consider the effect of man's warlike tendencies as described by Tyro's people. Use the Forecasting Worksheet on page 11.

Writing Activities

1. Tyro and Erik developed a bond between them even though their time together was short. Have the children imagine that they are either Erik or Tyro and write each other a letter. Encourage them to include something about their feelings.

2. Once Erik's father notified the authorities about the spaceman, there were numerous television broadcasts. Have the children write TV or radio broadcasts and deliver them as though they were broadcasters or TV anchorpersons.

3. Bring in newspaper articles of various spectacular events to share with the children. Discuss how newspaper articles include the who, what, when, where, and how of a happening. Have the children write a newspaper article about the events in *The Fallen Spaceman*. Some children might choose to write about the spaceship landing; others might write about its journey through the forest or about Erik's rescue or the spaceship's departure. Have them create a headline for their article.

4. Robots as we know them are only about thirty years old. The idea for "intelligent" machines that can do humans' work first came from the pages of science fiction novels. Have the children write a science fiction story. They might begin by generating current problems, current solutions, and future solutions (see figure 11.4). Then let them use the planning sheets in figures 11.5 and 11.6, pages 118 and 119.

Fig. 11.4

Current problem	Current solution	Future solution
People who are blind and need guidance	Seeing-eye dogs	Robots to lead them around

5. Share some science fiction picture books with the children. Using these as models, have them write a science fiction picture book. Some examples:

Brewster, Patience. *Ellsworth and the Cats from Mars*. Boston: Houghton Mifflin/ Clarion Books, 1981.

Counsel, June. *But Martin!* London: Faber & Faber, 1984.

Glass, Andrew. *My Brother Tries to Make Me Laugh*. New York: Lothrop, Lee & Shepard Books, 1984.

Marshall, Edward. *Space Case*. New York: Dial Books Young, 1982.

Marzollo, Jean, and Claudio Marzollo. *Jed and the Space Bandits*. New York: Dial Books Young, 1987.

Sadler, Marilyn. *Alistair in Outer Space*. New York: Prentice-Hall, 1984.

Fig. 11.5

The Fallen Spaceman Solution Planning Sheet

1. What will it look like?

_____

_____

_____

_____

_____

2. How will it work?

_____

_____

_____

_____

_____

_____

3. How will people use it?

_____

_____

_____

_____

_____

Fig. 11.6

The Fallen Spaceman Story Planning Sheet

1. Who are the main people in your story?

2. Where does the story take place?

3. What is main person's problem?

4. How does main person feel about the problem?

5. How is the problem solved?

6. How does the main person feel or how do things change after the problem is solved?

6. Have the children imagine it is the year 2075 and write a description of and illustrate their job as a:

teacher	pilot
librarian	police officer
doctor	occupation they choose

Et Cetera Activities

1. (Math) On page 25, the spacesuit is described as being seventy feet tall. Have the children locate some things inside or outside the school that are 70 feet tall so the children can actually visualize the size of the spacesuit. Have the children lie down with their feet touching each other's shoulders. Determine how many children it would take to stand seventy feet tall.

2. (Research) Stephen commented that the falling object might be a UFO (p.13). Have the children research unidentified flying objects. Some resources to use are:

Collins, Jim. *Unidentified Flying Objects*. Milwaukee, Wis.: Raintree Publishers, 1977.

Thorne, Ian. *U.F.O.'s*. Mankato, Minn.: Crestwood House, 1978.

Wilding-White, Ted. *U.F.O.'s*. Tulsa, Okla.: Educational Development Corporation, 1977.

3. (Math) On page 57, the author says, "The city was more than twenty miles away—a half an hour drive." If it took 30 minutes to travel 20 miles, ask the children how far they would go in sixty minutes. This can be explained graphically as in figure 11.7.

Fig. 11.7

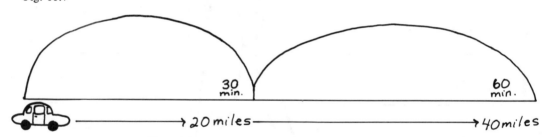

4. (Art) The illustrations in this text appear to be done with pen and ink. They are abstract to create the feeling of mystery, suspense, and the unknown. Discuss the illustrations. Have the children illustrate a scene from the story that the illustrator has not done. In order to simulate the illustrations in the book, use turkey feathers as pens and black tempera mixed with white glue for ink.

5. (Art) Have the children make a large mural of their community or neighborhood as it looks today and then as it might look like in the year 2050.

6. (Research) This story might prompt some children to want to do research about robots. One good source is Art Kleiner's *A Look inside Robots* (Milwaukee, Wis.: Raintree Publishers, 1981).

7. (Art Appreciation) Show the children Vincent van Gogh's painting *The Starry Night*. Explain that color was to van Gogh what words are to writers. They were the descriptors that enabled him to set the mood and feeling of his work. This painting expresses the artist's understanding and appreciation of the wonder of the universe. His brush strokes and use of color convey the immensity of the heavens and invite us to wonder what lies beyond. This painting can be used

to demonstrate van Gogh's style and use of color and to initiate a discussion about life on other planets and the effect this might have on life as we know it. This painting and additional information about Vincent van Gogh can be found in Adeline Peter and Ernest Raboff's, *Vincent van Gogh: Art for Children* (Garden City, N.Y.: Doubleday, n.d.).

The Author Says ...

Lee Harding was born February 19, 1937, in Colac, Victoria, Australia. Van Ikin describes him as "Australia's most versatile science fiction writer."[2] He has worked as an editor and writer and has written both adult's and children's books. He is keenly aware of the problems confronting today's youth and says, "They are living in a world I merely wrote about." He goes on to say, "it honestly terrifies me sometimes to imagine what it must be like for them in today's world." His concern for today's youth and for the world condition is very evident in *The Fallen Spaceman*.

A master storyteller, his plots are always a result of his character's plight. He has a gift for writing narrative that helps make his characters so believable.

His interests include travel, cooking, gardening, music, and reading. At one time he worked as a photographer only to realize that he would "rather work from inside of people rather than concern myself with surfaces." It is this ability to "see within" that enables him to create such realistic, sensitive characters. One need only to read one of his stories to understand why he has been awarded numerous honors. Among these awards is the Ditmar Trophy (1972) for the best science fiction story of the year. The winning novel was *The Fallen Spaceman*.[3]

Author Activities

1. *The Fallen Spaceman* was first published in *If* magazine. Harding is a regular contributor to periodicals. *Odyssey* is a magazine for young people interested in astronomy and outer space. Each month they feature a section called "Future Forum." Readers are encouraged to send in their opinions on various topics such as "How would you talk to an alien?" "Should NASA send non-astronauts into space?" "Should the U.S. develop robot technology?" In addition, this periodical publishes young people's illustrations and puzzles done on space themes. Encourage the students to submit a letter, illustration, or puzzle to *Odyssey* magazine. Submissions should be sent to *Odyssey*, 1027 North 7th Street, Milwaukee, WI 53233.

2. Harding worked for many years as a photographer. Taking pictures of portions of objects or close-up shots can sometimes distort a subject and often make it appear to be something from outer space. Have the children search for objects to photograph, such as the bottom of a stapler, the teeth on a comb. Let them experiment and shoot objects from different angles. Have them choose their best photograph, the one most difficult to identify, and give it a science fiction name. Display the photos with their titles and let other classes try to identify what is in the photo.

3. Harding has won several awards for his books. *The Fallen Spaceman* won the Ditmar Trophy in 1972 as did *Dancing Gerontius* (out of print) in 1970. Have the children design a trophy or plaque that would be appropriate for a science fiction award. Students could judge each other's science fiction stories done in Writing Activity 5 (page 117). This award could be presented to the best science fiction picture book. Students could use the Evaluation Worksheet on page 15 to select the best picture book.

[2]Curtis C. Smith, ed., *Twentieth-century Science-Fiction Writers* (New York: St. Martin's Press, 1981), 245.

[3]Frances C. Locher, ed., *Contemporary Authors*, vol. 106 (Detroit: Gale Research, 1982), 227.

The Funny Little Woman

Retold by Arlene Mosel. New York: E. P. Dutton, 1972.

SUMMARY

This story is about a little Japanese woman who loves to make rice dumplings and to laugh. One day one of her dumplings rolls down a hole in her floor. The little woman follows her dumpling down under the ground where she runs into the wicked *oni*. Despite the fact that the statues of the gods try to hide and protect her, the *oni* captures her and takes her home to cook for him. Many seasons pass and the little woman grows lonely for her home. She narrowly escapes, taking the *oni*'s magic paddle with her. The paddle enables her to make quantities of dumplings that she is able to sell and she becomes very wealthy.

Possible Student Outcomes

Expand reading vocabulary.

Recognize the characteristics of and to write an "incident story."

Compare two or more selections having the same plot pattern.

Identify and understand the meaning of the prefix *un-*.

Practice the thinking skills of fluency, flexibility, elaboration, originality, evaluation, forecasting, decision making, and risk taking.

** *CHOOSE A LIMITED NUMBER OF ACTIVITIES FROM EACH SECTION* **

Before Reading Activities

1. Play a recording of Japanese music to set the mood for this story. Explain to the children that this story takes place in Japan a long time ago. Ask the children what they know about Japan. Draw a pyramid on the chalkboard. Write the words *Old Japan* in the center of the pyramid and add the headings Language, Food, Religion, and Clothing. (See figure 12.1.) Ask the children what they know about each of these headings. List the words that the children generate beside the appropriate word on the pyramid. After reading the story, go back and make additions and changes with the student's new knowledge.

Fig. 12.1

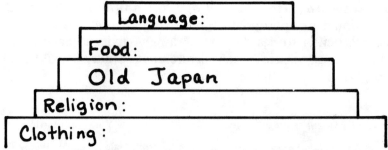

2. Some children will have little background knowledge of Old Japan. Have the children close their eyes and imagine that they are living in a Japanese village a long time ago. Their ability to visualize might be enhanced if Japanese music were played softly in the background. Help them picture in their minds a village in Old Japan. Paint a verbal scene of men, women, and children working and playing. Focus the scene on a woman in a small house. Describe the house and the woman cooking. Use as much detail as possible Try looking at a scene in the book and describing it to the children. After about five minutes, ask the children to open their eyes and draw a picture of what they saw in their minds. Discuss their pictures. See if the children understand the setting in which this story takes place.

3. Ask the children if they know what a dumpling is. If not, be certain that dumplings are discussed before reading the story. A recipe for rice dumplings is given in Et Cetera Activity 1 (page 127). These could be made up and the children could taste them before reading the story.

4. Put the following vocabulary words from the story on the chalkboard.

lantern	rice	paddle
woman	*Jizo*	laugh
dumpling	*oni*	wicked

    Discuss the words with the children explaining that these words will play an important part in the story they are about to read. Two words that are unique to this story are *Jizo* (one of numerous deities in the Buddhist religion whose responsibility it is to protect all sufferers especially small children) and *oni* (a devil or demon in Japanese folklore).

Predicting Activities

1. At the end of page 7[1] where the dumpling rolls down the hole, ask the children what they think the little old woman will do. Ask why they think that. Ask them if this reminds them of another story that they have heard. (Some children might mention *The Gingerbread Boy*.)

2. Have the children stop reading at the end of page 15 where the little woman hides behind the *Jizo*. Ask the children what they think the little woman will do. Ask why they think that.

3. After the children read to the end of page 26 where the little woman has decided she wants to return home, ask them to predict how they think she will escape. Ask how the illustration on page 27 might help them decide what she is going to do.

4. Have the children read to the end of page 28 where the wicked *oni* returns home and discover the little woman is missing. Ask the children to predict what the *oni* will do. Ask why they think that.

5. Have the children read to the end of the story.

Post Reading Activities

1. On page 9, the author says the little woman tumbled "head over heels" down the hole. Ask the children how the illustration differs from the text.

---

[1]Pagination begins on the title page of the text.

2. On page 9, the little woman said, "Ungrateful dumpling." Write the following sentences on the chalkboard.

> The dumpling was not grateful.
>
> The dumpling was ungrateful.

Ask the children if these two sentences mean the same thing. Ask them what word is added to the first sentence and therefore what the prefix *un-* means. Write the following words on the chalkboard.

happy	made	clear
healthy	usual	cooked
grateful	changed	curled

Go over the words with the children and identify the word meanings. Have the children add the prefix *un-* to each word and then identify the new word meanings. Have them use the new words to complete the following sentences.

> The girl left her bed _____ when she went to school.
>
> The clown was so _____ he did not smile.
>
> The girl's hat looked very _____ with the flowers all over it.
>
> The children said they were _____ about how to work the math problem.
>
> The rain _____ the girl's hair.
>
> When I went to visit my aunt, her house was _____.
>
> The vegetables were very hard as though they were _____.
>
> The old woman said the dumpling was _____.
>
> The children are so small and thin, they looked _____.

3. This story takes place over a long period of time. The author and illustrator have their own techniques for portraying the passage of time. Discuss the time phrases used by the author. For example:

"Long ago" (p.5)	"three minutes ago" (p.13)
"One morning" (p.7)	"the weeks and months passed" (p.24)
"soon" (p.13)	"one afternoon" (p.26)

Ask the children how the illustrator shows the passage of time. Point out the weather conditions shown in the illustrations. Encourage them to incorporate these types of words, phrases and/or illustrations in the stories they write in Writing Activity 4 (page 126).

4. The funny little woman is dressed in native Japanese attire. Discuss the lady's clothing, for example, kimono, obi, geta. Discuss the fact that today most Japanese people dress just as we do. Traditional costumes are usually worn only for celebrations.

5. The stories listed below are all similar to *The Funny Little Woman* in plot and theme. Have the children compare and contrast these stories.

> Galdone, Paul. *The Gingerbread Boy*. Boston: Houghton Mifflin Co., 1983.
>
> Jarrell, Randall. *The Gingerbread Rabbit*. New York: Macmillan Co., 1964.
>
> Lobel, Anita. *The Pancake*. New York: Greenwillow Books, 1978.
>
> Sawyer, Ruth. *Journey Cake, Ho!* New York: Viking Penguin, 1953.

6. Point out the well beside the little woman's house and discuss why the rock is tied to the handle.

7. This book was awarded the Caldecott Award for the most distinguished picture book for children in 1973. The illustrations are very cleverly done so as to focus the viewer's attention on where the action is taking place. Encourage the children to discuss the events taking place above ground in the black and white line drawings. Ask the children to verbalize what the visitor to the old woman's house might be saying or thinking. Discuss reasons why he might be going to the little woman's house.

8. As a vocabulary building activity, explain to the children that in Japan there is a card game called "Songs of a Hundred Poets." In this game there are two sets of cards. One set contains the first part of an ancient poem. The other cards contain the second part of the poem. One player reads the first part of the poem and the other player(s) try to locate the rest of the poem. Make a set of cards, each card containing a vocabulary word from the story. Make a second set of cards containing the word meanings. Shuffle all the vocabulary word cards and lay them face up in front of one or two players. Shuffle all the definition cards and lay them face up in front of the other one or two players. Have the player(s) with the vocabulary words pick up a card and read a word. The player(s) across from them should locate the card containing the word meaning. Some vocabulary words to use might be: dumpling, rice, ungrateful, *oni*, *Jizo*, wicked, woman, paddle, laugh, earthen, lantern.

10. Read other Japanese stories to the children such as:

> Laurin, Anne. *Perfect Crane*. New York: Harper & Row Junior Books, 1981.
>
> Yagawa, Sumiko. *Crane Wife*. New York: William Morrow, 1981.
>
> Yashima, Taro. *Crow Boy*. New York: Viking Penguin, 1976.

Thinking Activities

1. (FLEXIBILITY, ORIGINALITY) Have the children invent creative ways that the little woman could get a letter (asking for help) out of the *oni*'s home. (Writing Activity 1 on page 126 has the children write such a letter.)

2. (DECISION MAKING) Have the children compare and contrast various versions of the story as listed in Post Reading Activity 5 (page 124). Have them use the Decision Making Worksheet on page 14 to decide which version they like best.

3. (DECISION MAKING) Blair Lent won the Caldecott Award in 1973 for this book. Have the children look at other Caldecott Award winning books and decide which illustrations and/or story they like best. Use the Decision Making Worksheet on page 14 for this activity.

4. (RISK TAKING) The little woman took the *oni*'s magic paddle. Ask the children to discuss whether she should have done this. The children need to give reasons for their viewpoint.

5. (FLUENCY, FLEXIBILITY) After reading and discussing this book have the children list all the words they have learned that relate to Japan, for example, rice, kimono, lanterns.

6. (FLEXIBILITY, ORIGINALITY) Ask the children to devise other ways the little woman might have escaped from the *oni*.

7. (FLEXIBILITY) Ask the children to list all the ways their life would be different if they lived in Japan.

8. (ELABORATION) The flag hanging outside the little woman's home is advertising her business. Translated the sign reads *Dango*, which means dumplings. Have the children design a business card, a telephone book advertisement, or sign to advertise her business.

9. (EVALUTION) Japanese people do not wear shoes inside their homes. Use the Evaluation Worksheet on page 15 to discuss the pros and cons of this custom.

10. (FORECASTING) The little woman became "the richest woman in all of Japan." Ask the children what they would do if they came into good fortune like the funny little woman. Have the children use the Forecasting Worksheet on page 11.

Writing Activities

1. The little woman is being held prisoner by the wicked *oni*. Have the children imagine that they are the little woman and write a letter asking someone to help rescue them.

2. An old style of Japanese storytelling is called *kamishibai* (*kami* means paper and *shibai* means pray). Years ago Japanese storytellers would ride around on their bicycles carrying storytelling boxes. They would announce their arrival by clapping sticks together. The children would gather to hear their stories. The storyteller used a box with slits on both ends through which he would slide the pictures for each story. The text was written on the back of the preceding card. The box had flaps on the front that would open to reveal the stage. (See figure 12.2.) Let the children use a cardboard box with slits in both ends. The story of *The Funny Little Woman* can be illustrated on several tagboard cards. Beginning with the title card, the text for the first scene should be written on the back of the title card. After the title card is pulled through the slots, it should be placed behind the box so that the storyteller can read the words for the next scene. Each scene should be pulled through the slots and placed behind the stage box. Each card has the text for the next scene written on the back of it.

Fig. 12.2

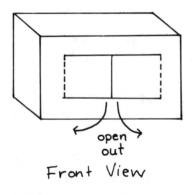

Front View

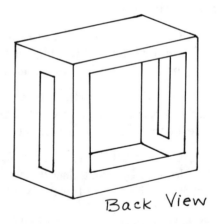

Back View

3. Japanese verse that consists of three lines and seventeen syllables is called *haiku*. *Haiku* are usually about something in nature. Have the children discuss the colorful scenes on pages 36 through 38 where the little woman is returning home. Have the children write a *haiku* describing this page. This could be done as an individual or class activity. For example:

> Spring, flowers bloom
>
> Bees buzz, squirrels chatter
>
> Birds sing, the earth awakens.

4. This type of story is called an "incident story." In her book *How to Write for Children and Young Adults*, Jane Fitz-Randolph (Boulder, Colo.: Johnson Books, 1987) explains the "incident excursion" plot, which takes the main character into familiar settings, and the "incident-adventure" plot, which takes the main character to an unfamiliar setting. Help the

children decide which type of plot this story is. Read some other "incident plot" stories to the children and let them write a story using this kind of plot. The children could use the story map in figure 12.3, page 128, to plan their stories. Discuss how their stories would differ if they were set in the United States, Mexico, Hawaii, Italy. See Post Reading Activity 3 (page 124) for ideas about words and illustrations. Other "incident stories" similar to *The Funny Little Woman* are listed in Post Reading Activity 5 (page 124).

5. Blair Lent cleverly allows us to view what is happening above and below ground in this story. Two other books that present a parallel plot in this way are *Humbug Rabbit* by Lorna Balian (Nashville, Tenn.: Abingdon, 1974) and *When the Root Children Wake Up* by Helen D. Fish (San Diego, Calif.: Green Tiger Press, 1989). Share these books with the children and have them write a story with a parallel plot.

Et Cetera Activities

1. (Cooking) The Japanese have a famous proverb, "Dumplings rather than flowers." The proverb demonstrates their realistic respect for food and the pleasure of eating. Rice is an important staple in the Japanese diet. Let the children use the following recipe to make rice dumplings or make the dumplings and let the children taste them.

Rice Dumplings
(Rice dumplings are called *dango*, which means round.)

Ingredients:	Utensils:
sweet rice flour	pan
water	shishkabob sticks
soy sauce	
sugar	

Directions: Moisten and stir the flour until it becomes the consistency of dough. Take a small amount of dough and form balls 1- to 1½-inches in diameter. Drop the rice balls into a pan of boiling water. Cook for 10 to 15 minutes. Remove the rice balls and place them on shishkabob sticks. Put five dumplings on a skewer. (Never place four dumplings on a stick as four is an unlucky number in Japan.) Flatten the dumplings on the skewer and serve with soy sauce sweetened with sugar.

A box of sweet rice flour can be purchased in a Japanese import store or ordered directly from KODA FARMS, INC., South Dos Palos, CA 93665. Because the dumplings resemble little moons, rice dumplings are often made on August 15 to celebrate the Moon Festival.

2. (Art) Lanterns are scattered throughout the illustrations in the text. Even the *oni*'s houses are shaped like lanterns. Lanterns are a very popular decoration in Japan. There is a festival in mid-July called the Bon Festival or the Feast of Lanterns. At this time, people of the Buddhist faith honor their ancestors. The streets are lined with lighted paper lanterns as are the entrances of homes. The lanterns are used to light the way for the spirits of their dead relatives whom they believe come to visit over this three-day period. Let the children make paper lanterns. Give each child a piece of colored construction paper 18"×12". Have the children fold their construction paper lengthwise (see figure 12.4, page 129). Draw a limit line approximately 1 inch from the outer edge. Have the children cut a fringe up to the limit line. Their fringe should be 1 inch wide. Have them open their papers and glue the 12-inch sides

Fig. 12.3

Main Character(s)

The Funny Little Woman Story Map

Incident
or Object

Event 1

Event 2

Event 3

Event 4

Solution :

together. They can use different colored strips (1"×12") for a handle or (1"×18") for decoration around the top and bottom of the lantern.

Fig. 12.4

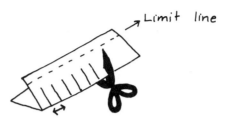

one inch between cuts

4. (Drama) Theater plays an important part in the lives of the Japanese. *Kabuki* plays were developed during the time the Tokugawa shogun ruled Japan. *Kabuki* was entertainment for the common folk. Before this time, only the noble classes enjoyed the theater. Let the children perform a readers theater production of this story. When adapting a text for readers theater:

a. Delete lines that tell who is speaking, for example, "said a very stern *Jizo*" or "roared the *oni*."

b. Delete lines that tell the characters what gestures to use, for example, "laughed the little woman" or "she tucked the magic paddle in her belt."

c. Rewrite narrative into dialogue if possible. For example:

"And soon after the wicked *oni* left she tried it out. One grain of rice and then stir! And as she stirred the one grain became two, two became four, then eight, sixteen, thirty-two, sixty-four, one hundred and twenty-eight, two hundred and fifty-six and the pot was full."

becomes

Narrator: After the wicked *oni* left, the little woman tried out the magic paddle.

Little Woman: First I'll drop in one grain of rice and stir. Oh my, one grain is becoming two, two are becoming four, four are becoming eight, and sixteen, and thirty-two, and sixty-four, and one hundred and twenty-eight, and two hundred and fifty-six. Look the pot is full!

d. Delete description that does not enhance the story or is not vital.

e. Divide narration among different speakers: Narrator 1, Narrator 2, or allow several children to read the narrator parts in chorus. This adds variety and allows more children to participate in the performance.

f. Feel free to change a few lines if it will enhance the story.

g. Repetitive lines or phrases can be done in "chorus."

Kabuki actors wear thick makeup. The book *Painting Faces* by Suzanne Haldane (New York: E. P. Dutton, 1988) contains striking examples of Japanese *kabuki* makeup patterns. Another option would be to have the children make masks. The masks could be mounted on tongue depressors and held up in front of their faces. The children could use the outlines in figures 12.5 and 12.6, pages 130 and 131, to make their masks.

(Text continues on page 132.)

Fig. 12.5   *The Funny Little Woman* Little Woman Mask

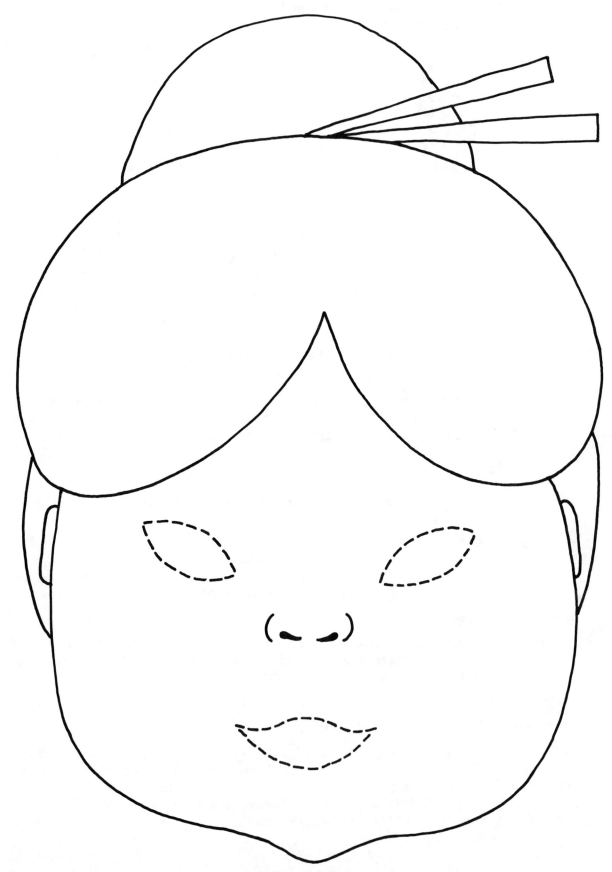

Fig 12.6   *The Funny Little Woman* Wicked *Oni* Mask

The Author Says ...

It is not at all surprising that Arlene Mosel (pronounced Mo-zel) grew up to be a storyteller. Born August 27, 1921, she has fond memories of the many hours her mother spent reading fairy tales to her as a child. *Tikki Tikki Tembo* was one of the tales she loved so well.

Mosel says she was an extremely shy child, so shy that a doctor recommended that she study dancing. Ten years later, she danced with the Metropolitan Opera Company when they performed in Cleveland.

She graduated from Ohio Wesleyan University and later studied Library Science at Western Reserve University where in 1967 she joined the staff as an assistant professor, later becoming an associate professor and retiring emeritus in 1981.

A children's librarian for many years, she says, "as a librarian, my greatest pleasure came from telling stories and planning story-hour programs. My books have grown from these experiences." *The Funny Little Woman* was one of the stories she loved to tell. She likes stories that have a "quiet subtle humor."

Her two books have received numerous awards. *Tikki Tikki Tembo* was awarded the 1968 Boston Globe-Horn Book Award and it was named an ALA Notable Book for the years 1940-1970. In addition to the 1973 Caldecott Medal, *The Funny Little Woman* was runner-up for the 1973 Hans Christian Anderson Award. It won the University of Wisconsin's Little Archer Award in 1976 and was selected to be on the 1974 Books for Young People Honor List. This book was an ALA Notable Book in 1973 and was also included in the Children's Book Showcase.

Mosel spends her summers in Aurora, Ohio and her winters in South Florida. She loves her plants and traveling.[2]

Author Activities

1. Mosel says that as a librarian her greatest pleasure came from telling stories to children. Help the children select a story that they enjoy. Encourage them to read the story over and over until it becomes their story. Discourage them from memorizing it. Instead they should say it over and over until they are able to tell it in their own words. Have them tell it to their classmates or to children in other grades.

2. Invite a professional storyteller to visit the classroom to tell *The Funny Little Woman* and other tales.

3. The author says that her parents spent a great deal of time reading to her. This particular story is one that Mosel's mother told her when she was a child. Have the children ask their parents to tell them a story that their parents told to them or read to them. Have the children learn the story and tell it to their classmates.

BIBLIOGRAPHY

Another book by Arlene Mosel for children grades 1 through 3.

Tikki Tikki Tembo. New York: Henry Holt, 1968.

---

[2]Sally Holmes Holtze, *Fifth Book of Junior Authors and Illustrators* (New York: H. W. Wilson, 1983), 224-25.

The Laziest Robot in Zone One

Lillian Hoban and Phoebe Hoban. New York: Harper & Row Junior Books, 1983.

SUMMARY

Sol-1 thinks he is overworked. His mother says he is lazy. When his mother scolds him and tells him to walk the dog, he is astonished to learn that due to his negligence the dog is loose. Frantically he tries to organize a search party to help him locate Big Rover. He soon realizes that his friends have their own chores to do and that if he wants their help, he will have to help them first. When all of his friends' problems are solved, everyone bands together to help Sol-1 find his dog and finish his chores.

Possible Student Outcomes

Expand reading vocabulary.

Identify the theme of the selection.

Interpret examples of figurative language.

Practice the thinking skills of planning, evaluation, originality, decision making, and communication.

*** CHOOSE A LIMITED NUMBER OF ACTIVITIES FROM EACH SECTION ***

Before Reading Activities

1. Place the word *robot* on the blackboard. Ask the children to tell you anything they know about robots. List what they know. Ask them how they know about robots.

2. Have the children compare and contrast robots and humans.

3. Sol-1 and his friends have numerous chores to do. Ask the children what household chores they are responsible for. Have them compare and contrast their chores with the robot's chores. (See also Thinking Activity 2 on page 137).

4. Ask the children if they know anyone who is lazy. Ask them to share some problems that can arise from people's being lazy. Ask them how they feel about work.

5. Ask the children if they have ever lost a pet and what they did. Ask them to list some ways people go about finding lost animals. Explain that this is a story about a lazy robot who has lost his pet.

6. List the following words from the story on a transparency.

Zone One	space garden	helped
robots	Down Time	Search Party
lazy	Big Rover	work
windmill	weeds	lost

List the following headings on a separate transparency: Setting, Characters, Problem, Solution. Have each child list the same headings on a piece of paper. Show them the list of words on the transparency and ask them to predict how the author will use these words in the story. Have the children list the words on their papers under the headings they think the author will use. After they make their own predictions, have the children share their ideas as a class. Place the words on the second transparency where the majority of the class feel each word should go. Throughout this procedure try to focus the children's attention on why they have chosen to place the words as they have. This activity is called a predict-o-gram.[1]

Predicting Activities

1. Have the children read through page 15. Ask them to predict how the space children might go about finding Big Rover.

2. Have the children read through page 29. Again the robots speak of "Down Time." Ask the children if their previous predictions have now changed.

3. Have the children read through page 33. Micromax cannot join the search party for Big Rover until he checks the temperature in the solar pond. Neither Micromax nor Sol-1 can get to the bottom of the pond. Have the children predict how they will solve their problem.

4. Have the children read through page 46. Ask the children to predict how the robots will get the cat, Power Puss, down from the windmill.

5. Have the children read to the end of the story.

Post Reading Activities

1. Sol-1 decides that if he organizes a search party, looking for Big Rover will be fun. Let the children discuss ways to make the following responsibilities more fun.

   Learning math facts

   Doing dishes

   Cleaning your room

2. When Rocko hears there is going to be a "party," he gets excited. There are lots of meanings for the word *party* depending on what words are combined with it. See how many words children can combine with the word *party*, for example, dinner party, birthday party, political party, quilting party, hunting party, search party.

3. On page 38, Sol-1 said if he had looked for Big Rover by himself he "wouldn't be in hot water." The author used this expression for two reasons. Ask the students if they can explain these reasons. (The robot is actually in the hot water and "being in hot water" means you are in trouble.) Have the students explain two meanings for the following expressions:

   "in over your head"

   "get on top of things"

   "don't let it get you down"

   After completing this activity, the students could complete Writing Activity 2 (page 138).

4. As a vocabulary building activity have the children complete the Word Search in figure 13.1.

---

[1]The idea for this predict-o-gram was taken from Camille L. Z. Blachowicz's article "Making Connections: Alternatives to the Vocabulary Notebook," *Journal of Reading* (April 1986): 648.

Fig. 13.1

The Laziest Robot Word Search

```
C F G J L P M O W E H S K U Q V J Y R Z F
J Q L A N Q R Z P Y D X W I H J L P Q Z V
Y Z O E A X C K Z U G O F B I D Z F G N B
K M V I O N J A D Y C E W X C W X M I V P
T W C P H E L R L O S T Q N G U E F V M D
C R T I Z U G A S B W S H E F K A D W Y Q
E G J H L S I B E I I P T K U Z C S L X U
I O Y M A C X D A G N A Z O M T Y Z N S R
S V T Q R N E X R R D C Q O Z K T S F M A
P D G H Y P Q P C O M E A C N B Q M R Z Q
Z W H O L Q F O H V I G M Y X E S N O Z T
X P D E G H J K P E L A L P F X O B T S I
F I H W E E D S A R L R R O B O T N B X N
M A V B T C Y X R D E D N G C L A R E B V
S T U Q D V M Z T A P E A N O R L B C X U
O E S G B L O D Y R K N V A N Q F Z P N Z
L D Q N A Z P S W O R K T N A B L T R E G
```

(Answers on page 196.)

Read the sentences below. Fill in the blanks with the correct answers from the story. Locate the answers in the Word Search puzzle and circle them. The words may run horizontally, vertically, or diagonally, but they will always be in a straight line. If you locate and circle the words correctly, they will form a picture.

Everyone in the story is a _____.

What did Sol-1 not like to do? _____.

The dog in the story was called _____ _____.

Super Scan had to weed the _____ _____.

Sol-1 invited the other robots to a _____ _____.

The robots found the cat on the blade of the _____.

All the work had to be done by _____ Time.

The robots lived on _____ _____.

The word Sol-1's mother used to describe him was _____.

The children looked for the dog because he was _____.

Sol-1 _____ the other robots do their work.

It was hard for Super Scan to catch all the _____ in the space garden.

5.   Make vocabulary cards for the children to use in their vocabulary robots suggested in Et Cetera Activity 4 (page 140). To make a vocabulary card, put a fill-in-the-blank sentence and three choices of words for an answer on the front of a 2"×3" card. Put the answer on the back. Let the children select a card and decide which word goes in the blank. Have the children place their card in their robot question box with the question side up. When the card comes out, the answer will be on the back of the card (see figure 13.2).

Fig. 13.2

Vocabulary Card

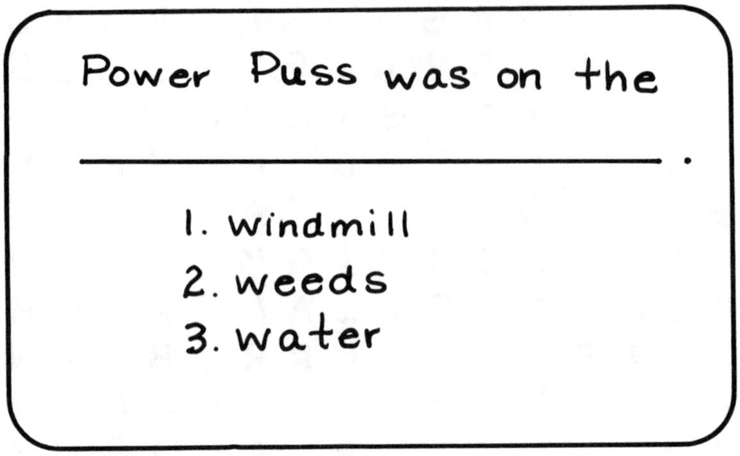

Power Puss was on the

_____ .

1. windmill
2. weeds
3. water

(front of card)

windmill

(back of card)

Other sentences might be:

a.   Mama-Sol wanted Sol-1 to _____ the space garden.
     (walk, watch, weed)

b.   Sol-1 did not like to _____ .
     (work, want, wave)

c.   The robots had to finish the work by _____ _____ .
     (Laser Tone, Game Time, Down Time)

6. Theme is what the story is about. There are usually several themes to a story; the most obvious theme is referred to as the *primary theme*. Other underlying themes are referred to as *secondary themes*. Ask the children what they think is the theme of this story. (It is important to note that because of their diverse backgrounds, it is unlikely that all children will always agree upon exactly the same thing.)

7. Discuss how robots are used today in business and industry. An excellent resource on this topic is Vol. XII No. 92 of *Scienceland* magazine. *Scienceland* is available from *Scienceland*, 501 Fifth Avenue, New York, NY 10017-6165.

Thinking Activities

1. (PLANNING) Have the children plan a space party for themselves and the characters in the story. Divide the class into groups. Each group should be given a particular portion of the party to plan, for example, refreshments, entertainment, decorations. Have each group use the Planning Worksheet on page 10 to plan their portion of the party. The children should be taught to foresee problems and discuss how they might handle them.

2. (EVALUATION) Sol-1 and his friends had several chores for which they were responsible. Have the children use the Evaluation Worksheet on page 15 to evaluate the advantages and disadvantages of having chores.

3. (ORIGINALITY) Ask the children to think of things they will *not* expect to see in the twenty-first century. They could list or draw what they think will replace them.

4. (PROBLEM SOLVING) The robots encountered several problems in this story, for example, finding Big Rover, testing the temperature of the solar pond, rescuing Power Puss from the windmill. Have the children select one of these problems. Have them use the Problem Solving Grid on page 17 to find a different solution for the problem than the robots used.

5. (ELABORATION) Have the children design one of the following:

    a. spaceship interior and exterior

    b. space home

    c. space bedroom

    Students can draw a picture or make a model of their design.

6. (ORIGINALITY) Place two objects for each student in a sack. The objects might be an eraser, pencil, small box, chalk. Divide the children into groups of four or five. Pass the sack around to each group and ask them to select two objects from the sack. Each group should try to place the two objects together so that they invent something that can be used *in the future*. They should give their new invention a name and explain how it will be used. Each group should select a spokesperson to explain their invention to the class.

7. (DECISION MAKING) Sol-1 says that the Laser Tones are his favorite music group. Ask the children what their favorite rock groups are. Select three groups. Play something that each group has recorded. Do not identify the groups for the children. Develop some criteria for deciding which group is best. Let the children use the Decision Making Worksheet on page 14 to complete this activity.

8. (COMMUNICATION) Raps are a rhythmic form of communication. Have the children say the tunes that the robots sing on pages 29, 43, and 63 as though they are raps. Children could work in groups and present their rap to the class. A variation of this activity might be to have the children rewrite the story as a rap.

9. (EVALUATION) Have the children discuss the advantages and disadvantages of using a robot as a friend, a housekeeper, a teacher, a doctor. Use the Evaluation Worksheet on page 15 to complete this activity.

10. (FLEXIBILITY) Have the children brainstorm to come up with ways robots can be used in the future. Have the children evaluate the advantages and disadvantages of using robots in these capacities. See what conclusion they draw from their discussion. Use the Evaluation Worksheet on page 15 to complete this activity.

11. (ORIGINALITY) Sola plays with her Uni-Doll. Have the children design a toy of the future.

12. (FORECASTING) Have the children forecast the causes and effects of robots in our lives. Use the Forecasting Worksheet on page 11.

Writing Activities

1. Rocko played several tunes on his jukebox. Select a melody that is familiar to the children such as "Down by the Station" and have them write lyrics for the tune that tell the story. For example:

   A lazy little robot, wouldn't get his work done.

   He played his favorite music, watched his favorite

   disc.

   Found he needed help to find his dog, Big Rover.

   Helped his friends and they helped him.

2. Have the children write a paragraph using the expressions in Post Reading Activity 3 (page 134) to show that they understand both the literal and figurative meaning of the expression. For example for the expression "in over his head":

   Sam went to the swimming pool with his friends. They were all good swimmers. Sam did not want to admit that he could not swim. All of his friends dove into the deep end of the pool. Sam was embarrassed, so he dove into the deep end with them. Down he went like a heavy stone. Before he could rise to the top, he panicked. He needed air. He realized that he was "in over his head."

   A variation of the activity might be for the students to draw a picture that would indicate that they understood both meanings of the expression.

3. Have the children begin on page 63 and write a different ending for this story.

4. Have the children describe Sol-1 in their own words. Encourage them to talk about his appearance, actions, and personality. Have them use the following Story Frame to create a Space Friend of their own and write a story about him or her.

Laziest Robot Story Frame

My Space Friend

_____ is _____ and
      (name)   (appearance)

_____ . He/She is _____
      (appearance)   (personality)

because he/she _____

_____

_____

_____

_____

Sometimes he/she _____

_____

_____

_____

_____

but he/she never _____ .

I like my friend best because _____

_____

_____

_____

_____

_____

_____ .

Et Cetera Activities

1. (Science) Neither Micromax or Sol-1 could get to the bottom of the solar pond due to the water's salt content. Ask the children why salt water would prevent them from getting to the bottom. (Salt increases the density of the water.) In order to help the children understand the problem faced by the robots, fill an 8-ounce glass three-quarters full of water. Gently drop a raw egg in the shell into the glass. The children will note that the egg sinks. Take the egg out and add three tablespoons of salt to the water, stirring after each tablespoon to dissolve the salt. Now set the egg in the water. The children will note that the egg floats. (You could use a felt tip pen and paint eyes, ears, and a mouth on the egg to make it resemble Sol-1.)

2. (Science) Sol-1 measured the temperature at the bottom of the solar pond at 1000°. Let the children use a thermometer to measure a variety of temperatures. Any standard liquid alcohol thermometer will do for these experiments. Children can work in groups or individually, depending on the number of thermometers available. Have the children measure the temperature in various parts of the classroom or school. Have the children measure the outside temperature on days that are cloudy, sunny, and so forth. Give the children two styrofoam meat trays, one that is white and one that is spray painted a dark color. Place thermometers in both trays. Place both trays in the sun and then both in the shade. The children will note the increase in the temperature due to the dark background. Water can also be placed in the trays and the water temperature can be measured. Have the children cover the trays with plastic wrap and note the difference in temperature. Results can be placed on a graph.

3. (Science) The weight on Sol-1 was tied with a slipknot. Demonstrate for the children how a slipknot is tied. Explain that there are several kinds of knots. See how many the children know. Descriptions of knots and how to tie them can be found in *The World Book Encyclopedia*.

4. (Art) Have the children make a vocabulary robot similar to the one in figure 13.3. The children should bring a shoebox to use as a base. The box will serve as the robot's body. A head can be made from a styrofoam ball. Stand the box up lengthwise. The shoebox lid should be the front of the robot. Cut two slits in the lid, one at the top, the other at the bottom. Inside the lid place a strip of tagboard. (See figure 13.3.) The tagboard serves as a chute to guide the vocabulary cards so that they can come out the bottom of the box. Instructions for vocabulary cards can be found in Post Reading Activity 5 (page 136).

Fig. 13.3

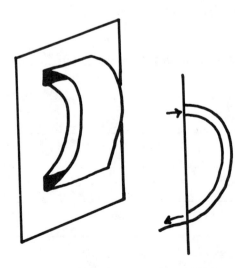

5. (Science) On page 14, the robots looked for Big Rover on top of the sun shield. Ask the children why it is necessary to have a sun shield. Ask them if they know what serves as a sun shield for the Earth (ozone layer). Discuss the importance of using sunscreen lotion as a protection from the sun when playing, swimming, and boating.

6. (Art) Have the children make a robot as a class project or have each child make his or her own robot. The children could use cardboard boxes, tubes, or plastic egg-shaped containers for this project.

7. (Art) Have the children draw a robot doing some chore that they do not like to do.

The Author Says ...

Lillian Hoban (1925-) has had several careers. She has been a professional dancer, a wife and mother, and an author/illustrator. She says she remembers reading at age four, and drawing before that. Her parents were extremely supportive of her artistic talent. At seven she was allowed to leave the regular classroom in the Philadelphia school she attended to participate in special art classes for gifted and talented children. She feels it is extremely important to provide opportunities for children to develop their talents at an early age. "It is more difficult to learn how to draw as an adult than it is to learn as a child. Drawing is a skill that can be learned; however, like anything we do well, it takes lots of practice," she says. She makes the observation that many illustrators become authors, but few authors become illustrators. She feels this might be because art is not stressed in schools in this country.

Hoban has always wanted to write and illustrate children's books. Her first book was published when she was eighteen years old. In addition to writing and illustrating her own books, she illustrates for her husband, Russell, as well as for other authors.

She has no preference for writing or drawing. "Whatever I'm doing at the time is what I like best." When asked how she begins her illustrations, she says she does her homework by going to the library and looking at pictures of real animals. She studies the distinctive features of the animals she is going to draw and then she begins. She jokingly states that she has drawn so many badgers, she does not need to look at badger pictures any more.

Her coauthor for *The Laziest Robot in Zone One* was her daughter, Phoebe. The story was written while Phoebe, a free-lance writer, was visiting her mother in her country home. At the time, Phoebe was doing a feature article on robots for a New York magazine. Robotics was just emerging as a new technology. Phoebe's knowledge and experience on this subject had enabled her to attend a European technological symposium to observe the newest advances in the field. As the two of them visited, the story began to emerge. "It was Phoebe's understanding of robots and their workings that enabled me to do the illustrations in this book," Hoban recalls. The story did not just emerge from their imaginations but rather from Phoebe's experience in the field of robotics. The book was a cooperative effort with both contributing to the text. The two authors enjoy working together. Because they are good friends, they feel comfortable sharing, brainstorming, and elaborating on each other's ideas. "I would think it would be difficult to just sit down and be told you were to write with someone else. It would seem more likely that children would share ideas at a sleepover or in some casual, informal setting if they wanted to jointly create a story," she says.

When asked what trade secrets she could share with children to help them improve their writing, she responded, "children should learn not to be afraid to write and rewrite. Too many people want to just dash things off. They are not willing to polish and rework their writing. You need to train yourself to stay glued to the chair hour after hour if you want your work to be good."

Author Activities

1. Lillian Hoban both writes and illustrates children's books. She has drawn such characters as Frances in *Bread and Jam for Frances* (New York: Harper & Row Junior Books, 1964) and Arthur in *Arthur's Honey Bear* (New York: Harper & Row Junior Books, 1974). Her drawings are quite often done in pencil. Show the children several books that she has illustrated and let them do a pencil drawing. Before they begin, show them how pencil can produce a variety of effects depending on how it is used. Shading can be done by using the side of the lead.

2. Many characters that Lillian Hoban draws have been created by her husband, Russell Hoban. Characters like Frances and Arthur have many different adventures. Select one of Russell and Lillian Hoban's characters and have the children write and illustrate a new adventure for the character. A bibliography of other books by this author/illustrator team is listed below in the Bibliography.

3. Lillian Hoban and her daughter, Phoebe, coauthored this book. Let the children coauthor a book.

BIBLIOGRAPHY

Some books written and illustrated by Lillian Hoban for grades 1 through 3.

Arthur's Christmas Cookies. New York: Harper & Row Junior Books, 1972. (RL 2   IL 1-3)

Arthur's Funny Money. New York: Harper & Row Junior Books, 1981. (RL 2   IL 1-3)

Arthur's Halloween Costume. New York: Harper & Row Junior Books, 1984. (RL 2   IL 1-3)

Arthur's Loose Tooth. New York: Harper & Row Junior Books, 1985. (RL 2   IL 1-3)

The Case of the Two Masked Robbers. New York: Harper & Row Junior Books, 1986.
    (RL 2   IL k-3)

Mr. Pig & Family. New York: Harper & Row Junior Books, 1980. (RL 2   IL k-3)

Silly Tilly & the Easter Bunny. New York: Harper & Row Junior Books, 1987.
    (RL 2   IL k-2)

Another book written and illustrated by Lillian and Phoebe Hoban.

Ready ... Set ... Robot! New York: Harper & Row Junior Books, 1985. (RL 2   IL 1-3)

Some books illustrated by Lillian Hoban.

Baby Sister for Frances. Russell Hoban. New York: Harper & Row Junior Books, 1964.
    (RL 2   IL k-3)

Bargain for Frances. Russell Hoban. New York: Harper & Row Junior Books, 1970. (RL 3   IL k-3)

Bedtime for Frances. Russell Hoban. New York: Harper & Row Junior Books, 1960.
    (RL 3   IL k-3)

Best Friends for Frances. Russell Hoban. New York: Harper & Row Junior Books, 1969.
(RL 3   IL k-3)

Birthday for Frances. Russell Hoban. New York: Harper & Row Junior Books, 1968.
(RL 3   IL k-3)

Bread and Jam for Frances. Russell Hoban. New York: Harper & Row Junior Books, 1964.
(RL 3   IL k-3)

Rosie's Walk

Pat Hutchins. New York: Macmillan Co., 1968.

SUMMARY

Rosie the hen sets out for a walk around the barnyard. Seemingly unaware that the fox is following her, she leads him on a merry chase and meanders back to her roost unharmed, which is more than can be said for the fox.

Possible Student Outcomes

Expand reading vocabulary.

Predict what might happen next in the story.

Increase observational skills.

Practice the thinking skills of fluency, flexibility, elaboration, evaluation, decision making, and planning.

*** CHOOSE A LIMITED NUMBER OF ACTIVITIES FROM EACH SECTION ***

Before Reading Activities

1. Draw a *Fox* and a *Hen* on the chalkboard (see figure 14.1, page 144). Place the subheadings Food, Description, Habitat, and Characteristics on lines extending from the drawings. Let the children tell you what they know about each word. Add the information they give you under the subheadings. Ask the children what they think of when you mention foxes and hens. Ask what they are basing their ideas on. Conclude the discussion by telling the children that they are going to read a story about a fox and a hen. Ask them to be prepared to see if their predictions were accurate.

Fig. 14.1

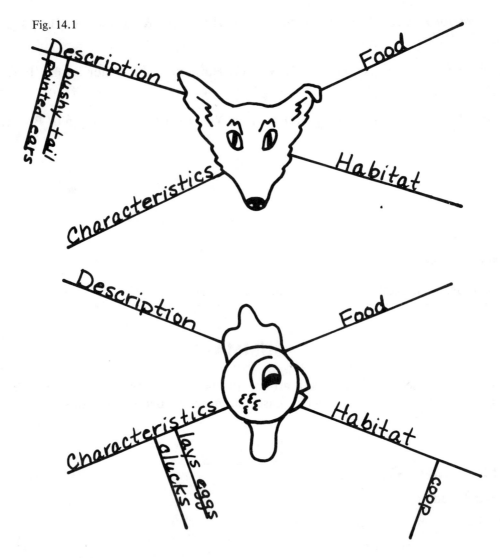

2. Ask how many children have been to a farm. Discuss what they saw on a farm. Put the headings Animals, Buildings, Crops, Tools on the chalkboard. Have the children name the things they saw or could see on a farm. List the items under the proper headings. Tell the children that they are going to read a story about a fox and a hen that live on a farm. Ask them what they think might happen.

3. Have the children look at the cover of the book. Ask them to predict what they think might happen in this story.

4. Have the children draw a picture of a farm. Have them include as many things as they can think of that might be on a farm, for example, tools, machinery, animals, buildings, people, people doing chores. Tell the children you are going to read a story about a farm. After reading the story, ask them to see what they included on their farm that is in the story and what is in the story that they left out.

5. The following words are ones the children should understand in order to comprehend the story. Include these words in your discussion before reading the story.

coop	walk	mill
rake	fox	beehives
hen	farm	

Predicting Activities

1. Have the children stop reading after page 7.[1] Ask them what they think might happen to the fox next. Ask why they think that.

2. Have the children stop reading after page 11. Ask them what they think might happen to the fox next.

3. Have the children stop reading after page 24. Ask what they think will happen when the fox lands in the wagon. Have them explain their responses.

4. Have the children read to the end of the story.

Post Reading Activities

1. Discuss the expressions "sly as a fox" and "outfoxed."

2. Ask the children what season this story takes place in. Have them explain their answer.

3. Have the children look at page 5. Ask them how they know that there are probably cows on this farm.

4. Have the children look at page 11. Discuss whether the leaves are actually touching the water. Ask the children how they know that they are.

5. Discuss the flour on page 20. Bring some flour and let the children see and feel it. Discuss what flour is used for.

6. Talk about the beehives on page 23. Bring some honey and a honeycomb and let the children taste it.

7. Have the children look at page 27 and tell why there is a ramp going up into Rosie's chicken coop.

8. Let the children play the game "Renard" (fox) as a vocabulary extending activity. Make a set of playing cards (39 cards) using the illustrations in figure 14.2, pages 146-49. Print the animal's name on nineteen of the cards and put the animal's picture on the other nineteen cards. The thirty-ninth card is reserved for the picture of the "Renard." The game can be played by 2 to 6 players. The object of the game is to match the animal picture with the animal name and discard the matching set. The last player holding a card is the "Renard" or fox.

Rules for "Renard"

One player shuffles and deals all the cards, face down, one at a time to the players. The players look at their cards, and if they have a matched set (name and picture), they lay them down *face up*. These matched cards are out of the game. The unmatched cards stay in the players' hands. Starting with the player to the left of the dealer, each player in turn picks one card from the player on his or her right. If the player selects a card that matches one in his or her hand, the set is placed down with the other sets, face up for all to see. The game continues with players picking one card from each player on the right. When a player has matched and discarded all his or her cards, he or she is out of the game. The game is over when there is only one player holding the "Renard." (This game can be varied by having three cards to match. Sets could be made of male, female, and baby animals. For example: rooster, hen, chick; bull, heifer, calf; ram, ewe, lamb; gander, goose, gosling.)

---

[1]Pagination begins on the title page of the text.

(Text continues on page 150.)

Fig. 14.2

Rosie's Walk Playing Cards

(Figure 14.2 continues on page 148.)

Fig. 14.2—*Continued*

goat

Spider

9. The author uses numerous prepositional phrases in this story. Put the following prepositional phrases on the chalkboard. Ask the children to use one of these phrases to complete the sentence "Rosie is walking _____."

across the _____   to the_____

around the _____   on the _____

over the_____   in the_____

under the _____

Ask the children the following questions:

a. Where is Rosie walking if the ground is sandy, water is lapping up on her feet, people are lying around on beach towels, and a boat is out in the water? (Rosie is walking on the beach.)

b. Where is Rosie walking if there are tall buildings all around her, cars honking, and traffic lights flashing? (Rosie is walking in the city or across the street.)

c. Where is Rosie walking if there is a train going over her head? (Rosie is walking under the train track or under the trestle.)

d. Where is Rosie walking if she is watching for the street light to change? (Rosie is walking across the street.)

e. Where is Rosie walking if she comes to the end of a row of houses and makes a sharp turn to the right? (Rosie is walking around the corner.)

10. Have the students make prepositional phrases of their own using the phrases in the story.

11. Discuss why the fox was following Rosie. Ask the children if they think Rosie was aware of the fox. Have them explain their opinion.

Thinking Activities

1. (ELABORATION) This text is very simply written. Have the children use the worksheet in figure 14.3 to elaborate on the text. Discuss each noun. Ask them to brainstorm adjectives that describe how a yard, pond, haystack, mill, fence, and dinner might look, smell, feel, taste. Have them use the adjectives to complete the worksheet.

2. (FLUENCY) Ask the children to name all the animals they can think of that live on a farm.

3. (FLEXIBILITY) Have the children categorize the farm animals listed in the previous activity in as many ways as they can.

4. (FLEXIBILITY) The fox is stalking Rosie. Explain what it means when an animal "stalks its prey." Have the children name other animals that stalk their prey.

5. (EVALUATION) Compare the fox in this story to the fox in Steven Kellogg's version of *Chicken Little* (New York: Morrow, 1985). Ask the students how they are alike and how they are different. Use the Evaluation Worksheet on page 15.

Other fox stories are:

Galdone, Paul. *What's in Fox's Sack?* New York: Clarion Books, 1982.

Spier, Peter. *The Fox Went Out on a Chilly Night.* Garden City, N.Y.: Doubleday, 1961.

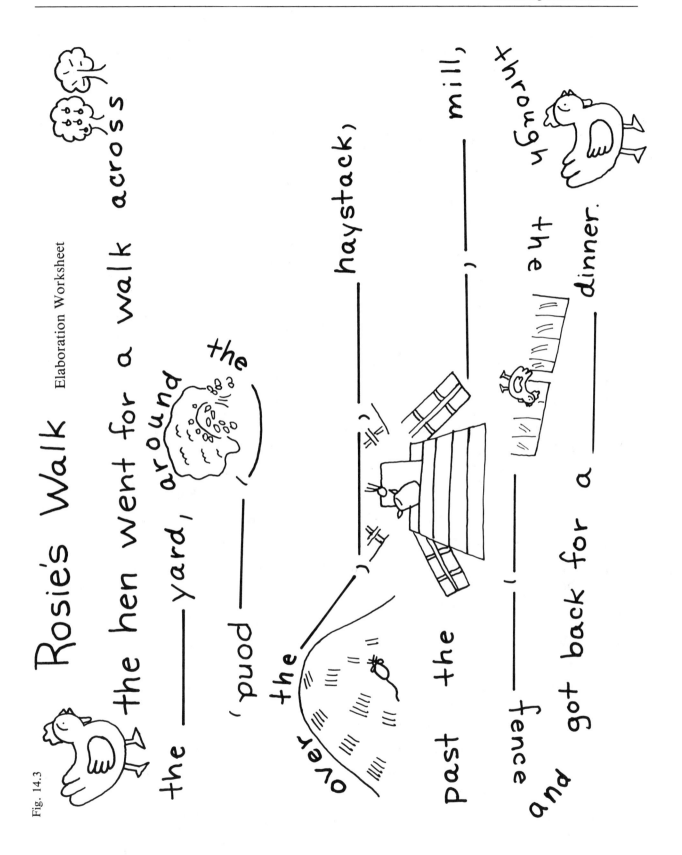

Fig. 14.3   Elaboration Worksheet

Rosie's Walk

the hen went for a walk across the ———— yard, around the ———— pond, over the ———— (haystack), past the ———— mill, through the ———— fence to go back for a ———— dinner.

6. (PLANNING) This is an example of a circle story. In a circle story, the character must end up back where he or she started. Have the children work individually or in groups to plan a circle story of their own. (See figure 14.4 for an example.)

Fig. 14.4

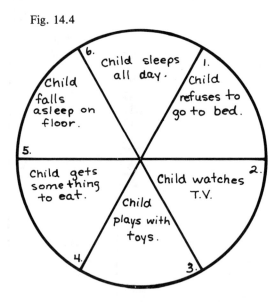

7. (EVALUATION) Janina Domanska's version of *The Little Red Hen* (New York: Macmillan Co., 1973) is illustrated in much the same style as *Rosie's Walk*. Compare and contrast the two books.

    Other hen stories are:

    Dabcovich, Lydia. *Mrs. Huggins and Her Hen Hannah*. New York: E. P. Dutton, 1985.

    Mathers, Petra. *Maria Theresa*. New York: Harper & Row, 1985.

    Paul, Jan S. *Hortense*. New York: Thomas Y. Crowell, 1984.

8. (FLEXIBILITY) Plan another walk for Rosie. She might go to the jungle, city, ranch. Have the children brainstorm to come up with things she might walk around on her new walk.

Writing Activities

1. This book is an example of a circle book in which the character starts off in one place and weaves a way through the story and right back to where he or she started. Have the children write a circle story. See Thinking Activity 6 (above). Other examples of circle stories are:

    Henkes, Kevin. *Once around the Block*. New York: Greenwillow Books, 1987.

    Hutchins, Pat. *Where's the Baby?* New York: Greenwillow Books, 1988.

    Numeroff, Laura J. *If You Give a Mouse a Cookie*. New York: Harper & Row Junior Books, 1985.

2. In Thinking Activity 8 (above), the children planned another walk for Rosie. Write about the new walk that Rosie could take. Use the wheel in figure 14.5, pages 153-54. The story can be written on the wheel or scenes depicting where Rosie is walking can be drawn on the wheel or both. Encourage the children to use as many prepositional phrases from the story as possible in their story.

Fig. 14.5

Rosie's Walk Circle Story Planner

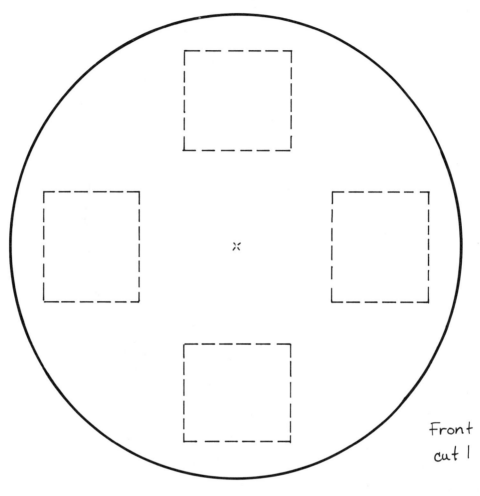

Front
cut 1

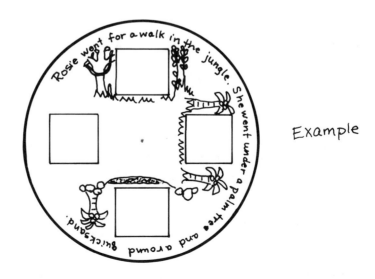

Example

(Figure 14.5 continues on page 154.)

Fig. 14.5—*Continued*

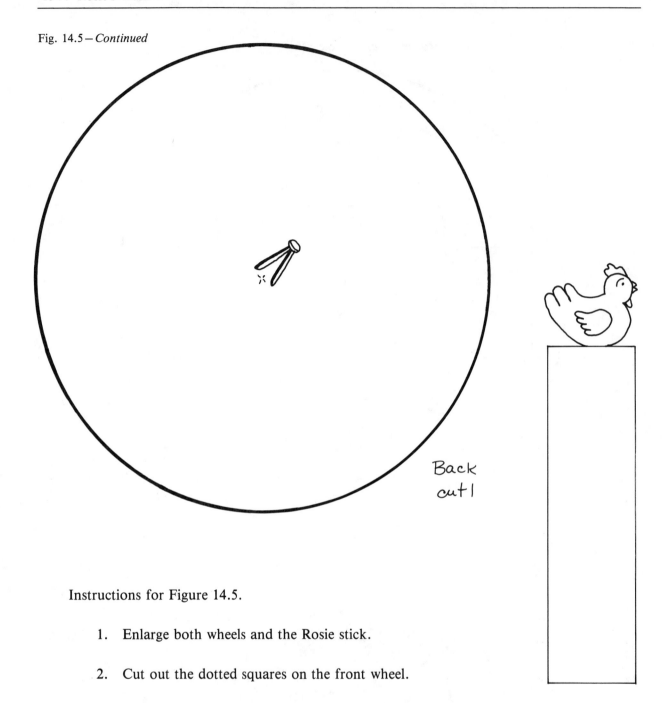

Back
cut 1

Instructions for Figure 14.5.

1. Enlarge both wheels and the Rosie stick.

2. Cut out the dotted squares on the front wheel.

3. Have the children draw scenes and/or write the words around the wheel.

4. Place the long Rosie Stick in the middle between the two circles halves. The bottom of the stick with Rosie on it should extend about ½" below the wheel.

5. Put a brad in the center of the two halves and move Rosie around to the different scenes.

3. This book is an example of a parallel plot. While Rosie is proceeding on her walk, the fox, independent of Rosie, is stalking her. Have the children write a parallel plot story where two different characters have experiences independent of one another.

   Other examples of parallel plot stories are:

   Balian, Lorna. *Humbug Rabbit*. Nashville, Tenn.: Abingdon, 1974.

   McCloskey, Robert. *Blueberries for Sal*. New York: Viking Press, 1948.

   McPhail, David. *The Bear's Bicycle*. Boston: Little, Brown and Company, 1975.

4. Have the children write to a farmer. They might ask him questions about farming, for example, what he grows, animals on his farm, if he likes to farm, problems he has.

Et Cetera Activities

1. (Art) Have the class make a large replica of Rosie to display in the class. Use an opaque projector or an overhead projector to enlarge the pattern in figure 14.6, page 156). Make two copies of the pattern and staple the edges together. Leave an opening and let the children stuff the stapled form with crumpled newspaper to give it a puffy effect. Have the children make large construction paper feathers to glue on the figure for its tail and wings.

2. (Science) On page 20, Rosie passed the mill and knocked the flour on the fox. Show the children what wheat looks like before it is refined into flour. Get some wheat berries from a wheat farm or from a health food store. Wheat berries can be ground in a flour mill or ground between two smooth stones to make flour.

3. (Music) Teach the children the familiar farm melody "Old McDonald Had a Farm." The children can add verses for the animals on Rosie's farm. For example: "And on this farm, he had some frogs, ee−i−ee−i−o! With a croak croak here, and a croak croak there, here a croak, there a croak, everywhere a croak croak."

4. (Rhythm) Teach the children the rhythmic speech activity in figure 14.7, page 157. Divide the class into five groups. Group 1 begins and softly repeats the two lines of Phrase 1 throughout the entire chant as an ostinato. (An ostinato is a pattern repeated over and over again.)

5. (Music, Art Appreciation) Teach the children the song "The Fox." The words and music can be found in *Go In and Out the Window* by Dan Fox and Claude Marks (New York: Henry Holt, 1987). This same volume contains an interesting tapestry designed by John Henry Dearie (1860-1932) depicting a wily fox longingly gazing at his prey.

6. (Art Appreciation) Pat Hutchins's vivid colors and symmetrical pattern are reminiscent of the work of Henri Matisse who in his later years worked with colored paper and scissors. Due to an illness, Matisse was bedridden for the last thirteen years of his life. Unable to work at a canvas, he began cutting paper and placing his cutouts on white or multicolored backgrounds. He is a master of color and design. Let the children compare Hutchins's work with designs done by Matisse. His work can be found in *The World of Matisse* by John Russell and the Editors of Time-Life Books (New York: Time-Life Books, 1969).

SCHOOL OF EDUCATION
CURRICULUM LABORATORY
UM-DEARBORN

(Text continues on page 158)

Fig. 14.6

SCHOOL OF EDUCATION
CURRICULUM LABORATORY
UM-DEARBORN

Fig. 14.7.

Rosie's Walk Rhythmic Activity

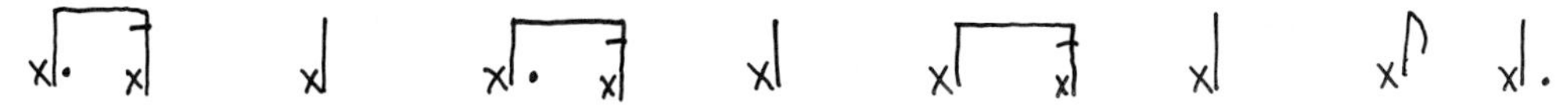

Phrase 1

Ro sie   walked   and   she   walked   and   she   walked   a   round
Ro sie   walked   and   she   walked   and   she   walked   a   round

(After Group 1 repeats Phrase 1 twice, Group 2 begins Phrase 2 saying it one time.)

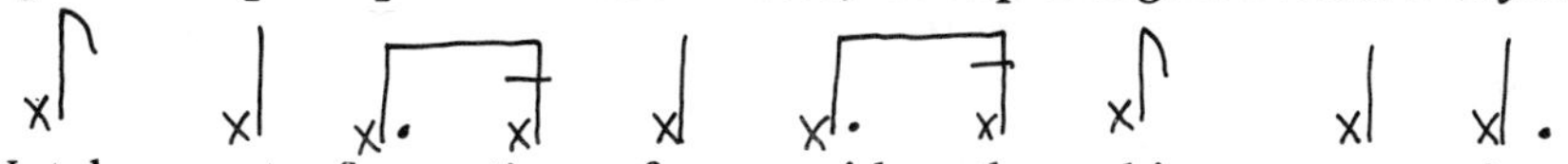

Phrase 2

Watch   out   for   the   fox   said   the   big   green   frog
Watch   out   for   the   fox   said   the   big   green   frog

Phrase 1

Ro sie   walked   and   she   walked   and   she   walked   a   round
Ro sie   walked   and   she   walked   and   she   walked   a   round

(Group 3 begins Phrase 3 saying it one time.)

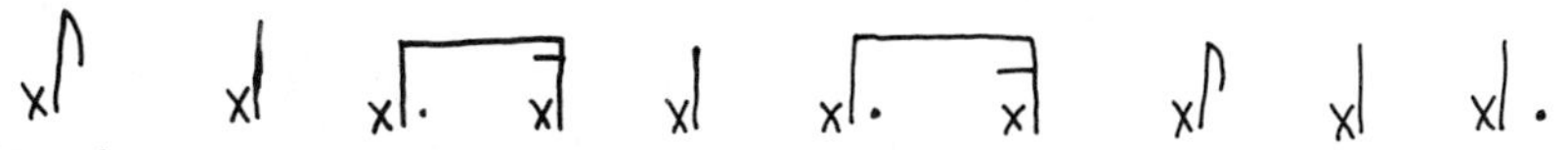

Phrase 3

Watch   out   for   the   fox   said   the   fat   red   bird
Watch   out   for   the   fox   said   the   fat   red   bird

Phrase 1

Ro sie   walked   and   she   walked   and   she   walked   a   round
Ro sie   walked   and   she   walked   and   she   walked   a   round

(Group 4 begins Phrase 4 saying it one time.)

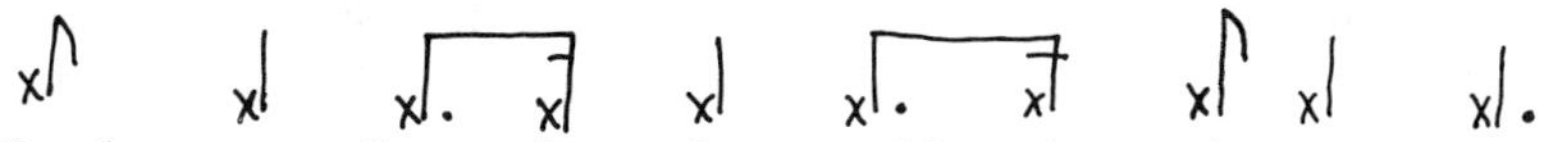

Phrase 4

Watch   out   for   the   fox   said   the   shaggy   goat
Watch   out   for   the   fox   said   the   shaggy   goat

Phrase 1

Ro sie   walked   and   she   walked   and   she   walked   a   round
Ro sie   walked   and   she   walked   and   she   walked   a   round

(Group 5 begins Phrase 5 saying it one time.)

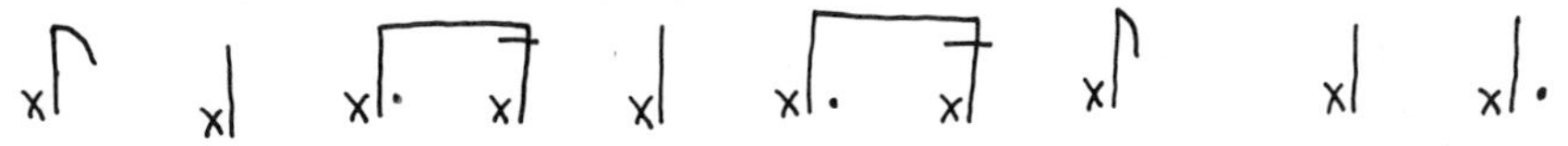

Phrase 5

Watch   out   for   the   fox   said   the   brown   groundhog
Watch   out   for   the   fox   said   the   brown   groundhog

(All groups together decrescendo to fade out.)

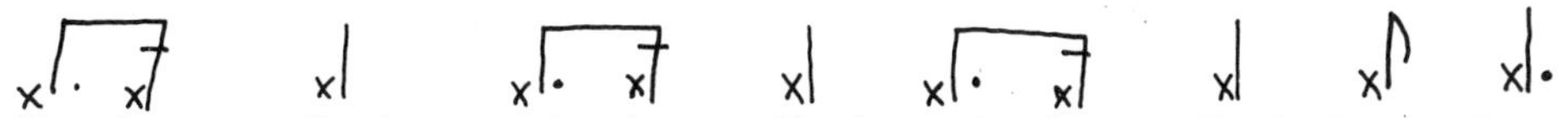

Phrase 6

Ro sie   walked   and   she   walked   and   she   walked   back   home.

The Author Says ...

Born in a village in Yorkshire in northern England, Pat Hutchins (1945-) writes about the people and places she knows. As a child, she spent lots of time tramping around the woods and fields that surrounded her home. The second from the youngest in a family of seven, she and her brothers and sisters often played nursemaid to wounded birds and animals. She fondly remembers finding a baby crow that became a unique family pet.[2] Her knowledge and love of nature is reflected in many of her books, particularly *Rosie's Walk*. As a child she drew pictures of her surroundings — the farms, houses, churches, and the animals she knew and loved. Encouraged by an elderly couple in the village, she continued to work on her drawing. At sixteen, she won a scholarship to Darlington Art School. Continuing her studies at Leeds College of Art, she specialized in illustration. Completing her studies there, she worked for a time in London as an assistant art director in an advertising agency. There she met her husband, Laurence. Soon after their marriage, the couple was transferred to New York. Although their stay in New York was brief, Hutchins seized the opportunity to do some free-lance work in the area of children's literature. Portfolio in hand, she visited several publishing houses. Pat recalls one publisher commenting about *one* line in a piece she had done about farmyard sounds. The line read, "This is the fox. He never makes a noise." "Try and write a story about that," the editor said. One year and numerous revisions later, *Rosie's Walk* was born. The editor said, "This is going to be a classic."

Hutchins believes that children are capable of understanding difficult concepts if they are presented to them logically and simply. Her stories and illustrations are carefully planned to heighten children's anticipation and to pique their curiosity. When she gets an idea, which for her she says is the most difficult part of writing, she spends a great deal of time laying out the words and pictures very logically. Her desire for order and sequence make her a master at circle books, which must be planned very carefully. She hopes that children enjoy reading her books as much as she enjoys writing them. She tries to draw her readers into her stories. In *Rosie's Walk* everyone but Rosie is in on the joke from the beginning. Pat wants children to enjoy anticipating the fox's misfortunes. She hopes her readers feel a certain satisfaction in being able to turn the page and make something happen. In *The Surprise Party* (New York: Macmillan, 1986), the reader knows that Owl is having a party before the story characters know it. This way the reader feels "in on the secret."

The Hutchins have two sons, Morgan and Sam. The boys have had a tremendous influence on Pat's work. Observing Morgan as a child playing with older children sparked the idea for *Titch* (New York: Macmillan, 1971). Morgan's afternoon playtimes often disturbed his Granddad who liked to take an afternoon nap. This frequent occurrence prompted *Goodnight, Owl!* (New York: Macmillan Co., 1972), Pat's favorite. *The House That Sailed Away* (New York: Greenwillow Books, 1975) was written for Morgan. She says it is her favorite because it contains her entire family, including her "Mum." This book was illustrated by her film director husband. Since that time, the two have collaborated on several other pieces. "Sam felt left out," said Hutchins, "so I wrote *Happy Birthday, Sam* (New York: Greenwillow Books, 1978) for him. The book is about Sam who liked to carry his chair around and use it to get into mischief. *The Wind Blew* (New York: Macmillan Co., 1974) won the Kate Greenaway Medal in 1974. This coveted British prize, like the Caldecott Award, is given to the outstanding picture book of the year.

Pat's illustrations are "inseparable from the text." Her illustrations vary depending on the story and her intended audience. The illustrations in *Rosie's Walk*, *The Surprise Party*, and *Titch* are simple because they were written for very young children. The illustrations in *One-Eyed Jake* (out of print) and *The Wind Blew* are more sophisticated because they are intended for a slightly older audience.

---

[2]Anne Commire, *Something about the Author*, vol. 15 (Detroit: Gale Research, 1979), 141-43.

Her style totally changed in *The Very Worst Monster* (New York: Greenwillow Books, 1985). Pat says that this story is reminiscent of her niece's response to an inquiry about her new baby brother. Like many children with a new sibling, her niece felt she would like to give the baby away. When asked why the characters are monsters, Pat said, "A real child giving her baby brother away isn't funny, whereas it's quite acceptable behavior for a monster."

Author Activities

1. Pat Hutchins's illustrations resemble stamp printing. Pattern art is simple and direct. Have the children find various repeated patterns in her work, for example, the fox, trees, Rosie. Have them experiment and create two formal patterns that they like (see figure 14.8).

Fig. 14.8

$$(3\ 3\ 3\ 3\ /\ || \ || \ || \ || \ )$$

$$(3\ || \ 3 ||\ 3|| \ 3|| \ 3|| \ 3|| \ )$$

Let them combine their patterns keeping them in a straight line. They could use their design to decorate a bookmark, dust jacket, greeting card.

2. Discuss the pattern Hutchins uses to make feathers, fur, and so forth on the animals. Have the children make a pattern printer. Have them use styrofoam meat trays to cut out the shape of an animal. Use the point of a lead pencil or some other blunt instrument and press a pattern into the styrofoam to simulate feathers, fur, and so forth (see figure 14.9). Paint the styrofoam animal with a washable felt pen or marker. The pattern will have to be recolored with the pen before each print. If children intend to use several colors in their picture, they should begin with the lighter color and end with the darkest color. Press the painted styrofoam animal onto a piece of paper and print the animals. (The first print may not be good. For the finished product, use the second print.) The children could create an animal scene using this technique.

Fig. 14.9

3. Let the children locate Pat Hutchins's childhood home on a map of England.

BIBLIOGRAPHY

Other books by Pat Hutchins for children in grades 1 through 3.

Changes, Changes. New York: Macmillan Co., 1971. (RL wordless   IL ps-1)

Don't Forget the Bacon! New York: Greenwillow Books, 1976. (RL 2   IL k-3)

The Doorbell Rang. New York: Greenwillow Books, 1986. (RL 2   IL ps-3)

Good Night Owl. New York: Macmillan Co., 1972. (RL 2   IL ps-3)

Happy Birthday, Sam. New York: Greenwillow Books, 1978. (RL 2   IL ps-1)

King Henry's Palace. New York: Greenwillow Books, 1983. (RL 2   IL 1-3)

One Hunter. New York: Greenwillow Books, 1982. (RL 2   IL ps-1)

The Very Worst Monster. New York: Greenwillow Books, 1985. (RL 2   IL k-3)

The Wind Blew. New York: Macmillan Co., 1974. (RL 2   IL ps-2)

The Stories Julian Tells

Ann Cameron. New York: Pantheon, 1987.

SUMMARY

Written from the first-person point of view, this brief chapter book relates five episodes in the life of seven-year-old Julian and his little brother, Huey. The boys are full of mischief, so there is seldom a dull moment in their household. The chapters are filled with family warmth and love and lots of humor.

Possible Student Outcomes

Expand reading vocabulary.

Recognize the correct use of quotation marks and commas in writing dialogue.

Identify a story written in the first-person point of view.

Identify and construct similes and metaphors.

Practice the thinking skills of fluency, flexibility, forecasting, originality, imagination, evaluation, and planning.

*** CHOOSE A LIMITED NUMBER OF ACTIVITIES FROM EACH SECTION ***

Before Reading Activities

1. Ask the children to think about a funny incident that happened to them in their home. They might want to relate a time they got in trouble, or a time they did something foolish. Their incident may or may not include someone else in their family. After the children relate their incidents, explain that the book they are going to read is about a boy named Julian and his family. Each chapter is about an everyday happening at Julian's house. Suggest that they listen throughout the stories for incidents similar to events in their households.

2. In order to be certain that the children understand the meaning of the following vocabulary words from the story, have them respond in writing to the questions in figure 15.1, page 162.

handkerchief	raft	catalog
evened	quiver	fertilizer
mustache	pliers	fig
genuine	ancients	ignorant
visible		

   If some children do not comprehend certain vocabulary words, have other children pantomime or draw pictures demonstrating the meaning of the unfamiliar words.

3. Have the children examine the book's cover. Read the title. Ask them to speculate about what they think this book is about.

4. Bring in a lemon, a package of lemon pudding, a seed catalog, a package of seeds, a bowl of figs (fresh, dried, or canned), a kite, and a paper tooth with a string tied around it. Let the children identify each object. They might want to taste the figs. Put the title of the book on the chalkboard and let the children discuss how the title of the book might relate to the objects. Let them see the cover of the book. Tell them that all these objects appear in Julian's stories. The children might want to have a contest to see whose prereading idea is closest to what actually happens in the book.

5. Before reading chapter 4, "Because of Figs," let the children eat a Fig Newton cookie.

Predicting Activities

1. Have the children read the title of chapter 1 on page 1. Ask them to predict what this story might be about. Ask them what kind of pudding they think this is. Ask what makes them think this.

2. Have the children read to page 6 where the boy's father says he is going to take a nap. Ask the children to predict what they think will happen. On what do they base their prediction?

3. Have the children read to the bottom of page 9. Ask them to predict what Julian's father will do. Ask them what their parent would do and what they think the parent should do.

4. Have the children read the title of chapter 2. Have them predict what this chapter might be about. Ask what makes them think this.

5. After the children read to the bottom of page 22, ask them what they think is going to happen next. Ask what Julian, Huey, and their father will do. On what do they base their prediction?

6. Have the children read to the bottom of page 37. Ask the children to predict the trouble that Julian might have because of figs.

Fig. 15.1

The Stories Julian Tells Vocabulary Worksheet

Words Words Words

The underlined words on this page are all found in the book *The Stories Julian Tells* by Ann Cameron. Write answers to the following questions about the words.

1. What are two things someone might do with a handkerchief?

    a.

    b.

2. What happens to you when you quiver?

3. Tell something pliers might help you do.

4. Where is a mustache located?

5. Why would you use fertilizer?

6. How would you know if you like figs?

7. What would you do with a raft?

8. If something is *not* genuine, it is _____ .

9. If something is considered ancient, that means it is _____ .

10. What is the purpose of a catalog?

11. What does it mean if something is visible?

12. If a person is ignorant, what is wrong with that person?

13. If you evened something, what would you do to it?

7. Have the children read to the middle of page 47 where Julian's father says he will take care of the loose tooth. Ask them to predict ways Julian's father might suggest pulling his loose tooth.

8. Have the children read to the end of the book.

Post Reading Activities

1. Ask the children who is telling this story. How do they know? This book is an example of a story written in the first person. This means that the story is told using the first person "I." Let the children read portions of the story as if it were written from someone else's point of view.

2. Have the children read the title of the book. Explain that *stories* is the plural of *story*. Remind the children that when singular words end in a consonant followed by *y*, we usually change the *y* to *i* and add *es*. Place the following words on the board and let the children write their plurals.

baby	fly	puppy
cherry	city	pansy
sky	lady	berry

3. After they complete chapter 1, ask the children to discuss the way that Julian, Huey, and their father handled the pudding episode. Ask them if they agree or disagree and why.

4. There is a great deal of dialogue in this text. Explain to the children that quotation marks are used to set apart direct speech or conversation. Discuss the sentences containing quotation marks. Point out how commas and capital letters are used with quotation marks. Put the following sentences on the chalkboard. Let the children practice placing quotation marks, commas, and capital letters in the appropriate places.

    Julian's father said the pudding is for your mother.

    Huey said I wonder how the pudding tastes.

    Julian's mother said would you like some pudding, boys?

    I want to see the catalog cats jump said Huey.

    Julian asked the fig tree are you growing?

    Can you turn a cartwheel? Gloria asked.

    Place some passages from the story on an overhead transparency. Leave out the commas, capital letters, and quotation marks. Let the children add them in the correct places.

5. Sometimes authors use a figure of speech called *hyperbole*. *Hyperbole* is exaggeration used to make a point. It is not meant to be taken literally. On page 2, Julian says about his father, "when he is angry, me and my little brother Huey shiver to the bottom of our boots." On page 6, the author writes "he wiped the counter so fast his hair made circles around his head." On page 33, she says, "she said we were dirty enough that she could grow plants on our hands and knees." Let the children create *hyperbole* using the following phrases:

    It was so cold _____.

    The desk was so messy _____.

    She ran so fast _____.

6. The author uses lots of similes to paint a picture for us. Similes are comparisons of unlike things using *like* or *as*. The title of chapter 1 contains a simile, "The Pudding Like a Night on the Sea." Explain similes to the children. Help them locate the similes in the story. Discuss the author's comparisons and let the children write their own. Let the children make simile

mobiles. Place the word they are describing in the center of the mobile. Hang new cards or phrases that describe that word to construct a mobile.

7. Discuss Julian's response to his brother on the bottom of page 19. Ask the children why Julian told Huey that he asked his dad too much. Let the children relate some things they have learned on their own and from their parents, brothers, sisters, friends. Ask who may be the best teacher and why. Discuss the advisability of learning from a variety of sources. Ask the children if they think it is best to learn certain things from certain people. Why? Have them give examples.

8. Gloria and Julian become good friends. Discuss friendship. Ask the children what they feel are the most important qualities in a friend. Ask what Julian and Gloria like about each other. Ask the children if they would like to have Julian or Gloria for a friend. Why or why not?

9. The illustrator tells us a lot about Julian and his family through visualization. Have the children examine the illustrations in the book. Ask them what they know about the characters, plot, and setting of the story by examining the illustrations.

Thinking Activities

1. (FLUENCY, FLEXIBILITY) Julian's family is happy. Have the children brainstorm to come up with words that describe happy families, for example, cooperation, love, kindness, consideration, laughter.

2. (FORECASTING) Have the children list the causes and effects of this family's compatibility.

3. (FLEXIBILITY, ORIGINALITY, IMAGINATION) In chapter 2, Julian tells Huey that "A catalog is a big book that is filled with cats." Let the children match the words to the make-believe meanings on the worksheet in figure 15.2. Let them write imaginary definitions for the words at the bottom of the page. The children can also select their own words to define.

4. (FLUENCY) Have the children list as many adjectives as they can to describe Julian, Julian's father, and Huey.

5. (ORIGINALITY) Let the children suppose that they were the main character in this story. Ask them how the story would be different. Substitute someone the children know for Julian's father. Ask the children how the story would be different, for example, suppose the school principal was the father in the story.

6. (EVALUATION) Have the children list similarities and differences between Julian's household and their own household.

7. (PLANNING) Let the children plan how they will make the lemon pudding in Et Cetera Activity 1 (page 169). Use the Planning Worksheet on page 10.

8. (ORIGINALITY, IMAGINATION) On page 32, there is a description of the corn and the house of flowers that the boys planted in their garden. Let the children create a new vegetable or flower and write a description. The plant should not be anything that currently exists.

Fig. 15.2

angelfish

The Stories Julian Tells
Make-Believe Meanings

catalog cats

Match the following words and their make-believe meanings. Place the letter from in front of the definitions in column B on the line after nouns in column A.

A	B
1. breakfast _____	a. an insect that takes long graceful strides
2. dandelion _____	b. a slippery yellow container from which to drink
3. cheapskate _____	c. a Chinese pastry
4. angelfish _____	d. a small frozen town
5. iceberg _____	e. a tree made of soft cushy floor covering
6. icicle _____	f. quickly ruin something
7. buttercup _____	g. a fancy jungle animal
8. cakewalk _____	h. a sharp object made for cutting grass
9. carpentry _____	i. inexpensive shoes to use on ice
10. antelope _____	j. a heavenly ocean animal

(Answers on page 196.)

Write make-believe meanings for the words below.

1. bottlenose _____

2. retreat _____

3. pintail _____

4. pilot _____

5. herringbone _____

Writing Activities

1. This book is an example of a first-person narrative. When a story is written in the first person, readers feel as though they are living or experiencing the main character's feelings, thoughts, and actions as they are happening. First-person point of view is limiting in that the author is not at liberty to share other character's thoughts and feelings without losing credibility. Have the children write a story about a favorite incident in their lives using the first-person point of view. Other examples of books written in the first-person are:

    Alexander, Sue. *Lila on the Landing*. Boston: Little, Brown and Company, 1987.

    Hazen, Barbara Shook. *Tight Times*. New York: Viking Press, 1979.

    Orgel, Doris. *My War with Mrs. Galloway*. New York: Penguin Books, 1986.

    Viorst, Judith. *Alexander and the Terrible, Horrible, No Good, Very Bad Day*. New York: Atheneum, 1980.

    Viorst, Judith. *Rosie and Michael*. New York: Atheneum, 1975.

    Whelan, Gloria. *Next Spring an Oriole*. New York: Random House, 1987.

    Zolotow, Charlotte. *Someone New*. New York: Harper & Row, 1978.

2. Review the main idea of each chapter in the book. Talk about the fact that each chapter is based on an incident that happens to most children. Point out that the simplest event can be the basis for a story. Explain that our stories are best when we write from our own experience. Ask the children to share some experiences in their lives that might be similar to Julian's experiences. Have them brainstorm to come up with five or six events that they might write about and list them on a piece of paper. Pair them up with a classmate. Have them verbally share one or two of these incidents with each other. After about an 8-minute sharing time, let them choose one of the topics to write about. Periodically during the writing time, have them stop and share what they have written with their partner, each posing questions to the other in order to make their stories clear.

3. Julian's family gets along well. They all appear to have high regard for one another. Have the children use the recipe card in figure 15.3 to write a recipe for a happy family. Before they begin, be certain that the children understand the various measurements. Show them a cup, one-half cup, teaspoon, tablespoon. Also discuss terms such as fold, beat, whip, mix, add. This will help make their recipes more accurate.

4. Share some verses about home and families with the children. Verses can be found on plaques, in greeting cards, and on posters. Have the children write verses about families and home. Use a web to plan words and ideas to create their verses. Place the verses on the wall hangings described in Et Cetera Activity 2 (page 169).

5. On page 2, Julian describes his father. Have the children use paragraph 2 as a model and write about their father or mother. (Handout follows on page 168.)

6. In chapter 6, Julian and Gloria list their wishes on strips of paper and attach them to the kite tail. Have the children write their wishes and hang them on the tail of the kite they make in Et Cetera Activity 4 (page 169).

Fig. 15.3

The Stories Julian Tells Recipe Card

Recipe from _____

Serves _____

Ingredients

_____   _____

_____   _____

_____   _____

_____   _____

_____   _____

_____   _____

Directions_____

_____

_____

_____

_____

_____

_____

The Stories Julian Tells
Character Description Worksheet

My father/mother is _____
                                              (size)

with _____
                        (physical description)

_____

_____ .

When he/she _____ , the _____

_____

_____

_____

_____ .

When he/she _____ , you can

_____

_____

_____

_____ .   When

he/she is _____

_____

_____

_____ , I _____

_____

_____

_____ .

Et Cetera Activities

1. (Cooking) Have the children make pudding similar to Julian's father's recipe in chapter 1.

Lemon Pudding

Ingredients	Utensils
4 tablespoons lemon juice	Double boiler
3 eggs (separated)	Two medium-sized bowls
1/2 cup sugar	Whisk
1/8 teaspoon salt	Egg beater or electric mixer
1/2 pint whipping cream (whipped)	Juice squeezer
Yellow food coloring	Large spoon
	Measuring cup
	Measuring spoons
	One large bowl

Squeeze the juice from the lemons. (Remove seeds.) Separate the egg yolks from the whites and place in the two medium-sized bowls. Slightly beat the yolks and add the sugar and salt. Place this mixture in the top of the double boiler and cook until smooth and thick, stirring constantly. Cool the mixture. Put the cooled mixture into a large bowl. Beat egg whites until stiff. Combine egg whites and whipped cream. Fold into cooled lemon mixture. Add several drops of yellow food coloring and stir well. Serves 8 to 10.

2. (Art) Have the children make a wall hanging or a refrigerator magnet and place the verse they wrote in Writing Activity 4 (page 166) on them. Cut out a square of cardboard approximately 3"×3" for a refrigerator magnet or approximately 6"×8" for a wall hanging. Cut a piece of heavy cardboard for the background. Cut a piece of fabric one-half inch larger than the cardboard. (A small print or polka dot fabric makes an attractive background). Glue the fabric to the cardboard. Miter the corners on the back. Glue lace or eyelet around the outside edge of the frame on the back. Have the children write their verse on a square of art paper and glue it on the front of the plaque. Small wooden animal silhouettes can be painted and glued on the side of the verse or the children could paint a picture on the side to make their plaque more finished. Attach small magnets, yarn, or cord to the back so that these can be hung. See figure 15.4.

Fig. 15.4

3. (Science) The boys enjoyed helping their father plant the garden. Let the children plant seeds in milk cartons.

4. (Art) In chapter 6, Julian and Gloria make a kite of folded newspapers and sticks. Have the children work in groups or pairs and make a kite. Let them hang their wishes (from Writing Activity 6 on page 166) on the kites' tails.

5. (Art) Select some black and white pictures from magazines of a house, an animal, a piece of clothing. Give each child a picture. Have them cut off a piece of their picture and glue the remainder on a plain piece of paper. Have them use the piece they cut off as their guide to help them try to draw that portion they cut off onto the picture they pasted down. Encourage them to get as many details of shading and texture as they can.

6. (Art Appreciation) Julian's family is very close. Discuss the kinds of behavior that nurture close-knit family relationships. A contemporary artist, Charles Alston (1907-) has captured this mood or feeling in his painting called *Family No. 1* (1955). In this painting, Alston portrays a loving family through composition rather than through words. The figures are placed together tightly; their gestures portray their kindness and sensitivity to one another. A black and white reproduction of this painting can be found in *The Shorewood Art Reference Guide* by Matila Simon (New York: Shorewood Reproductions, 1970).

The Author Says ...

Ann Cameron's stories about Julian were originally inspired by anecdotes a South African friend, Julian De Wette, told her about his childhood in South Africa. The original Julian did have a best friend Gloria and a little brother Huey, wishing kites, a fig tree he ate from, and a father who made a forbidden lemon pudding. But Cameron moved her character, Julian, to the United States and has invented many other stories about him.

"I still keep learning about my Julian," Cameron says. "For example, I don't know what his mother's name is yet. I don't know exactly where he lives. This is because what matters to me is not where he lives, but how he feels and what happens to him. In my next book about him, *Julian, Dream Doctor*, he catches two beautiful big snakes—corn snakes. These snakes can be found only in Louisiana and part of Texas—so now by chance I'm closer to knowing exactly where Julian lives."

For Cameron, the process of writing is like the process of living. "In life, a bad time can lead you on to a good time and even teach you things that will help you enjoy that good time. In writing, the stuff that's dull can lead you on to something exciting."

"When I write," she says, "I start from a feeling and a situation and see what develops. That means I sit and stare off into space, focus my mind on the situation, and wait for ideas to come to me. As the ideas come, I make notes. The notes are quick summaries of possible action and bits of dialogue: they're often messy and not spelled right because I'm in a hurry to keep up with my thoughts. I don't impose any order on these thoughts. I just note them down. Often I know the end of a book before I know the beginning. Sometimes I write the end first and work backward to find the beginning that would cause such an ending. I try to imagine myself actually living in my story. Sometimes this imagining becomes very real to me. When I wrote *More Stories Julian Tells* (New York: Knopf, 1986), the instant I realized that Huey was going to fall out of bed and land on his head, tears rolled down my face, I felt so bad for him!"

When Cameron begins a book, she usually spends an hour or two on it each day. "Then as I try out and abandon different ways of developing character and action, I gradually become more sure what will work. When I have this structure in my head, I work longer."

She says she used to be very self-critical and "very afraid of paper—afraid to see what was going to come out of my mind and land on it! But now I don't think about the paper or even see it. It is just there as a place to note down what I am seeing in the theater of my mind. My paper is my tool to use whatever way I want. My mistakes are also my tools."

"I think of a story," she says, "as the island a writer makes in the ever-changing river of time. A writer's first ideas for it may never show in the end, but they have served as its foundation stones— to keep time and unrelated thought from dissolving his island."

When asked if there were any trade secrets to writing, she said, "There are no secrets to writing, but honesty, relaxation, and thoughtfulness about life. You need to live your story, to write what you believe are really the deepest feelings of people, and to portray what you care about in words that are the most exact and truest you can find."

She suggested that in teaching the writing process, teachers read aloud stories and poems that they themselves like, even to older children, about fifteen minutes each day, "so that they become sensitive to the richness of words and their rhythms and learn that they can see things in their minds without the aid of TV. This read-aloud time should be simply a regular relaxation and a treat, with no questions asked by the teachers about what is read and no interruptions of the narrative by teachers' comments. Children should be free to listen or not listen, to clean their desks, or draw, or just put their heads down and rest during the reading. There is very little privacy in the world, and almost none in school. So it's important to give children a sense that not everything in life is followed by a question or a test, that they have the right to dream, the right to pleasures that are both shared and private. Only without pressure can they discover that literature is enchantment, and it's from this enchantment that the desire to write can begin."

She does not believe in teachers assigning topics to be written about. Rather she suggests that teachers encourage students to use a daily writing period to "write about what makes them happy, and write about what makes them sad; write about mistakes and successes, fights and fears and joys, friends and family, people and places they miss and things they are curious about, and things they hope to do one day." She thinks children should be introduced to examples of various literary forms—fables, haiku, prose poems, autobiography—very early.

"Above all," she says, "teach them about metaphors and encourage their use—the wilder the metaphor the better," she says. "Kids could even have a 'wild metaphor' competition and vote for the best one. The teacher could join the competition, too."

She proposes that teachers encourage poetry by having children as a group suggest words that are especially beautiful, mysterious, or scary and write those words on a blackboard and then individually combine some of them in a poem. Another suggestion is that children interview older family members to learn about their childhoods and write a story from the point of view of their own parents as children.

She suggests teachers not judge children's work but encourage them to evaluate it: "Have they said exactly what they feel? All that they have to say? Have they said it in a way that they and others can understand? Is there another way they could say it that might have more impact? Could they say it better or differently in a poem? Teachers should not exclaim over 'best' writing or frown over 'bad' writing. Rather they should help the child to feel that everything they write is valid as an expression of their life and growth."

Cameron has lived in Massachusetts, New York, Iowa, and California, as well as in Mexico and Central America. She has been a teacher of creative writing in universities, an editor of fiction and nonfiction, and a camp cook on a Mayan dig in the jungle of Belize, sleeping for four months in a hammock while at night boa constrictors hunted mice in the thatched roof of her hut. Her hardest job ever was babysitting twenty-three cats, including two sick ones who needed eye drops and kept hiding from her in kitchen cabinets.

For the past six years, Cameron has lived much of the time in Panajachel, a small village on the shores of a volcanic lake in the highlands of Guatemala.

"Mostly," Cameron says, "I like to write about strong and happy people. I want to learn their secrets!"

Author Activities

1. Ann Cameron uses a great many metaphors in her work. Encourage the children to use metaphors in their writing. Hold a "Metaphor Contest" as suggested by Cameron. Establish criteria by which to judge the metaphors and have the children vote for the best one.

2. Cameron likes to write about strong and happy people. Have the children select people that they think are strong and happy and write a story about them.

BIBLIOGRAPHY

Other books by Ann Cameron for grades 1 through 3.

Julian, Secret Agent. New York: Random House, 1988. (RL 3   IL 2-5)

Julian's Glorious Summer. New York: Random House, 1987. (RL 3   IL 2-5)

More Stories Julian Tells. New York: Alfred A. Knopf, 1986. (RL 3   IL 2-5)

The Most Beautiful Place in the World. New York: Alfred A. Knopf, 1988. (RL 3   IL 3-5)

The Seed. New York: Pantheon, 1975. (RL 3   IL k-4)

A Story A Story

Retold by Gail E. Haley. New York: Atheneum, 1970.

SUMMARY

Long ago in Africa, there were no stories because they all belonged to the Sky God, Nyame. Ananse, the Spiderman, spun a web up to the heavens and humbly asked the Sky God how he could purchase his stories. Amused that such a tiny creature would even dream of asking this question, the Sky God gave Ananse three tasks to perform in return for the stories. Clever as he was, Ananse accomplished all of the tasks and returned to Nyame, with the price he asked. The Sky God was a man of his word and he gave the stories to Ananse who scattered them throughout the world.

Possible Student Outcomes

Increase basic reading vocabulary.

Recognize the characteristics of, and to write, a "pourquoi" story.

Increase understanding of the Ashanti people through reading a folktale.

Practice the thinking skills of fluency, flexibility, originality, evaluation, forecasting, and decision making.

*** CHOOSE A LIMITED NUMBER OF ACTIVITIES FROM EACH SECTION ***

Before Reading Activities

1. Have the children examine the cover of the book. Ask them where the story takes place and what clues tell them this. Ask what questions come to their minds as they look at the picture. They might wonder why everyone is looking up. Ask them what this might mean. Discuss the spiderweb in the left-hand corner. Ask them where the spider might be and why. After this discussion, explain that this story is one of numerous spider stories brought to this country from Africa by slaves. Share Gail Haley's detailed explanation in the front of the book about the origin of these tales.

2. Play African music softly in the background while showing a transparency of a map of the world. Point out the continent of Africa. Put up a transparency of Africa and point out Ghana, which is just east of Ivory Coast. This area is where the Ashanti people live. Explain to the children how the Portuguese named this the Gold Coast because when their explorers arrived they were met by the Ashanti who were adorned in gold ornaments. Call their attention to the jewelry worn by the Sky God in the story. Explain that this story is one told by the Ashanti people and it explains the origin of storytelling in their culture. Gail Haley spent a year studying the African people and their culture before she began writing this story. Ask the children what they learn about these people from her words and pictures.

3. Put the following vocabulary words from the story on the chalkboard:

royal	frond	latex
hornet	yams	leopard
Ananse	calabash	Africa
fairy		

   Ask the children how much they know about each word. Allow them to discuss the words. Then ask them what they think this story is about. Ask them to predict how these words will fit into the story.

Predicting Activities

1. Have the children read to the bottom of page 8[1] where Ananse climbs down to earth. Ask the children how they think he will capture the leopard-of-the-terrible-teeth. Ask how they would catch him.

2. After the children read to the end of page 13 where Ananse captures the leopard, ask them how they think he might capture the hornets.

3. Have the children read to the bottom of page 23 where Mmoatia asks the Gum baby, "Don't you reply when I thank you?" Ask what they think Mmoatia will do and why they think that.

4. Have the children read to the end of the story.

Post Reading Activities

1. Explain to the children that African storytellers often repeat words to help the listener visualize what is being described. The Sky God describes Ananse as "a weak old man — so small, so small, so small" and he says Ananse tied the leopard "by his foot, by his foot, by his foot, by his foot." Discuss how we would write or describe these people or events. Have the children

---

[1]Pagination begins on the title page of the text.

select something and describe it the way the African storyteller might say it. They might describe a body of water, a large person, someone riding a bicycle.

2. Discuss the epithets used to describe the characters, for example, "the leopard-of-the-terrible-teeth, Mmboro the hornets-who-sting-like-fire, and Mmoatia the fairy-whom-no-man-sees." Have the children write descriptive names for an animal, a weather phenomenon, a person.

3. African storytellers often mimic the sounds and movements of people or animals, for example, "Ananse ran along the jungle path—yiridi, yiridi, yiridi." Incorporating these sounds into the text enhances the mood or tone of the story. When it is done naturally, the listeners can hear and see the scene more vividly in their mind. Have the children find examples of sound words in other books. Have them imitate sounds they hear in their own environment and write original words for these sounds. (Excellent audio cassettes featuring narratives of the African stories *A Story A Story*, *Why Mosquitoes Buzz in People's Ears*, and *Who's in Rabbit's House* are available from Weston Woods, Weston, CT 06883-1199.)

4. Folktales are stories told by the common folk. They are tales that have been passed from generation to generation by word of mouth. These stories have been carried around the world by sailors, soldiers, minstrels, monks, scholars, and, in the case of many African folktales, by slaves. Sometimes the stories were combined, producing variants of the same story. Because folk literature contains elements of religious beliefs, superstitions, as well as past events of the culture of its origin, it allows us to gain insights into the various cultures from which these tales originate. Have the children examine the words and pictures in this text. Ask them to list what they learn about Africa, its people, art, religion, and animal and plant life.

5. On page 24, the fairy-whom-no-man-sees tells the Gum baby that she is going to slap her "crying place" if the Gum baby does not respond to her. Have the children explain what this means. Ask the children if this incident reminds them of another story they might have heard ("Brer Rabbit and the Tar Baby"). Brer Rabbit is the same folktale trickster hero in the southern United States as Ananse is in West Africa. Many Brer Rabbit tales parallel Ananse stories.

6. Ask the children to look at page 33 where the author says "Ananse took the golden box of stories back to earth." Call their attention to the doll that the one little girl is holding. In her book *The Art of Africa*, Shirley Glubok (New York: Harper & Row, 1965) explains that historically Ashanti women and girls kept flat wooden dolls with long necks tucked in the back of their waistcloths. It was hoped that these charms would ensure that the woman carrying them would have good-looking children.

7. Read aloud *A Story A Story* Rhythmic Activity using 4/4 meter and metronome marking of 144. Teach the children to read the story along with you. Teach the children the rhythmic activity in figure 16.1. While one group of children reads the story aloud, another group can provide the background rhythmic accompaniment and sound effects in figure 16.2, page 176.

Thinking Activities

1. (FLUENCY) Have the children brainstorm to come up with everything they know about Africa. This activity can be done before and after reading this story.

2. (FLUENCY) Have the children list as many adjectives as they can to describe Ananse.

3. (FLEXIBILITY) There are many sound words in this story. Have the children choose a sound and find a clever way to simulate it. They might simulate an animal walking through water by lapping their hand in a pan of water.

Fig. 16.1

A Story A Story Rhythmic Activity

A Rhythmic History of Stories

A long time ago in Africa,
The people were sad, the people were mad.
They had no stories to make them laugh or cry,
The stories belonged to the God in the sky.
Ananse knew just what to do
For he was smart and clever too,
He made a web up to the sky
And asked Nyame to let him try
To earn the stories He kept hidden away
To this Nyame had this to say,
"Bring me the leopard of the terrible teeth,   (Ratchet)
Bring me the hornets for me to keep (Buzz)
Bring me the fairy whom no man sees (Windtube)
Bring all these things back to me   (All)
And I'll give you the stories, you'll see, you'll see!"
Ananse bound the leopard by his feet, by his feet.
He tricked the hornets that he chanced to meet.
The fairy's pride was her downfall
When he captured her, he had them all.
The Sky God was pleased to see the prize
He said, "Ananse is very wise.
He earned the stories, they're his forever,
Ananse is surely very clever."
So this is how the stories came to be,
At least that's how it was told to me.

Fig. 16.2

A Story A Story Rhythmic Accompaniment
and Sound Effects

Tempo: Metronomic Marking: 144

Beat: Bongo Drum

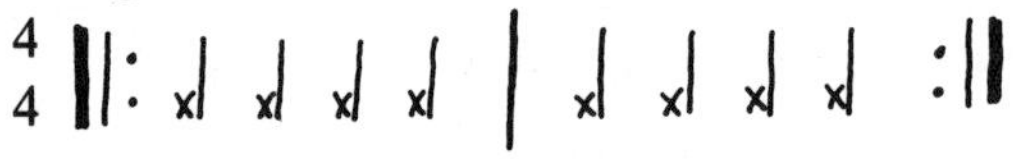

(To assist the children in developing the pattern, the children should quietly speak the words as they play the pattern.)

Ostinato Pattern I: Rhythm Sticks

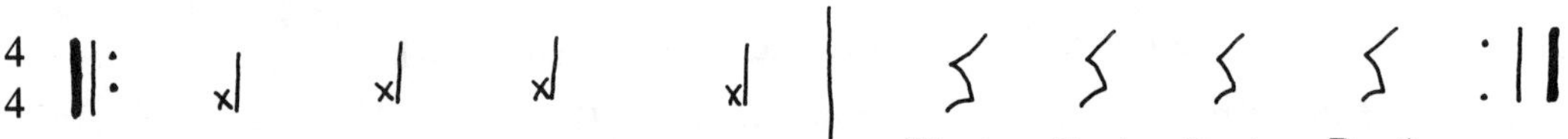

Speak: You'll see, You'll see (Rest Rest Rest Rest)

Ostinato Pattern II: Macaca played in palm of hand

Speak: God in the sky God in the sky

Special Effect Orchestration

Teeth = Ratchet (Slowly)

Hornets = Class makes "buzz" with voice

Fairy = Windtube

All these things = All of above

Incidental Sounds:

Sprinkle the reading with an occasional (use sparingly) quico, African thumb piano, Afuchel or Cabasa sounds to add flavor of African setting.

4. (FLUENCY, FLEXIBILITY) Have the children brainstorm to come up with colorful, descriptive words to include in their story planning for Writing Activity Activity 1 (below).

5. (ORIGINALITY) African storytellers often use clever beginnings and endings for their stories. Review the last page of the text where the author says, "This is my story which I have related. If it be sweet, or if it be not sweet, take some elsewhere, and let some come back to me." Have the children create original endings for the "pourquoi" stories in Writing Activity 1 (below).

6. (DECISION MAKING) Gail Haley won the 1970 Caldecott Award for this book. Have the children look at other Caldecott Award winning books and decide which illustrations and/or story they like best. Use the Decision Making Worksheet on page 14 for this activity.

7. (EVALUATION) Have the children discuss the advantages and disadvantages of living in Africa. Use the Evaluation Worksheet on page 15 for this activity.

8. (FORECASTING) Ask the children to imagine that all stories were taken away from us. Use the Forecasting Worksheet on page 11 to discuss this problem.

Writing Activities

1. Folktales that tell "how" or "why" something came to be are called "pourquoi" tales. These stories often explain various phenomenon in nature such as "how the elephant got his trunk." *A Story A Story* might be considered a "pourquoi" story in that it explains the origin of the African stories. Read other "pourquoi" stories to the children and let them write their own tale explaining how something came to be. The children could use the Pourquoi Tale planning worksheet in figure 16.3, pages 178-79, to plan their story. Other "pourquoi" stories to share with the children are:

   Aardema, Verna. *Why Mosquitoes Buzz in People's Ears*. New York: Dial, 1975.

   Kipling, Rudyard. *Just So Stories*. Garden City, N.Y.: Doubleday, 1912.

2. This is one of many African folktales that include Ananse, the spider. Ananse is a common cultural hero in a group of stories from the Ashanti people in which Ananse plays numerous roles. Sometimes he is cunning and sly, sometimes wise and sympathetic, and at other times he is greedy and unscrupulous. Most often there is a moral to the story and Ananse is punished for inappropriate behavior. Read other spider stories to the children and have them write a new episode or adventure for Ananse. Some spider stories to read are "How Spider Got a Thin Waist," "Why Spider Lives in Ceilings," "How Spider Got a Bald Head," "How Spider Helped a Fisherman," "Why Spiders Live in Dark Corners," "How the World Got Wisdom." All of these stories can be found in *The Adventures of Spider* by Joyce Cooper Arkhurst (New York: Scholastic, 1964). A variation of this activity would be to simply read the titles of these stories to the children and let them write their own version and then compare it to the original version.

3. The creation of some natural phenomena are said to be attributed to Ananse. Read Gerald McDermott's Caldecott Honor Book *Anansi the Spider* (New York: Henry Holt, 1972). Have the children write an original story in which Anansi (alternate spelling of Ananse) creates something else in nature, for example, the sun, stars, waterfalls, mountains.

4. The last illustration in the text shows many African artifacts emerging from the story box. Have the children identify the objects. Each child could then select one object and write a story about it.

(Text continues on page 180.)

Fig. 16.3

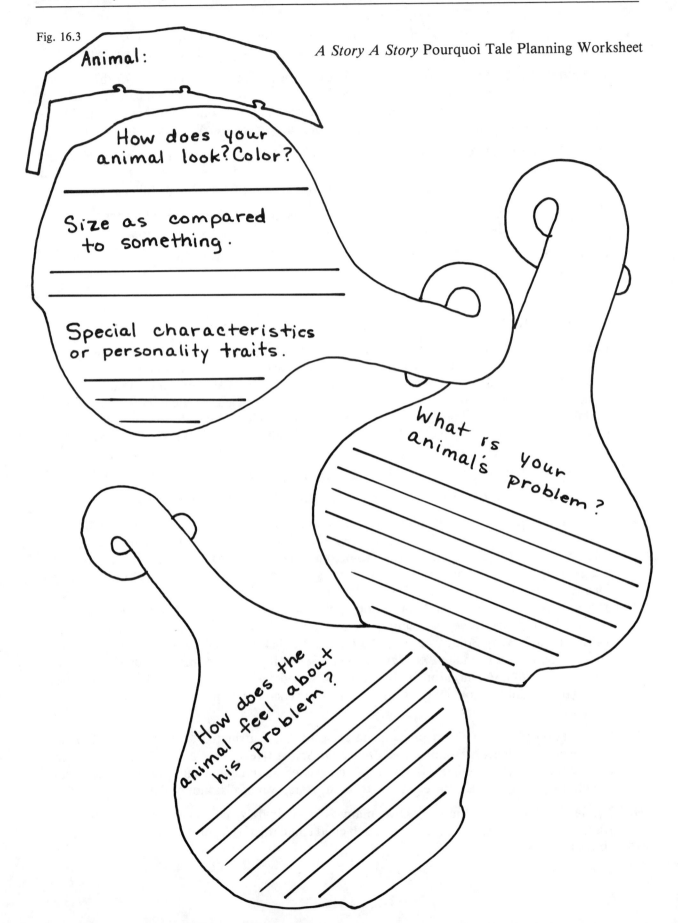

Animal:

How does your animal look? Color?

Size as compared to something.

Special characteristics or personality traits.

What is your animal's problem?

How does the animal feel about his problem?

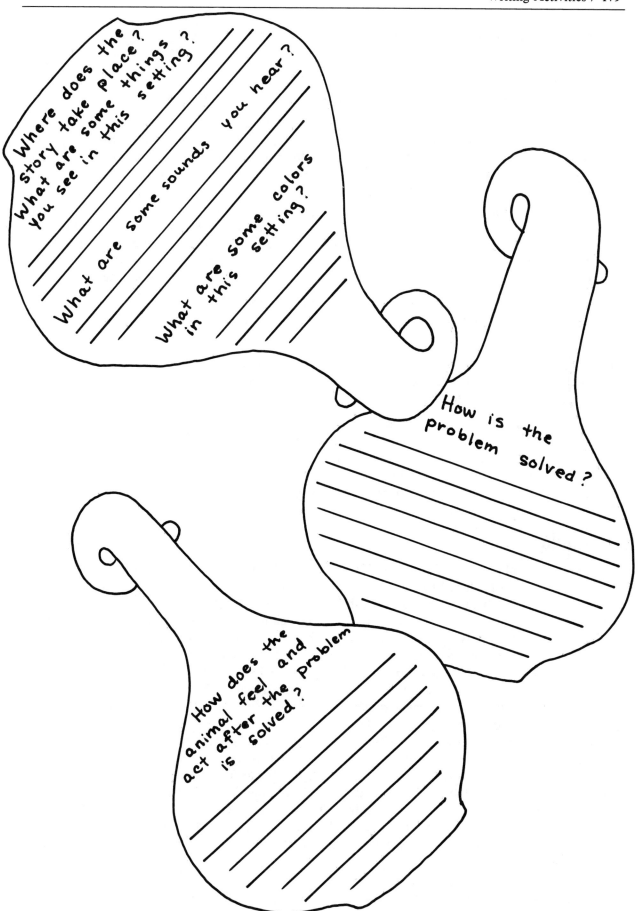

Where does the story take place? What are some things you see in this setting?

What are some sounds you hear?

What are some colors in this setting?

How is the problem solved?

How does the animal feel and act after the problem is solved?

Et Cetera Activities

1. (Art) After reading numerous "spider stories" to the children, have them make a mural depicting spider in his various predicaments. Some spider story titles from Arkhurst's *The Adventures of Spider* are listed in Writing Activity 2 (page 177).

2. (Storytelling) African storytellers use a variety of techniques to introduce their stories. Sometimes they have a box containing articles such as feathers, bones, leaves. The objects represent various stories in the storyteller's repertoire. The listener selects an item and the storyteller begins his tale. Another technique requires the storyteller to wear a hat with a variety of trinkets suspended from the brim. Each trinket represents a story. Again the listener points to a trinket and the storyteller begins. Have the children learn one or more stories and choose or make an object to represent their story. These items could be placed in a story box or hung from the brim of a hat. The children could be divided into groups. Each group could have a hat or a story box. Younger children could be invited to the classroom and they could select items from the box or the hat, and the child whose object was chosen could tell the story.

3. (Art Appreciation) Gail Haley's research is evident in her illustrations. Compare the photographs in Shirley Glubok's *The Art of Africa* with the illustrations in this text. Note the similarities.

4. (Research) On page 14, the author says "Ananse held the banana leaf over his head as an umbrella" and filled a "calabash with water." Have the children use an encyclopedia to do research about the size of banana leaves and how a calabash is made.

5. (Art) Discuss the repeated patterns in the illustrations, which are particularly evident in the foliage and trees. Let the children replicate pattern art by making sun prints. Cut leaves, insects, flowers, or geometric shapes from paper and place on light-sensitive paper. Expose it to the sun for five minutes then rinse and dry. Sunprint kits are available from Miles Kimball, 41 West Eighth Avenue, Oshkosh, WI 54906.

The Author Says ...

Although Gail Haley was born on November 4, 1939, in Charlotte, North Carolina, the city holds few memories for her. From age two until seventeen, she lived in Shuffletown, an "old-time rural village" in North Carolina. Her neighbors were hard-working folk who wore poke bonnets and dresses made of feed sacks. Their way of life was "simple and beautiful, if difficult," she says. For years she was an only child and because she had no playmates, she spent lots of time alone roaming barefoot through the woods that surrounded her home. Sally was her make-believe friend and the two of them spent endless hours playing games and sharing secrets. Being alone meant she had lots of time for "dreaming, exploring, reading, and drawing." She confesses that she did and still does talk to fairies. *The Green Man* (Blowing Rock, N.C.: New River Publishing, 1980) was someone she "saw" in the woods as a youngster.[2]

Her vivid imagination coupled with the homespun environment in which she grew up have influenced Haley's style of writing and illustrating. Her close relationship with her father was another contributing factor to her career choice. He was the art director of the Charlotte *Observer*. Gail loved to visit him at the newspaper and he taught her the skills of his trade. She can remember wanting to find folk stories and to be a children's book writer since she was seven or eight years old. All through elementary and secondary school, she drew and wrote. After high school, she attended Richmond Professional Institute and then studied graphics and painting at the University of

---

[2]"Gail Haley ... A Whimsical Visionary," *Early Years/K-8* (November/December 1985): 24-25.

Virginia. She herself bound and sold her first children's book, *My Kingdom for a Dragon*. Then for six years, she illustrated for other authors until she was able to sell her own first manuscript. She prefers doing her own writing and illustrating working back and forth between the text and the illustrations until they express what she wants them to say. She does not describe or illustrate everything, deliberately leaving some things to the reader's imagination.

She uses a variety of mediums, letting the story dictate the technique she will use. Sometimes she works in linoleum blocks or woodcuts and sometimes she paints on wood. *A Story A Story* is done with woodblocks that she cut herself, one block for each color. She felt that woodblocks best represented the African artifacts. The book was two years in the making. The first year she spent researching the African culture, the second in production.

Haley often writes with a cause in mind. Having grown up in an area where she witnessed a great deal of prejudice, she says she would "like to right wrongs." *A Story A Story* was the first book to have a black God. Sometimes she writes "to share something significant from folklore that she thinks children should know."[3]

Whatever her reason for writing, her extensive knowledge about folklore is evident. She has traveled extensively, living in England, New York City, and the Caribbean. In her travels, she has collected old children's books, toys, dolls, puppets, and numerous other artifacts from around the world. These items are valued at over $350,000 and are housed in The Gail Haley Collection of the Culture of Childhood in Boone, North Carolina.

She has won numerous awards for her books. *A Story A Story* won the Caldecott Award in 1970. The Japanese chose *The Post Office Cat* (New York: Scribner's, 1976) to receive the Kadai Tosho Award. Haley was also given the Caldecott Award and its English equivalent, the Kate Greenaway Medal, for *The Post Office Cat*. Although she acknowledges the importance of winning awards, in that they help to market her books, she says that even without the awards, she would continue to write and illustrate children's books because she thoroughly enjoys her work.

Author Activities

1. Gail Haley says she nearly always writes with a cause in mind. *A Story A Story* was the first book to have a black God. Ask the children what causes or injustices they think should be addressed in books.

2. Because children can learn so much about other cultures from their literature, the author feels that children should have lots of experiences with folklore. Have the children select folklore from other cultures and make posters showing what they have learned. An outline of the country or continent of the story's origin could be placed in the center of the poster. Illustrations depicting religious beliefs, language, food, dress, and art could be placed around the picture of the country.

BIBLIOGRAPHY

Other books by Gail E. Haley for children grades 1 through 3.

Birdsong. New York: Crown Publishers, 1984. (RL 5   IL 2-6)

Jack and the Bean Tree. New York: Crown Publishers, 1986. (RL 4   IL k-3)

Jack and the Fire Dragon. New York: Crown Publishers, 1988. (RL 4   IL k-4)

---

[3]Doris De Montreville and Donna Hill, eds., *Third Book of Junior Authors* (New York: H. W. Wilson, 1972), 117-18.

Swamp Monsters

Mary Blount Christian. New York: Dial, 1983.

SUMMARY

Two monster children have only read about "real children" in books. One day they dress up like children and go out to play in the swamp. Before long, they spy some school children on a field trip with a substitute teacher. Moving closer to get a good look, they are nabbed by the substitute who thinks they are part of her class. Whisked off to school, they are totally confused by the teacher's directions to her class. Their antics prove extremely funny to the children but not so funny to the teacher. Ultimately the swamp monsters decide that they like being monsters better than being children.

Possible Student Outcomes

Expand reading vocabulary.

Differentiate literal and figurative expressions.

Identify the moral of the story.

Practice the thinking skills of fluency, flexibility complexity, originality, and evaluation.

** CHOOSE A LIMITED NUMBER OF ACTIVITIES FROM EACH SECTION **

Before Reading Activities

1. Write the following lists of words on the blackboard.

Column I	Column II
substitute teacher	masks
monsters	noodles
school	field trip
lunch	finger painted
dress up	fountain
jumped	principal

    Go over the words with the children several times. Ask them to predict how the author might connect the words in Column I with the words in Column II to create a story.

2. Have the children look at the picture on the cover of the book. Read the title with the children. Ask the children to predict what they think this book might be about. Ask what makes them think this.

3. Have the children brainstorm to come up with as many school words and swamp words as they can. Put these words on two charts. After reading the story see how many of the words that are listed were actually in the story. Add words from the story to the list.

4. The monsters were curious about children. Ask the children what they are curious about. Ask them if they have ever been curious about a different place or about someone and how they satisfied their curiosity.

5. Chants are good ways to familiarize children with new vocabulary. Teach the children the following chant to the rhythm of "Baa, Baa, Black Sheep."

Two little monsters went to school

Curious little monsters didn't understand the rules

Picked up the chair, ate the lunch money

Made the children laugh and the teacher say, "Not funny!"

Predicting Activities

1. Have the children stop reading at the end of page 9. Have them predict what the swamp monsters are going to play. Ask the children why they think this.

2. Have the children stop reading at the end of page 21. Have them predict what they think will happen next. Ask why they think this.

3. Have the children read to the end of the story.

SCHOOL OF EDUCATION
CURRICULUM LABORATORY
UM-DEARBORN

Post Reading Activities

1. Discuss how illustrations help tell the story. Have the children look at the illustrations on pages 4 and 5. Ask them to find and read the sentences that best describe each illustration as they read through the book.

2. Ms. Mumfrey used a great many expressions that the swamp monsters misunderstood. Sometimes we use expressions that do not make sense if we interpret them in their *literal* (actual) sense. Explain the difference between literal and figurative expressions. Ask the children how they might say the following expressions so they would not be misunderstood.

     "Take your seats." (Sit down.)

     "Today we will finger paint." (We will paint with finger paints.)

     "Straighten you out."

     "Put your heads on your desks."

     "Put on the TV."

   Ask the children to think of some other expressions we use that do not always make sense, for example, pick up your room, empty your mouth before speaking.

3. Have the children compare and contrast the children and the monsters in the story.

4. On page 36, the author uses similes to describe some of the food. She says, "the noodles look like worms" the "ice cream looks like snow." Have the children create their own similes for the following words: jello, grass, snow, clouds, rope.

5. The author uses a great many "sound" words in this text. As the children read the story, list all the sound words, for example, whined, Shh, gronk, RRRRroarrr. Ask the children to demonstrate how and when they might hear or use these words. Write sentences on the chalkboard and let the children fill in the blanks with the appropriate words from the list. For example:

The silverware _____ as it fell on the floor. (clinked)

My daddy went _____ as he slept in the chair. (Zzzzz)

The lion let out a _____ when he saw the man. (RRRRroarrr)

6. The author uses the words *lunchtime*, *lunch money*, *lunchroom*. Ask the children to think of as many words or combinations of words as they can that go with the word *lunch*, for example, lunch pail, lunch box, luncheon, luncheon meat, lunch wagon, luncheonette.

Thinking Activities

1. (FLUENCY) The little monsters lived in the swamp. Have the children list as many things as they can that live in a swamp, as many things as they can that water is used for.

2. (FLEXIBILITY) Have the children examine the list of school words and swamp words they came up with in Before Reading Activity 3 (page 182). Have the children see how many ways they can group these words.

3. (ORIGINALITY) Have the children create their own three-dimensional monster. Have them give it an unusual name.

4. (EVALUATION) Have the children read another monster story and compare and contrast it with this story.

   Some other monster stories they might enjoy are:

   Christian, Mary Blount. *Go West, Swamp Monsters!* New York: Dial, 1985.

   Crowe, Robert L. *Clyde Monster*. New York: E. P. Dutton, 1976.

   Dinan, Carolyn. *The Lunch Box Monster*. Boston: Faber and Faber Limited, 1983.

   Parish, Peggy. *No More Monsters for Me!* New York: Harper & Row, 1981.

5. (COMPLEXITY) Have the children list some words that describe Ms. Mumfrey's personality.

6. (COMPLEXITY) The field trip did not seem to be well-organized. Have the students list five things that the children could have been asked to do during and after the field trip that would have made the trip more meaningful.

7. (PLANNING) Have the children plan a field trip using the Planning Worksheet on page 10.

8. (COMPLEXITY) Ask the children what qualities they think are important in a teacher. Have them make up sentences demonstrating how the teacher would manifest these qualities.

Quality	Ways to demonstrate the quality
kindness	When we fall down the teacher bandages our knee.

9. (COMPLEXITY) Ask the children what they would show or explain to these monsters if they came to their classroom.

Writing Activities

1. Have the children write a story about a make-believe monster. Before they begin writing, have the class discuss some monsters they have heard, seen, or read about. Talk about where these monsters lived, what they looked like, and what they did. Have the children create a monster they might like to write about. They could use the following form to create their monster.

Ideas for My Monster

Name	Setting	Appearance	Action

Some children might need more structure to complete this activity. After participating in the discussion, they could use the story frame on page 186 to write their story.

2. Have the children design and write a thank-you card or letter as though they were the monsters thanking the children for their exciting day at school. Before they begin writing, allow the class to discuss things they have thanked people for in the past. Discuss the fact that a thank-you letter says more than "thank you." Talk about the things that the monsters might mention that they enjoyed during their school visit. Read a thank-you note to the class as a model.

3. The monsters went on an adventure. Adventures involve doing something or going someplace that is unknown to us. Adventures can be as simple as going under a porch, opening a strange door, or meeting someone for the first time. Have the children write about an adventure that they have had.

4. Have the children reverse the plot and write a story as though they were dressed up like monsters and went to the monster's house.

Et Cetera Activities

1. (Science) Introduce the children to some nonfiction books about swamps. A good source to use along with this book is Wendy W. Cortesi's *Explore the Spooky Swamp*, which is part of the National Geographic Society series IV, "Books for Young Explorers" (Washington, D.C.: National Geographic Society, 1978). This book has excellent photographs and text about swamps. After they use this nonfiction book or any other book on swamps, have them generate lists of plants and animals that live in the swamp. Have each child make a paper animal and display it on a bulletin board.

2. (Art) Have the children finger paint a swamp picture. Encourage them to include as many plants and animals as they can that live in the swamp. They might want to use paper doilies and sponges to give the pictures a swampy appearance. Dried Spanish moss could be glued on their pictures to make them more realistic. (Dried Spanish moss is available at many stores that sell artificial flowers.)

Swamp Monsters Story Frame

My Monster

This story is about a monster named _____ who

lives _____ .

This monster is _____ and has

_____

_____

_____

_____ .

One day _____ decides to _____

_____

_____

_____

_____ .

Next _____

_____

_____

_____ .

The story ends when _____

_____

_____

_____

_____ .

3. (Art) The monsters had children masks. Ask the children to design their own mask. Two good sources to use are:

    Emberley, Ed. *Ed Emberley's Drawing Book of Faces.* Boston: Little, Brown and Company, 1975.

    Feller, Ron, and Marsha Feller. *Paper Masks and Puppets for Stories, Songs and Plays.* Seattle, Wash.: Arts Factory, 1985.

    McKay, Bob. *How to Draw Funny People.* Mahwah, N.J.: Watermill Press, 1981.

    The children could use a brown paper bag for their background. One interesting tip for making fur is to cut strips of construction paper and roll it on a pencil to make it curl. See figure 17.1. Place the strips close together or overlap them. Beans and/or aluminum foil might be used for teeth.

    Fig. 17.1

4. (Cooking) Have the children make Mud Pie to eat after they have finished reading this book. Place a snake egg on top of each individual pie or scatter several around a large pie, one for each child. (Yogurt-covered raisins or malt candy Easter eggs could serve as snake eggs.)

    Mud Pie Recipe

    1 frozen pie crust or 25 small ready made crusts

    Filling
    chocolate pudding

5. (Math) The monsters have definite foods they like and dislike. Have your students list the foods they like the least, the most. Make bar graphs listing their choices (see figure 17.2).

    Fig. 17.2

    Foods Students Like the Most

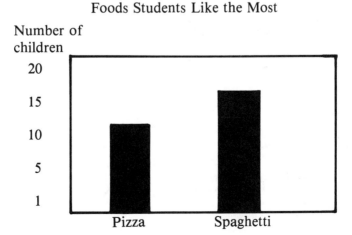

6. (Math) Have the children complete the Math Activity Sheet found in figure 17.3, page 188.

Fig. 17.3

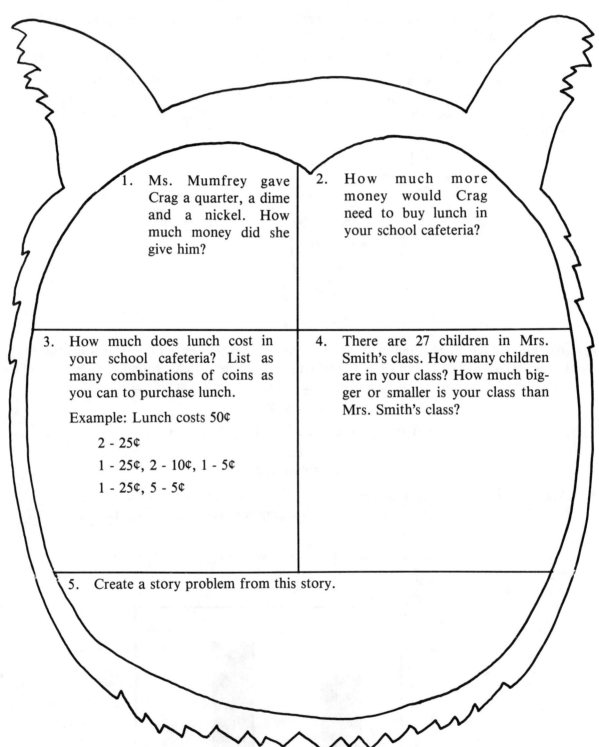

Swamp Monsters Math Activity Sheet

1. Ms. Mumfrey gave Crag a quarter, a dime and a nickel. How much money did she give him?

2. How much more money would Crag need to buy lunch in your school cafeteria?

3. How much does lunch cost in your school cafeteria? List as many combinations of coins as you can to purchase lunch.

   Example: Lunch costs 50¢

   2 - 25¢

   1 - 25¢, 2 - 10¢, 1 - 5¢

   1 - 25¢, 5 - 5¢

4. There are 27 children in Mrs. Smith's class. How many children are in your class? How much bigger or smaller is your class than Mrs. Smith's class?

5. Create a story problem from this story.

The Author Says ...

Everyone knows that a vivid imagination is a valuable asset to an author. Mary Blount Christian (1933-) has been honing her imaginative skills for many years. An only child, she loved to rewrite fairy tales and put on plays, which she often performed for her make-believe friends. She says the word *author* is a bit too fancy for her. "I write, therefore I'm a writer."

When she was about eleven years old, she read Carol Ryrie Brink's *Caddie Woodlawn*. It was then that she realized that she wanted to be a writer. An avid reader, she rollerskated to the public library where she read the shelves from A to Z.[1] Her formal writing career began in 1971 and her first book was published in 1973. With nearly eighty books to her credit, she continues to delight her readers with tales of mystery and humor. It is interesting to note that one of her minors at the University of Houston was Psychology/Criminology. When asked how she plots a mystery, she said, "I know the problem, the kinds of characters who need to "people' it, and before I finish the first draft, I know who did it. I like to sort through clues as I go, rather than have it too 'pat.'"

Christian teaches classes on writing for children. Her advice to children who are beginning their writing career is "to begin writing immediately by keeping a journal or diary. She suggests also that they be aware of others and why they act the way they do. Ask yourself what is in their past that makes them do things now. Don't be afraid to get inside your character and cry with them. If an idea makes you laugh or cry or feel happy, it will affect someone else that way too. Become the characters you are writing about; that is emotional commitment and it makes your reader live the story, instead of hearing about it. It's important to wonder and ask yourself questions. Why does that dark house at the corner make me feel creepy? What makes my best friend sometimes act so hostile? What would it take to change a person?" Answers to questions like these might well be the nucleus of a story.

She thought about *Swamp Monsters* for a year before she actually began writing it. It took her a week to write the first draft and approximately five weeks "to sharpen, delete, and enhance it into easy-read."

She says her stories are conceived as a result of "a deep inner feeling and/or experience of her own or someone else's." When asked what prompted her to write *Swamp Monsters*, she said it was "the feeling that many times I'm the innocent, and everyone but me, is in on the joke. But the deep inner feeling is that good will survive and thrive, despite everything." She enjoys playing with words and certainly *Swamp Monsters* gave her an opportunity to use words and phrases to entertain us.

Christian has received many awards for her books, such as the Edgar Allan Poe Scroll Award given to her by the Mystery Writers of America, the Ann Martin Award, and numerous "Classroom Choices," just to mention a few. Her books have been translated into French, Japanese, German, Swedish, and Braille. When asked which of the many books she has written is her favorite, she said, "it must always be the one I'm working on, else I wouldn't have the enthusiasm to face blank pages day after day. Writing is a one-person job, so you must love the characters trying to get your attention at the moment. Besides it's unproductive to look back with self-satisfaction."

Author Activities

1. Mary Blount Christian created and wrote a television program called "Children's Bookshelf." The program featured an author whose works were presented in whole or in part. The author was interviewed and reviews of his or her work were shared with the audience. Discuss with the children what a book review is. Read some reviews to them to model how critics judge books. Let the children write reviews of some books that they have read.

---

[1]Anne Commire, *Something about the Author*, vol. 9 (Detroit: Gale Research, 1976), 36.

Set up a Children's Bookshelf program to interview the authors in your classroom. Each week a different child who has written a book could be the featured author. The teacher or another student could be the interviewer. Make an author box where children can submit questions that they would like the featured author to answer. The author could read his or her work aloud. Classmates could review the work orally, or if they have read it previously they could share written responses that they prepared ahead of time. It is important to teach children to make positive comments about their classmates' work.

2. Mary Blount Christian said that reading the book *Caddie Woodlawn* by Carol Ryrie Brink convinced her that she wanted to be an author. Ask the children what their favorite book is. Set up a display of these choices in the classroom or library. Label it "Favorite Fiction." Children could design book jackets with end papers containing author information and a summary of their book. The book jackets could remain with the display to advertise the books when they are checked out.

3. The author recommends that children keep journals or diaries that record their own and others' feelings and activities. Have the children begin keeping a journal.

4. Christian says her stories come from her own personal experiences. Have the children write about one of their own experiences.

BIBLIOGRAPHY

Other books by Mary Blount Christian for grades 1 through 3.

April Fool. New York: Macmillan Co., 1981. (RL 3   IL 1-4)

The Doggone Mystery. Niles, Ill.: Albert Whitman, 1980. (RL 2   IL ps-3)

Go West, Swamp Monsters. New York: Dial, 1985. (RL 2   IL 1-3)

The Green Thumb Thief. Niles, Ill.: Albert Whitman, 1982. (RL 2   IL 1-3)

The Lucky Man. New York: Macmillan Co., 1979. (RL 3   IL 1-4)

Penrod's Pants. New York: Macmillan Co., 1986. (RL 3   IL 2-5)

The Toady and Dr. Miracle. New York: Macmillan Co., 1985. (RL 2   IL 1-3)

Two-Ton Secret. Niles, Ill.: Albert Whitman, 1981. (RL 3   IL 1-3)

The Undercover Kids and the Museum Mystery. Niles, Ill.: Albert Whitman, 1983. (RL 3   IL 3-4)

APPENDIX A:
PUBLISHING YOUR YOUNG
AUTHORS

As your students' writing improves, you may want additional audiences for their work. The following periodicals and organizations currently publish young children's writing.

Chickadee is a Canadian publication for children ages eight and younger. This magazine publishes ten issues each year. The "All Your Own" section features children's artwork and centers on a different theme each month. A "Puzzles and Fun" section prints children's jokes and riddles. "Ask Chickadee" prints questions posed by children and is part of the "Puzzles and Fun" section. For subscription information write to *Chickadee*, 56 The Esplanade, Suite 306, Toronto, Ontario, M5E 1A7, Canada.

Child Life publishes eight issues annually. It is intended for children ages seven to nine years and focuses primarily on health-related themes. This publication accepts children's poetry for its section "The Poet's Page." Children may also contribute to the "Jokes and Riddles and Cartoons" section, as well as the "Ask Doctor Cory" section, which prints questions on health topics from children and adults. Each issue features a "Young Writer's Story." The story may not exceed 500 words. For submission guidelines and subscription information write to *Child Life*, Children's Better Health Institute, Benjamin Franklin Literary & Medical Society, Inc., 1100 Waterway Boulevard, P.O. Box 567, Indianapolis, IN 46206.

Children's Digest publishes eight issues annually for children ages eight to ten years. Published by Children's Better Health Institute, the magazine focuses on topics such as exercise, nutrition, sports, and health. The "Page for Poetry" section prints children's poems. Readers' questions on health topics are printed in the "Ask Doctor Cory" section. "What Do You Think?" prints readers' opinions on specific situations. The periodical has a "Jokes and Riddles" section and also features a "Young Author's Story," which cannot exceed 700 words. For submission guidelines and subscription information write to *Children's Digest*, Children's Better Health Institute, Benjamin Franklin Literary & Medical Society, Inc., 1100 Waterway Boulevard, P.O. Box 567, Indianapolis, IN 46206.

Cobblestone: The History Magazine for Young People is a monthly publication. Each issue focuses on a different historical theme and features authentic historical and biographical fiction, adventure, and legends, all relating to the theme. Students may submit theme-related nonfiction activities, poetry, or puzzles. No submissions should be made without first writing for theme lists and writer's guidelines. The section "Dear Ebenezer" prints letters and poems written by children. Teachers can request information about upcoming themes by sending a self-addressed, stampled envelope to Teacher's Theme List, *Cobblestone Magazine*, 20 Grove Street, Peterbourough, NH 03458. For subscription information, write to the above address to the attention of the Subscription Department.

Cricket is a monthly publication for children ages six to eight years. Its purpose is to expose children to the works of writers and illustrators of children's books. Letters from children are published monthly in "The Letterbox." Art and poetry contests are sponsored each month and focus on a particular topic or theme. The winning entries are published. For subscription information write to *Cricket*, Box 52961, Boulder, CO 80322-2961.

Dolphin Log is a bimonthly publication offered by The Cousteau Society for children ages seven to fifteen. The magazine is designed to "delight, instruct and instill an environmental ethic and understanding of the interconnectedness of living organisms including people." Articles are on ocean or water-related themes or on experiments that can be done at home and demonstrate a scientific principle. Although the magazine is written by adults for children, each issue includes some children's illustrations. Children are invited to write stories on a particular water or ocean theme. These stories are not published, but The Cousteau Society offers to send information about sea life to contributors. In order to be knowledgeable about each month's topics, you would need to subscribe to this publication. For subscription information write to *The Dolphin Log*, The Cousteau Society, 8440 Santa Monica Boulevard, Los Angeles, CA 90069-4221.

Highlights is published monthly and is intended for children ages two to twelve. It accepts some poems, drawings, and stories from readers. Four times a year children are asked to submit creative endings for unfinished stories. A popular feature "Creatures Nobody Has Ever Seen" appears in some issues and features children's artwork. For subscription information and submission guidelines, write to *Highlights for Children*, 803 Church Street, Honesdale, PA 18431.

Humpty Dumpty's Magazine is another publication of the Children's Better Health Institute and is issued eight times a year for children ages four to six years. Children's artwork is featured in "You Draw the Pictures" section. For subscription information write to *Humpty Dumpty's Magazine*, Benjamin Franklin Literary & Medical Society, Inc., 1100 Waterway Boulevard, P.O. Box 567, Indianapolis, IN 46206.

International Arabian Horse Association Youth Essay Contest is sponsored annually by the International Arabian Horse Association. There are two age categories of entries, nine to thirteen and fourteen to eighteen. Children's essays in the ages nine to thirteen category should be between 500 and 900 words. Each year's contest has a different title. There is a first and second place prize in both the non-horse owner category and in the horse owner category. The first place non-horse owner prize is a purebred Arabian. All other awards are savings bonds. For specific contest rules, write to Essay Contest, International Arabian Horse Association, P.O. Box 33696, Denver, CO 80233.

Jack and Jill is published eight times a year by the Children's Better Health Institute. Its intended audience is children six to eight years old. The magazine publishes readers' contributions in the form of jokes and riddles, interesting letters, poetry, and artwork. Each issue features "A Young Writer's Story" not to exceed 500 words. For submission guidelines and subscription information, write to *Jack and Jill*, Children's Better Health Institute, Benjamin Franklin Literary & Medical Society, Inc., 1100 Waterway Boulevard, P.O. Box 567, Indianapolis, IN 46206.

National Written & Illustrated By ... Awards Contest for Students is sponsored by Landmark Editions, Inc. There are three age categories of entries: A—six to nine years old, B—ten to thirteen years old, C—fourteen to nineteen years old. Each book submitted must be both written and illustrated by the same student. Three books, one from each category, are printed as hardbound books.

Manuscripts are judged on the merits of originality and the writing and illustrating skills displayed. Guidelines for submission are very specific and can be obtained by writing to The National Written & Illustrated by ... Awards Contest for Students, Landmark Editions, Inc., P.O. Box 4469, Kansas City, MO 64127.

Odyssey is a monthly publication featuring articles on astronomy and outer space. In each issue children are invited to submit creative responses to new monthly topics. Some responses are printed in the "Future Forum" pages. Some puzzles and artwork created by children are also published. For subscription information write to *Odyssey*, 1027 North 7th Street, Milwaukee, WI 53233.

Owl is a Canadian publication issued ten times a year by The Young Naturalist Foundation. Its goal is to interest children eight years and older in their environment and the world around them. The December issue of this publication announces an annual children's writing contest. The topic changes each year. A photography contest is usually announced in the summer issue. The May issue announces a poetry contest, and a cover contest is announced each October. For subscription information and submission guidelines, write to *Owl*, 56 The Esplanade, Suite 306, Toronto, Ontario, M5E 1A7, Canada.

Raintree's Publish-A-Book Contest is sponsored by Raintree Publishers and is open to children in grades 4, 5, and 6. Four winning entries are published as hardbound books. Twenty writers are given honorable mention but not published. Each year a new theme is announced. The 1989-90 school year theme is Tall Tales, Folk Tales, or Fairy Tales. Stories should be between 700 and 800 words in length. Specific guidelines must be followed. For rules and guidelines, write to Publish-A-Book Contest, Raintree Publishers, 310 West Wisconsin Avenue, Milwaukee, WI 53203.

Ranger Rick is published monthly by the National Wildlife Federation and is intended for children ages six to twelve years. Each issue is devoted to nature and science. The magazine publishes children's questions about nature in the "Who Knows?" section. A yearly writing contest gives readers an opportunity to write an ending for a story. The best endings are published. For subscription information write *Ranger Rick*, 8925 Leesburg Pike, Vienna, VA 22184-0001.

Shoe Tree: The Literary Magazine by and for Young Writers is published for children ages six to fourteen by the National Association for Young Writers. A triannual publication, its purpose is to encourage children to "write to the top." Each issue contains about a half-dozen fiction and nonfiction stories and poems. All published pieces are of the finest quality. The cover artwork of this publication is done by children, as are some book reviews. For submission guidelines and subscription information, write to *Shoe Tree* Competition, c/o NAYW, 215 Valle del Sol Drive, Santa Fe, NM 87501.

Skipping Stones is a periodical designed to help children learn about the world and its people from each other. It is a multiethnic forum for children's original artwork and writing. It is published quarterly and accepts contributions from children of all ages. Each issue is unique. Suggestions for submissions are riddles, songs, stories, poems, recipes, customs, festivals, reports on projects, pen pal letters and requests, instructions for making things, book and movie reviews, photos, drawings, paintings, and puzzles. For submission guidelines and subscription information, write to *Skipping Stones*, 80574 Hazelton Road, Cottage Grove, OR 97424.

Stone Soup is published five times a year (Sept., Nov., Jan., March, May) by the Children's Art Foundation. The entire magazine is made of children's work, both art and writing. The editors say they want to "encourage children to use writing and art as a means of serious communication." They try "to encourage children to look to the world they can see and touch for the sources of their inspiration." For submission guidelines and subscription information, write to *Stone Soup*, P.O. Box 83, Santa Cruz, CA 95063.

Wombat is a journal of young people's writing and art. It is published six times a year and contains short stories, poetry, nonfiction articles, artwork, illustrations, puzzles, cartoons, and letters to the editor, all created by children ages six to sixteen. Professional adults are invited to submit articles on topics that might be of interest to young people. For submission guidelines and subscription information, write to *Wombat*, P.O. Box 8088, Athens, GA 30603.

Young Writer's Contest Foundation is a nonprofit, tax-exempt organization, dedicated to improving children's communication skills. The contest is open to children in grades one through eight. Entries are accepted in the areas of poetry, short stories, or essays, written in the English language. No joint or group-written entries are accepted. Schools may submit up to twelve entries and all twelve may be authored by the same student. A minimal registration fee must accompany the entries. For specific guidelines contact Young Writer's Contest Foundation, P.O. Box 6092, McLean, VA 22106.

APPENDIX B:
ANSWERS TO WORKSHEETS

Answers to *Amos and Boris* Crossword Puzzle (figure 4.3)

Answers to Railroad Words (figure 8.1)

R A I L R O A D

1. tracks   3. locomotive   5. train   7. coach

2. cowcatcher   4. flatbeds   6. caboose   8. shades

Answers to Galaxy of Words (figure 11.3)

(1) galaxy ☆
(2) tinge ☆
(3) whorl ☆
(4) buffet ☆
(5) cavort ☆
(6) harness ☆
(7) biped ☆
(8) whine ☆

(9) polarized ☆
(10) hull ☆
(11) coil ☆
(12) tread ☆
(13) rung ☆
(14) cleft ☆
(15) meteorite ☆
(16) urgent ☆

Answers to *The Laziest Robot* Word Search (figure 13.1)

The answers are: robot, work, Big Rover, space garden, search party, windmill, down, zone one, lazy, lost, helped, weeds.

Answers to *The Stories Julian Tells* Make-Believe Meanings (figure 15.2)

An insect that takes long graceful strides (antelope)

A slippery yellow container from which to drink (buttercup)

A Chinese pastry (cakewalk)

A small frozen town (iceberg)

A tree made of soft cushy floor covering (carpentry)

quickly ruin something (breakfast)

A fancy jungle animal (dandelion)

A sharp object made for cutting grass (icicle)

Inexpensive shoes to use on ice (cheapskate)

A heavenly ocean animal (angelfish)

INDEX

Cover Design
Michael Mancarella

CLTIP90#1